LEGENDARY LOCALS

OF

CROOKSTON

MINNESOTA

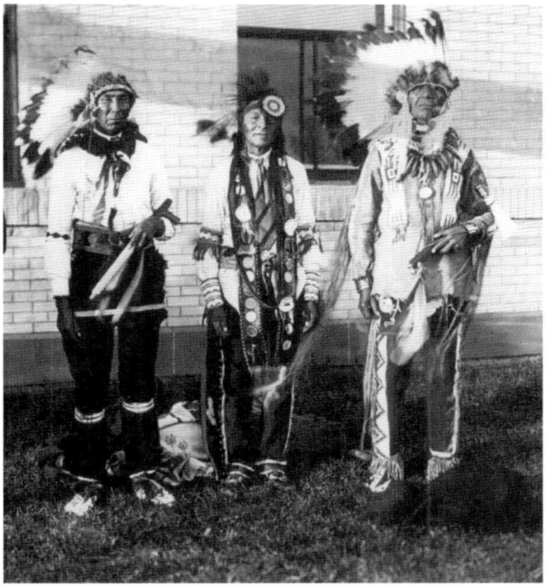

I0806128

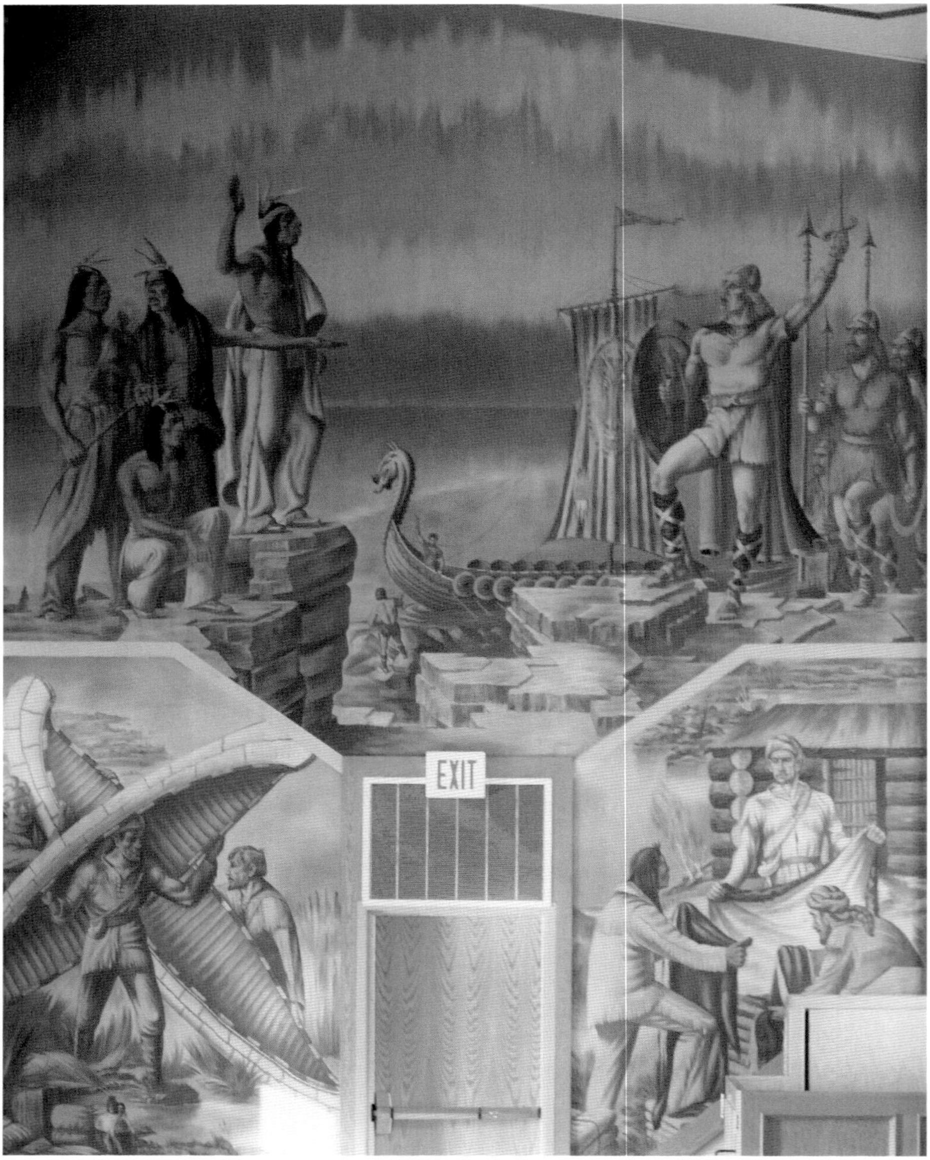

John Martin Socha's Art
The Northwest School of Agriculture (NWSA) class of 1932 gifted this wall mural commissioned to be painted by the highly acclaimed artist John Martin Socha. It was finally completed as a Works Progress Administration (WPA) project in 1942. Supt. Conrad G. Selvig got involved with this politically charged mural, which exists to this day. Situated on the west wall of the Kiehle Auditorium, Socha depicts a Vikings' ship with a tattered sail, as if they are seeking help from the Native Americans. (Photograph by Steve Hannah.)

Page 1: Chief Mays-Ko-Gwan
In the Red River Valley, the very first legendary locals of the Crookston area were the Chippewa and Sioux tribes. On the right is Chief Mays-Ko-Gwan in his elaborate headdress and warm buckskin clothes; the other two Native Americans are not identified. (Courtesy of Northwest Research and Outreach Center [NWROC].)

LEGENDARY LOCALS

OF

CROOKSTON

MINNESOTA

KRISTINA TORKELSON GRAY

LEGENDARY LOCALS

ISBN 978-1-4671-0157-8

Legendary Locals is an imprint of Arcadia Publishing
Charleston, South Carolina

Printed in the United States of America

Library of Congress Control Number: 2013956184

For all general information, please contact Arcadia Publishing:
Telephone 843-853-2070
Fax 843-853-0044
E-mail sales@arcadiapublishing.com
For customer service and orders:
Toll-Free 1-888-313-2665

Visit us on the Internet at www.arcadiapublishing.com

Dedication
To my parents, Glen and Lucile Torkelson, stalwart, longtime members of the Crookston community, and to my long-suffering and humble husband, Dr. Kenneth R. Gray

On the Front Cover: Clockwise from top left:
A Crookston parade with color guard represented with American flags (Courtesy of Polk County Historical Society [PCHS]; see page 27), Mae Rideout, multiyear recipient of the Woman of the Year Award (PCHS; see page 119), Victoria Dragseth Irwin, active community member (Courtesy of Judy Dragseth Ellingson; see page 120), May Mix (née Mary Lincoln Shapleigh), vaudeville actress (PCHS; see page 102), Ole O. Sundet and Bertha Morgan's wedding, the biggest and the most unique wedding in the northwest (Courtesy of Judy Sundet Keasler; see page 17), Edwin Widseth, College Football Hall of Fame member (Courtesy of Greg Widseth, see page 93), Evelyn Probstfield, Crookston High School teacher (PCHS; see page 117), Scott Janssen, Iditarod competitor (Courtesy of Bill and Lois Janssen; see page 100), Russell and Helen Sundet, Army first sergeant and WAVES member (Courtesy of Richard Sundet, see page 43).

On the Back Cover: From left to right:
The 1928 Crookston baseball champions at Central Park grandstand (PCHS; see page 90), Cliff Nelson of the Polk County Museum (Photograph by Twylla Altepeter; see page 124).

CONTENTS

ACKNOWLEDGMENTS

This book springs from face-to-face or virtual conversations with sons and daughters of Crookston now scattered from Alaska and Washington State, to Arizona and Florida—and towns and cities and farms everywhere within Minnesota's boundaries. Other conversations that fed the biographies herein took place first hand at the Carnegie building and everywhere else in Crookston. The mailing back and forth of precious family photographs kept the Crookston Post Office busy. Fortunately, other photographs used in this book were available in Crookston, with many from the archives of the Polk County Historical Museum. (All photographs are courtesy of the Polk County Historical Society archives unless otherwise noted.)

To create a book worthy of Crookston's heroes and tell their individual stories, I sought the best possible photographs available. Some of these were prepared by more contemporary photographers, listed here in alphabetical order: Twylla Altepeter, Wayne Anderson, Don Buness, Steve Hannah, Ken R. Johnson, Gene Miller, and John Zak. I am especially indebted to Steve Hannah for his willingness to go after the images I could not find in the archives but were needed to tell certain stories. The photographers producing the vintage, early-19th-century pictures are often unknown. We credit an indispensable profession, the true value of which we realize more and more as time progresses. In spite of all these efforts, present-day unavailability of photographs kept some people from being selected for this book of legends.

This book represents the collection and packaging of community knowledge of Crookston's history and many of its remarkable men and women who lived here from 135 years ago to today. Understandably, the length and depth of my encounters with the present-day community—by telephone, letter, e-mails, Facebook, or face-to-face dialogues—will be lost in any short and impersonal alphabetized list of acknowledgments. However, I hope each person listed will know how sincerely appreciative I am of their assistance in this project.

When women have provided information on legendary relatives, I included their maiden names to help identify the relationship. The following is my attempt to give credit: Cindy Brolsma Conklin; Margaret Childs Rose; Sally Dahlgren; Patti Dillabough; Judy Dragseth Ellingson; Paul Eickhof; Bette Ellingson Talbert; Cathy Erickson Johnson; Ron Gramer; Tim and John Hanson; Betty Heldstab; Chuck, Jeanie, and Matt Hiller; Bill and Lois Janssen; John Janssen; Kathy Jurchen Pissoneault; Sr. Laurian Lasha; Nancy Melby; Margie Keller; Kathy Kiewel Romuld; Sherry Kiewel Pratt; Nancy Maves Thomasson; Janna Miller Braun; Janet Moe Solheim; Gerry Moreno; Tom and Junice Mulvaney; Cliff Oftelie; Deanna Patenaude; Deb Kiel; Joy Riggs; Judy Sundet Keasler; Richard Sundet; Kenny and Bob Swenson; Tony Torkelson; Amber Wagner Bailey; Leah Warren Volker; Maggie Warren Nitti; Mary Lynn Warren Hoard; and Greg Widseth.

Finally, thanks go to our wonderful librarians at the Crookston Public Library for allowing me to scan photographs there. Also a thank-you goes to Sr. Eileen Beutel for her index work of many decades of the *Crookston Daily Times*. Kudos go to Twylla Altepeter's editing skills; she was very thorough in detecting the errors of my first draft. Also, high fives go to Maureen Aubol of the Northwest Research and Outreach Center and my sincere appreciation is given to the helpful staff at the University of Minnesota, Crookston Library. I am deeply humbled by all the amazing support.

INTRODUCTION

The 10 chapters of this book will bring out qualities of bravery, sacredness, talent, inventiveness, risk-taking, athletic prowess, volunteerism, kindness, and many other attributes that contribute to make men and women legends. Many readers will have previously recognized a name attached to a Crookston building, street, or social organization but not have known the story that honors that name. Others may know, as a relative, a person selected for this to represent a cross-section of our town, as a sports person, a cleric, a volunteer. Most of Crookston's legends have already left this sod. Some are still alive but have moved away from the Red River Valley. It is my desire that the information contained herein, about Crookston's homegrown legends, will make all who have called Crookston home, proud.

To understand the major players who helped form early Crookston, it is necessary to go back in time. Pretend as if you are using a time machine to know what obstacles these legends may have faced. The context of early Crookston from which its first legends emerged can be gained from primary sources written over a century ago. Therefore, what the writer of old intends for his reading audience to understand about Crookston is clearly spelled out. What became obvious to me was the early Crookstonites faced hardship and were very proud of their city and its accomplishments.

The first four chapters focus on Crookston's early pioneers, military, businessmen, and farmers. Henrietta Holte's *Album of Memories*, written in the 1950s, is a good source for background on the Native Americans present in the region in the early days (see Henrietta Holte on pages 37 and 116). Henrietta studied Native Americans and contributed a large collection of artifacts to the Polk County Museum when it was housed at the old McKinley elementary school. Many of these were later passed on to other area museums. She writes that although traces of prehistoric man have been found in the Crookston area, the most commonly known people to precede the early settlers were the Sioux and Chippewa Indians. These were enemies who fought among themselves for control of the region's wild rice resources. According to Holte, Governor Ramsey embarked on a treaty-making expedition to Pembina as early 1851, guided by Pierre Bottineau. Ramsey and the Indians made a treaty that was not, however, ratified by Congress. Lands here remained the property of the Native Americans. White men intruded, and the Indians resented this, which led to uprisings becoming common. By 1862, the great Sioux insurrection had depopulated Georgetown (a town of 120 about 60 miles from present-day Crookston). These were the trials that faced early settlers in the valley. Holte continued, writing that Governor Ramsey returned to meet with the two Indian bands in 1863 to try to arrive at a new treaty. This was the meeting at the old Treaty Crossing of the Pembina Trail and the Red Lake River.

Holte wrote, "Crookston's early settlers to the valley at first owed its growth to transportation. Homes followed the development of transportation. By 1858, the trade with Red River settlements had become so important to the then rising city of St. Paul, that the St. Paul Chamber of Commerce offered $2,000 as a bonus to anyone who would have a steamboat plying on the waters of the Red River in 1858. In 1874 and 1875, boats also ran up the Red Lake River to Crookston. One morning in 1872, while the railroad bridge was being constructed across the river, the piercing whistle of the steamer *Dakota* on its trial run aroused the couple of hundred Crookstonites."

After the slow ground transport and unpredictable water transport proved to not be reliable, the coming of the railroad caused Crookston to develop quickly. Crookston was blessed with being both a river and railroad town. The April 1922 journal of Alice Miller set down her thoughts about Crookston's history:

> Of course there was quite a rush of settlers taking up lands along the river, each one hoping that would be on the favored spot of the crossing. About May 1, 1872 the railroad located its crossing of the Red Lake River at the point where Crookston is now located. Of course, there were

> many disappointed squatters. Bob Houston was one of the first to take up claim on the land which was afterward the city's site. As Houston was one of a party who was with the railroad engineers, E.C. Davis, B. Sampson, John Darkow, Dick Hussey and W.H. Stewart were others of the favored ones. [All these names were applied to Crookston's streets and additions.]
>
> Soon a very lively little town was born and it grew quite rapidly. The crossing was named Crooks-ton after the chief engineer of the railroad, Col. William Crooks of St. Paul. Stewart started a saloon and hotel. E.C. Davis who had a large grading contract had supply stores, and other stores and saloons. Saloons grew up overnight. There were a great many men employed in railroad work, in steel and grading gangs and business was very brisk, gamblers and others of that ilk reaping part of the prosperity. Several stores were started and they had a large Indian trade. Indians used to come to town much in early days, especially in the summer, and their favorite camping place was the higher ground where the [Central] high school is located.

Chapter five of this volume focuses on the secondary education of the children of the farmers of the area. This Northwest School of Agriculture (NWSA) campus, which has now become a branch of the University of Minnesota at Crookston, is better known as "UMC." This institution has come a long way from the beginnings described by Henrietta Holte in her writings. The first school was started in Crookston in 1874 with Luella Thompson as the first teacher in a small building on Main Street between Third and Fourth streets.

The last five chapters of this book reveal more of Crookston's churches, politics, sports, theater, music, and other notable legends. Crookston grew to be a thriving city. This is detailed in the following newspaper account from *Northern Tier* dated October 21, 1893:

> It is a little more than a dozen years since the first building was erected on the spot where Crookston now stands. Today a thriving and prosperous city of brick and stone rests her foundation here, with her 5,000 souls, her six lines of railroad running in as many different directions, her miles and miles of graded streets, sidewalks, sewers and water mains, her array of manufacturing institutions, her water works and water power, her electric lights, her handsome three and four story business blocks, her magnificent opera house, her schools, her churches, her financial exchanges, her jobbing and mercantile interests, her beautiful natural parks and her comfortable homes for a happy and prosperous people. What a wonderful change in these short years? So short that it seems but yesterday since the foundation was laid upon which now stands the "Queen City of the Red River Valley". . . .
>
> Nature has favored Crookston with two splendid water powers, one of which is developed and furnishes 75,000 horse power which is used to run our large flouring mills, pump water for the city for fire and domestic purposes, run the machinery which furnishes the electric light, both arc and incandescent, with which our streets, business houses and residences are lighted and lastly to furnish the power through the medium of a water motor by which the presses are run that print this paper.

I apologize in advance for the lack of inclusion here of many deserving men and women who are also legends. In some instances, I did not have a quality photograph to go with a remarkable life. In other cases, I may have had a great photograph but did not have enough readily available information. Choices had to be made, and they were imperfect choices. My default preference was to present legendary characters from Crookston's more distant past, to memorialize whatever information there is left about them before we lose it entirely.

I feel very privileged to be on the Polk County Historical Society Board of Directors and to be chairing the Carnegie committee. As a result, I feel doubly thankful for having access to what has been preserved in the museum's archives and handed down to us from the past. We hope in the future to make more records and documents available to other researchers in the basement of the former Carnegie library.

CHAPTER ONE

Pioneers and Other Legends

In the early 1870s, Crookston had many settlers who arrived with high hopes. Crookston's heavily timbered and river-looped area soon housed more living legends than trees. The newly built railroad made all the difference. The community quickly blossomed from a fledgling town of makeshift tents, sod houses, and tarpaper shacks to a small city of commerce. Eventually, Crookston became known as the "Queen City of the Northwest." However, it required able-bodied people with gritty determination and hard work to forge ahead in spite of many obstacles. Many came, but many left, especially when the financial crisis hit. Some of those who stayed made names or fortunes for themselves.

Please note that many of Crookston's pioneers are not featured in this book because considerable space was given to them in the Images of America: *Crookston* book, published in 2013. Examples are photographer P.E. Lynne, responsible for many of the images in both books. Another is the Great Northern Railroad engineer and Civil War veteran Col. William Crooks, for whom Crookston is named. Also not included is Edmund M. Walsh, considered the "Dean of the Old Settlers." Bernhard and Petra Sampson, for whom Sampson's Addition is named, are other examples. Another important figure in Crookston's history is Tom Morris, longtime jeweler but more importantly Crookston's first fire chief, who was also featured earlier. Bert Keck, Crookston's early architect was portrayed alongside the Crookston buildings that he helped create. For a more complete story, purchase both books!

The Polk County Historical Museum houses important information about other Crookston legends. Because there are photographs to tell the story, this chapter will focus on Ole Sundet and his bride, Bertha Morgan, in "An Indian Wedding." Other writings digitally scanned from the *Polk County's Centennial* book, published in 1979, can be found online, such as stories of "Lucky O'Brien," and "Minnesota Man Two," which were written by E. Boh. Two more essays "Old Crossing Treaty" by Albany Capistran and a funny anecdote about "Honest Scottie" by Judge William Watts (see page 79) are all stories that need to be preserved. Younger generations can profit from learning about how the local legends survived the tough things in life.

Lack of space and available photographs explain why others were not chosen. For example, *Crookston Daily Times* editor William McKenzie is not featured explicitly, but his figurative fingerprints are all over this volume. McKenzie's photograph is included in the first Crookston book. The service of many of the others omitted is also written all over Crookston's history.

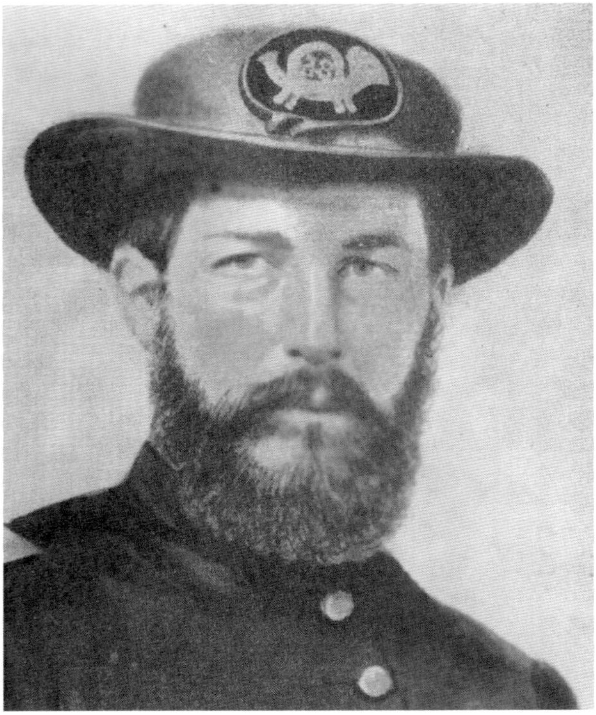

Ellery C. Davis, Master of All Trades

On June 11, 1872, Capt. Ellery C. Davis filed for a homestead near Crookston where he made his headquarters. He was involved in moving railroad supplies, providing railroad contracts, and selling general merchandise. Davis opened a real estate office on July 14, 1878 and became Crookston's first mayor in 1879. He had patents on a new railroad tie (1886) and a rubber horseshoe (1894).

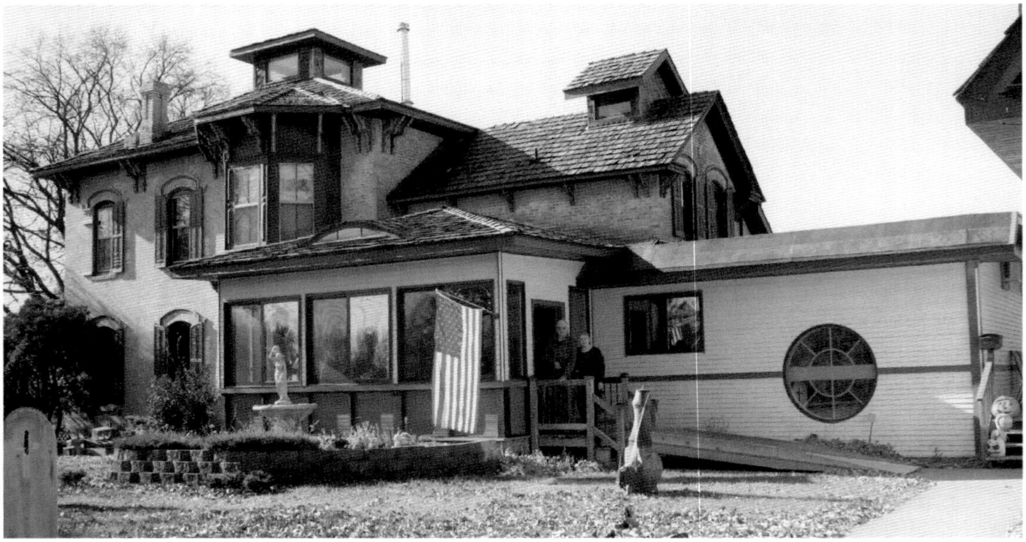

Gary and Jean Luckow

The current master and mistress of the Davis house on North Front and Grant Streets are Gary and Jean Luckow. They are pictured next to an American flag and have put much tender, loving care into the house Captain Davis built. Davis brought a brick kiln up the Red Lake River by steamboat to Fisher's Landing. In 1879, Ellery and Rachel Davis moved into their new home in the hill district. It was the first brick house in the Crookston area. The Davis family employed several servants, and the house has two different foundations with hidden passageways. The roof features a lookout tower, also known as a widow's walk. Rachel Davis was instrumental in starting the Congregational church. (Photograph by Steve Hannah.)

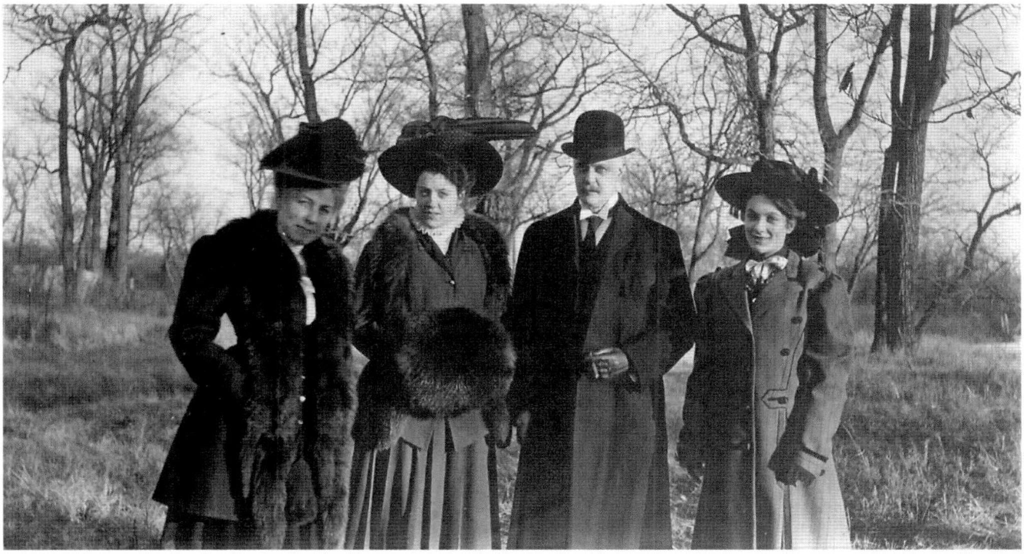

Ellsworth D. Childs and Carman Addition

In 1877, the St. Paul & Pacific Railroad lured Ellsworth D. Childs and his brother Albert M. Childs to invest in the Carman area. Large tracts of farmland were sold at $2.50 per acre. E.D. Childs bought 10,000 acres. In order to get others, who needed water, to buy his real estate, Childs's firm spent much money prospecting for an artesian supply well. By 1894, Ellsworth had established two flowing wells in Carman. One well was in the street north of Block 11 in Carman. The other was choked off when one of the Carman elevators burned, and it never reopened. Ellsworth, the wealthy developer of Carman Addition, was also known as the "Sidewalk Builder." He had three sons and three daughters (two of which are unidentified in the above image) from his marriage with Eliza (far left). She died in 1904. He lost his savings due to bad investments with his partner, railroad baron James J. Hill, and moved to Washington State as a widower in 1907. He married Henrietta Stevens in Yakima, Washington, on November 11, 1911. (Above, courtesy of Margaret Childs Rose.)

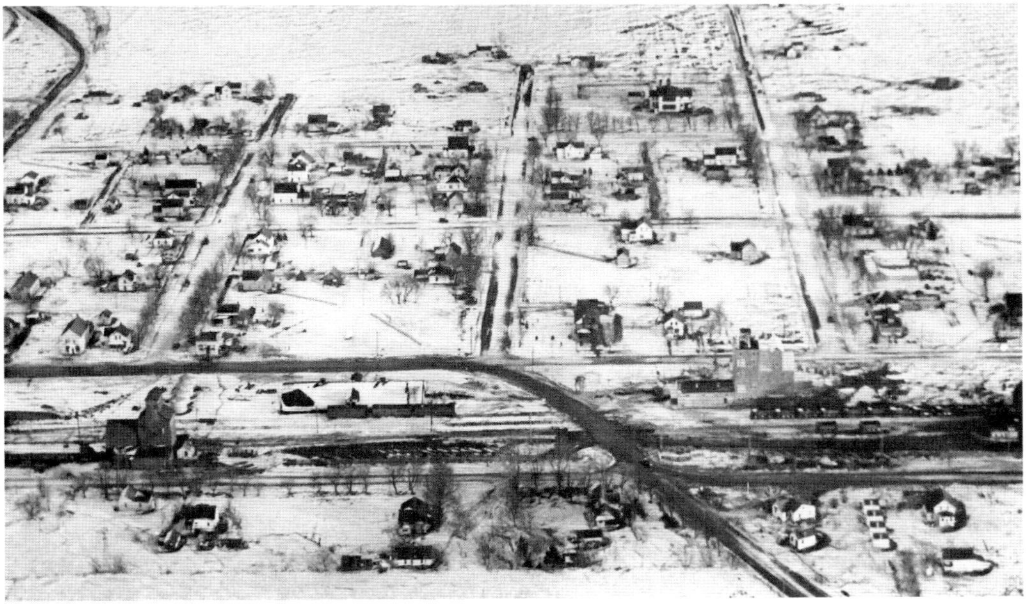

Louis Fontaine

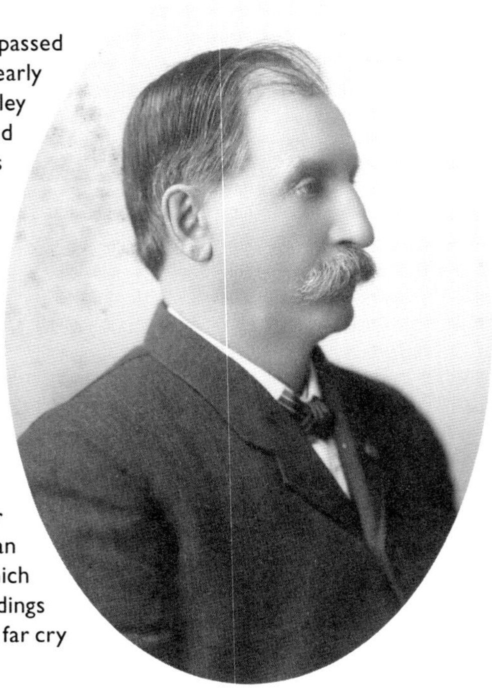

Louis Fontaine, born January 11, 1840, passed through Crookston as a fur trader as early as 1872. He traveled the Red River Valley by oxcart. Born in Quebec, he ventured to St. Paul when he was only 18 years old to help farm. In November 1861, he enlisted for the Civil War and was discharged in 1865. In the summer of 1878, he partnered with William Anglim to operate the Fontaine and Anglim Store on North Main and Second Streets. This consisted of three departments: dry goods, clothing, and groceries. The partners were in business for 25 years. He was married in 1866 and had nine children. Fontaine died in St. Paul on November 7, 1914. The photograph below is an aerial view showing Crookston, which is well built-up with many brick buildings concentrated in several city blocks—a far cry from Fontaine's early days.

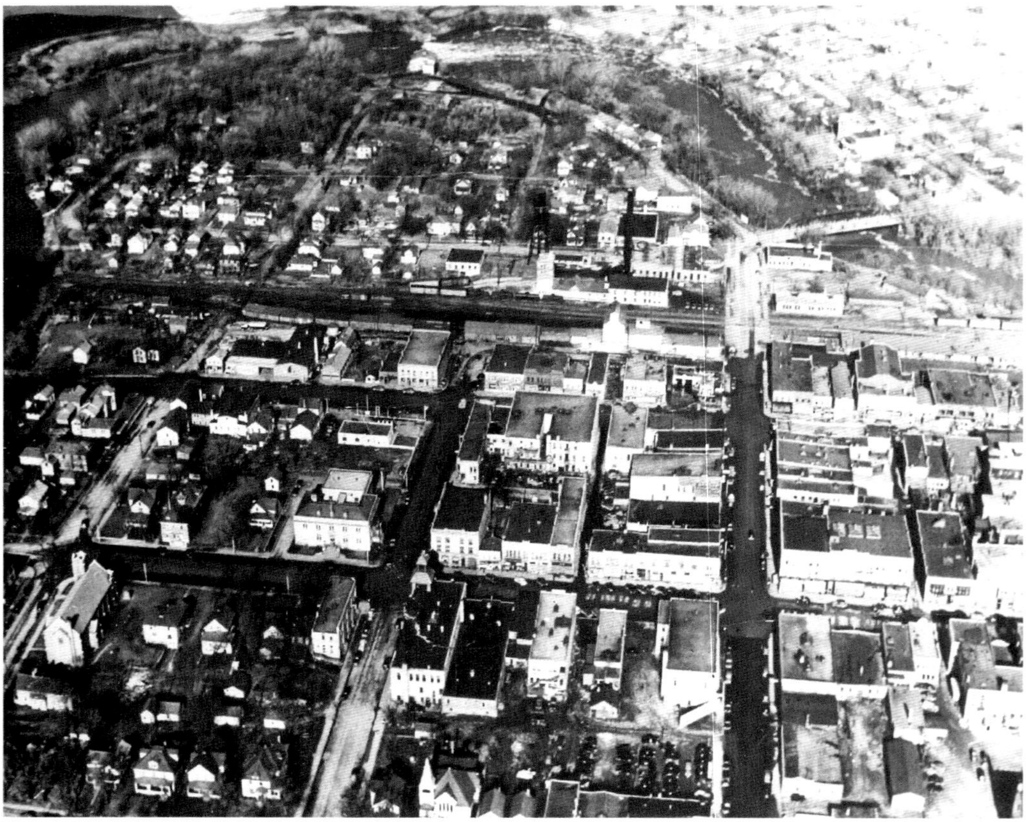

The Five McKinnon Brothers

Alexander (left), born in Ontario, Canada, on March 5, 1854, was one of five McKinnon brothers. Alex left school at age 14 and learned the trade of blacksmithing in Wisconsin. He came to Crookston in the fall of 1878. Through his own hard work and industry, he had saved $700 and started up a blacksmith shop on the corner of North Main and Robert Streets, where Crookston Paint and Glass is now. He was soon joined in business by his younger brother Allan. His older brother John (right), born in Scotland on September 13, 1851, arrived in Crookston on May 15, 1880. John was more involved with farm implements and got a patent for a ditching machine in 1904.

The McKinnon brothers not only had a successful business in manufacturing and farm implements, they also were involved in real estate, insurance, and local public service. As early as June 11, 1887, the McKinnon brothers broke ground for a new building on Main Street where the blacksmithing shop had been. It was a fine brick building, 125 by 140 feet costing $75,000. It contained McKinnon Hall, where annual balls were held. Some Crookstonites who had weathered the financial crisis years earlier thought the McKinnons had overextended. But by 1890, the McKinnons owned the Independent Order of Odd Fellows block. In April of that same year, Alex became Crookston's mayor. He was reelected without opposition the next year. Allan, who had earlier been an alderman, was elected Crookston's mayor on November 6, 1909.

There was such a need for buildings downtown that in May 1901 the McKinnons made plans to add an additional story on the brick McKinnon Block. Alex owned several hundred acres of land. In February 1904, the *Crookston Daily Times* stated there was a foreclosure on this farm. The newspaper reported, in August 1907, that Alex McKinnon had supposedly struck it rich in cobalt mining. Such were the business risks and rewards in those days.

Another enterprising brother was Archie McKinnon, who was manager of the Crookston racetrack. In 1899, Dan McKinnon was granted a patent for a buggy clip invented to keep harness traces in place. The same year, a patent was granted to Dan for his harness fastener. On March 10, 1900, the *Crookston Daily Times* reported Archie and Allan McKinnon were turning out a large number of vehicles from a factory. In February 1914, the McKinnons used the Farm Crops Show to display machinery they had for sale. Industry seemed to run in the family.

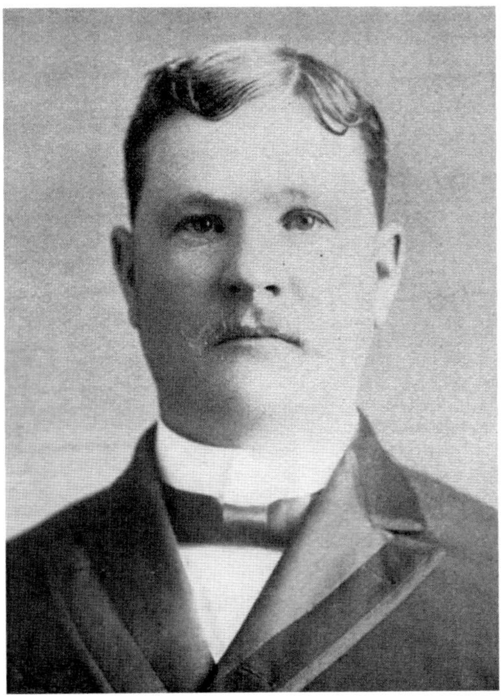

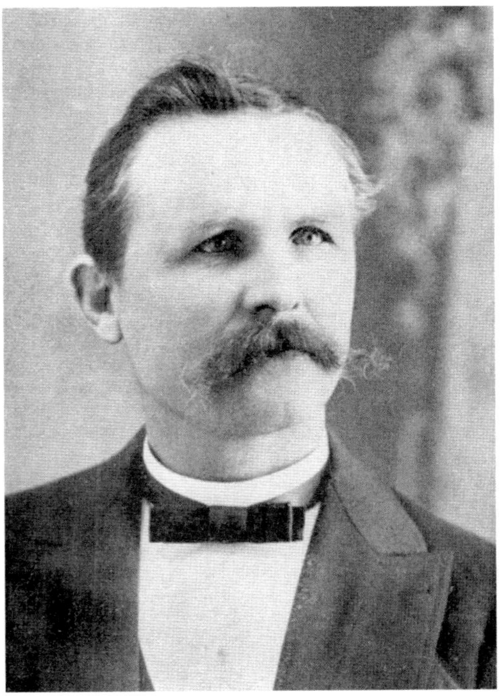

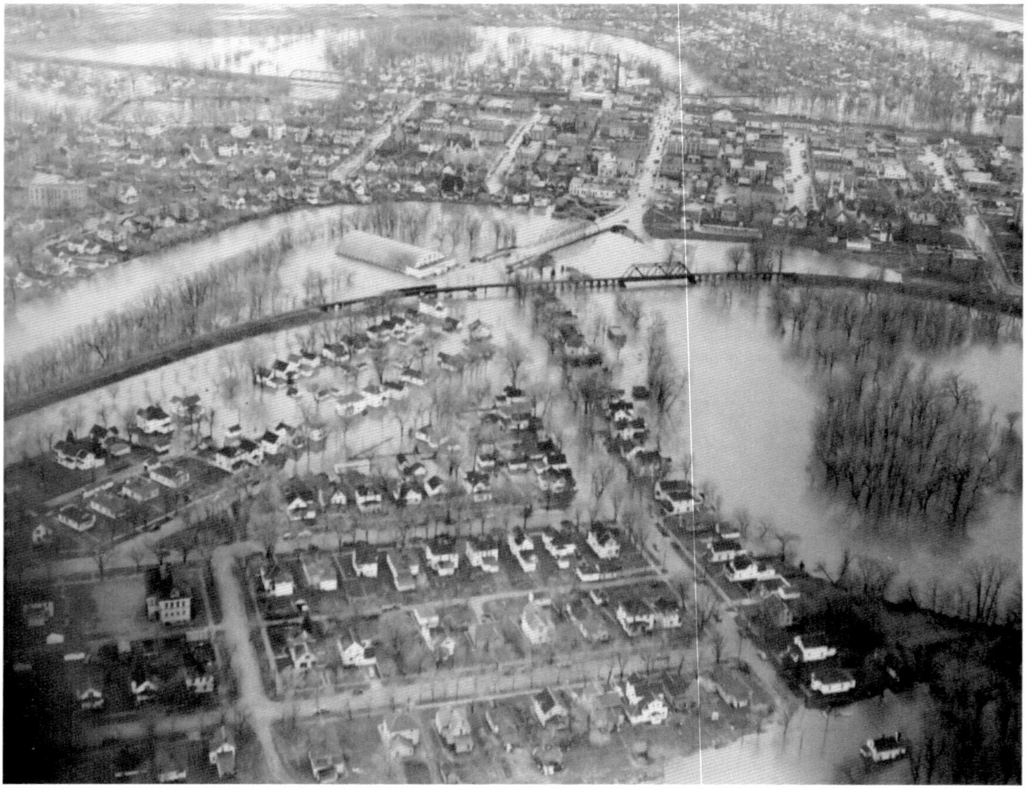

Frank Jerome's Addition

In June 1884, Frank Jerome built a large livery stable on Robert and Ash Streets, which was taken over by Bjoin and Carlson. Close to the same location, he built the Hotel Jerome in 1886. With railroad men and new settlers populating Crookston's railroad hub, there was a need for housing. In June 1888, Jerome built a three-story brick addition and renamed it the St. Louis Inn. After the 1893 flood, it was revamped to become the Crookston College, established in 1896 by Jacob C. Sathre (see page 22).

Simultaneous to the building up from the Jerome's Addition, the father of Mary Lincoln Shapleigh (also known as "May Mix") was cutting down trees in the Woods Addition in order to build a house for his family. Woods Addition was rightly named because it was heavily wooded. Eventually, many trees were felled, and the tree stumps were uprooted in order to create the residential area that exists today. Some of the lumbermen who worked across the river to the south for the T.B. Walker sawmill had sleeping quarters in the Woods Addition. They fashioned a wooden bridge to walk across the Red Lake River to the mill.

Because of the need for more living accommodations, Frank Jerome kept enlarging and adding to his hotel up to the year before the flood of 1893. This flood destroyed houses and his hotel in the Jerome's and Woods Additions. He was Crookston's street commissioner at the time of his death in 1908. Tragically, on January 26, 1901, Jerome's eight-year-old son died under the sled runner of a run-away sleigh.

An account of the history of "Aunt Polly's Slough" in the Jerome's Addition can be found in a *Crookston Daily Times* article dated December 5, 1923. Apparently, Polly Carelton would watch youngsters skate on the frozen slough and feed them cookies and warm them up when they got too cold. Some of the neighborhood fathers at the start of the ice season would skate across the slough from one end to another to make sure it was suitably frozen so no child would fall through. Supposedly, some of the best skaters and hockey players came from the Jerome's Addition. The Crookston Sports Arena was built by the WPA in 1938. In this photograph, a round-topped Quonset hut can be seen under water during the flood of 1950.

Charles and John Kiewel

Charles Edward Kiewel (pictured) came to Crookston and established the Kiewel Brewing Company in 1899. He also owned 600 acres of farmland, located 3.5 miles west of Crookston. Kiewel married Catherine Blake of Little Falls on November 17, 1896. They had three sons, some of whom carried on the brewing tradition. The Kiewel family had deep roots in Minnesota. John Kiewel, shoe merchant in Crookston, recorded the following memories of his Kiewel ancestors:

> I remember when there was not a foot of railroad in the state. I came here with my parents in 1857. We located in Carver County, which was then in a wild state and neighbors were few and far between. It was the hunting ground of the Indian and all kinds of game abounded. Where these hunting parties put in their camps, I have seen piles of hair as big as hay cocks from the hides of the game that the Indians killed, and which they shaved off to lessen the weight of their prizes.
>
> It cost something to move a family in those days. We had no team, and father paid a neighbor who had an ox team $20 to move us 20 miles, a $1 a mile and yet we kick now on paying 3¢ a mile to travel in luxury. I remember the famous treaty made between General Cooke and the Sioux Indians which involved what was known as the great Sioux reservation on the west side of the Missouri River, comprising 11,000,000 acres of land. The pow-wow lasted several weeks before General Cooke succeeded in getting two-thirds of the Indians to sign, which was necessary to make the treaty valid.
>
> In 1865 our people moved to Stearns County, near the now thriving city of St. Cloud. There was a small hamlet there at the time and the St. Paul & Pacific Railroad, the first railway west of St. Paul, was built to that point. This road, as you know, was the beginning of the greatest transcontinental line, the Great Northern. This railroad was built in little sections in the then northwest, but not much progress was made until the master mind of Jim Hill got behind it. The great country to the west and north of St. Cloud was then almost an unexplored wilderness, occupied only by the Indians and fur traders. Once a year, the traders from the Red River and Assiniboine River used to rendezvous at St. Cloud to barter furs for supplies and I have seen as many as one hundred Red River carts come in at once, drawn by oxen and cows. The latter were used oftener than oxen when on a long journey.

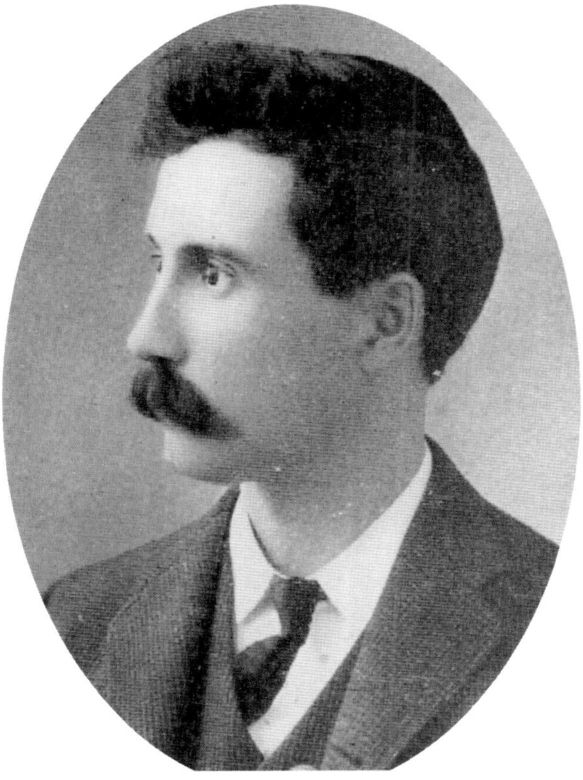

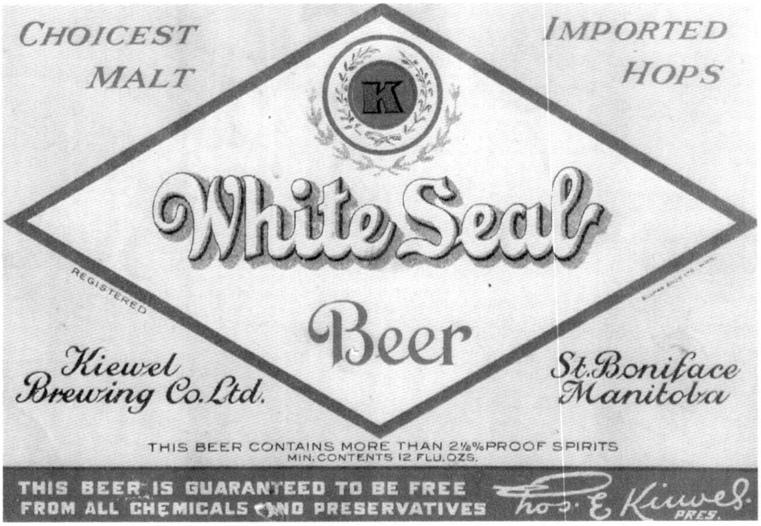

Kiewel's White Seal Beer and Brewery
Kiewel's White Seal Beer was produced at the Charles Kiewel Brewery located on the corner of Fifth and North Front Streets, right next to the Great North Railroad track. He and his sons sold White Seal Beer throughout Crookston's thriving saloons. They promised the best quality beer, free from chemicals and preservatives, using imported hops. Kiewel built two saloons; the one on North Broadway was a billiard hall, millinery, and music shop in 1889. The second saloon was built at 203 North Main Street in 1907. Olaf Bakke and Ole O. Sundet were a few of the many bartenders in Crookston who served Kiewel's beer. Competition to Kiewel were Hamm Theo Brewing and Minneapolis Brewing Company, both situated close by on North Main Street. Opposition was on the rise by some Crookstonites, who believed beer flowed all too freely.

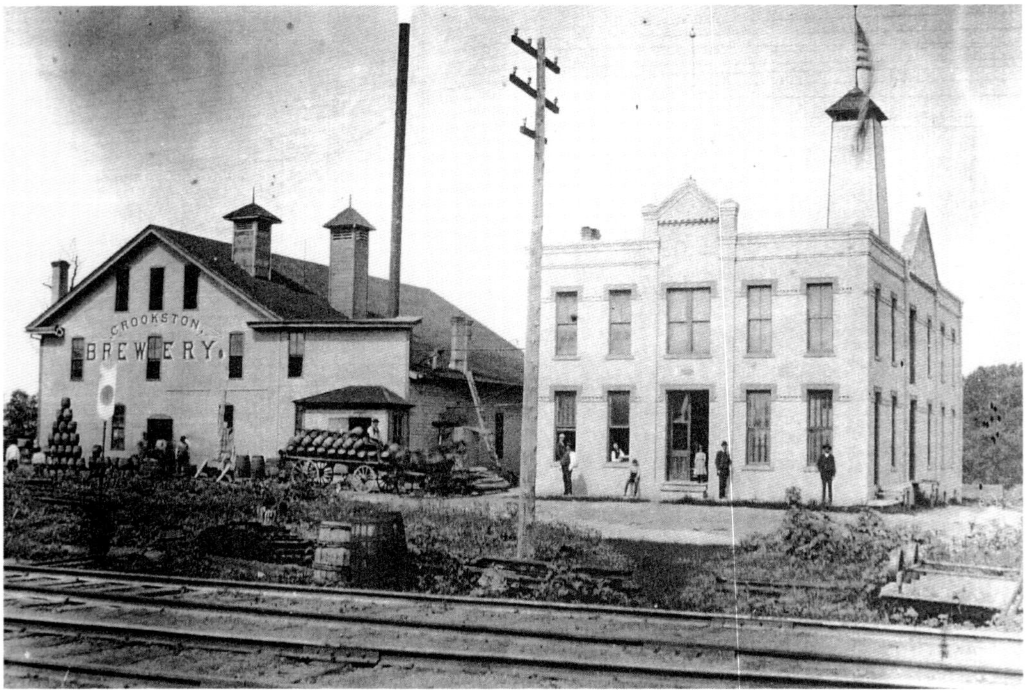

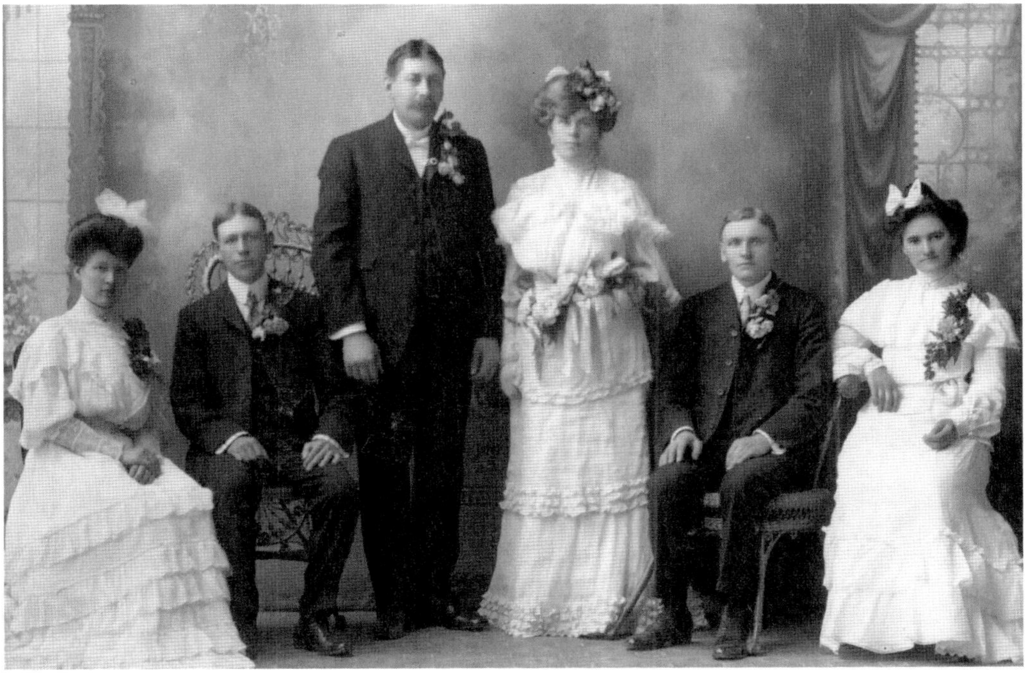

Ole Sundet and Bertha Morgan

Ole O. Sundet was born on November 18, 1868. After a three-month journey, he arrived by oxcart, at age four, at Climax, Minnesota. Ole Sundet and Bertha Morgan had perhaps the biggest and the most unique wedding in the Northwest. The event was witnessed by almost 350 people. They were driven to the Odd Fellows Hall on May 10, 1904, where a band of 24 members of the Improved Order of Red Men of Crookston led a Native American marriage ritual. They offered greetings that translated to, "May the new teepee be ever pitched in pleasant places among forests filled with game." Charles Kiewel gave the couple a dining room set and Mayor Chesterman gave a short address. The G. Oliver Riggs orchestra and Silken Strings played for the dancers upstairs. (Both courtesy of Judy Sundet Keasler.)

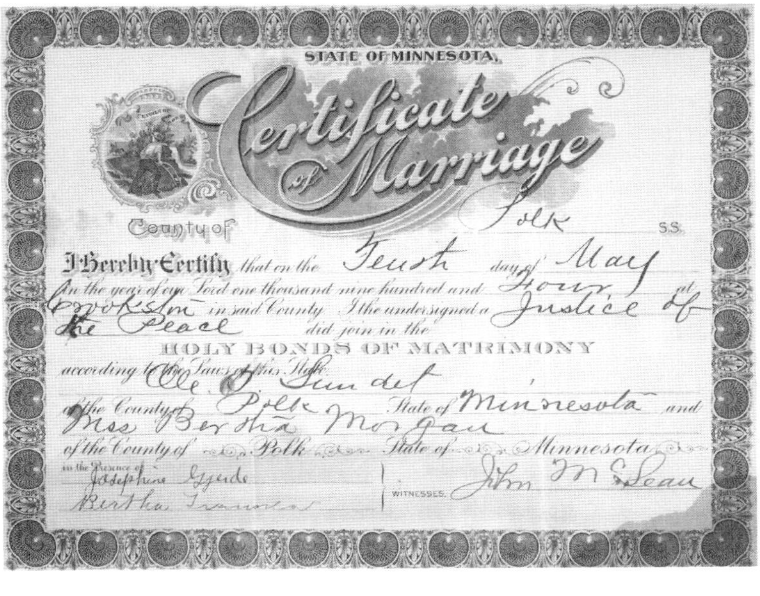

STATE OF MINNESOTA

Certificate of Marriage

County of Polk ss.

I Hereby Certify that on the Tenth day of May
In the year of our Lord one thousand nine hundred and Four at
Crookston in said County I the undersigned a Justice of
the Peace did join in the
HOLY BONDS OF MATRIMONY
according to the Laws of this State
Ole O. Sundet
of the County of Polk State of Minnesota and
Miss Bertha Morgan
of the County of Polk State of Minnesota
in the Presence of
WITNESSES. John McLean

Sam Rosenthal Sr. and Maurice Rosenthal

A prominent Jewish name in Crookston was the Rosenthal family. These Crookston pioneers only have a grave marker at Oakdale Cemetery to serve as a reminder of them. Samuel Rosenthal Sr. was born in Württemberg, Germany, in 1857 and came to America at age 15 in 1872. He married Mollie Falk (1861–1932) of Peru, Indiana, and a few months later they came to Crookston in 1882. He and his brother-in-law Harry L. Falk were the founders of C.O.D. (Clothing of Distinction) at the site of what is now JJ's Body Shop.

They sold House of Kuppenheimer suits for men, considered the highest grade of clothing in America. C.O.D. opened on July 13, 1882, which made it Crookston's oldest continuously running establishment of 40 years when Sam Sr. died on December 13, 1922. The Rosenthals entertained a great deal in their apartment above the C.O.D. store. Harry Falk and his wife, who lived next door, owned the first air conditioner in Crookston.

According to Crookston lore, there was only one grandson, Samuel Rosenthal Jr., who lived above the C.O.D. store with his parents, Maurice and Nella Rosenthal. Maurice had married a Gentile woman, and so all the Rosenthal money was to be passed on to Sammy and a Jewish synagogue. Sammy, born on January 2, 1925, also became the heir of his Uncle Harry Falk's estate since the Falks had no children, but he died in the Army as a private soldier in Texas on June 15, 1944, under mysterious circumstances.

According to an August 5, 1948, *Crookston Daily Times* article when Maurice died, his will stated, "His widow is to be permitted to disperse 35 per cent of the trust as she desires. The remaining 65 per cent is to be distributed by the trustees to exclusively charitable corporations . . . they must agree to expend the proceeds of such property as they may get for charitable purposes in Crookston or in the vicinity of the city." Lee R. Boyd was the will's executor and brother-in-law to Rosenthal. He was also Crookston's engineer and street commissioner.

Maurice's widow, Nella B. Rosenthal, got at least $150,000 and whatever of the remaining wealth once it was all inventoried. The rest of the estate was divided up and kept in a trust at Crookston National Bank and Trust. Some of this Rosenthal money was donated to help build Crookston's new public library in the 1980s. Reverend Oelschlager, representing Friends of the Library, was presented a check for the library's fund on behalf of the Rosenthal estate. (Photograph taken by Steve Hannah.)

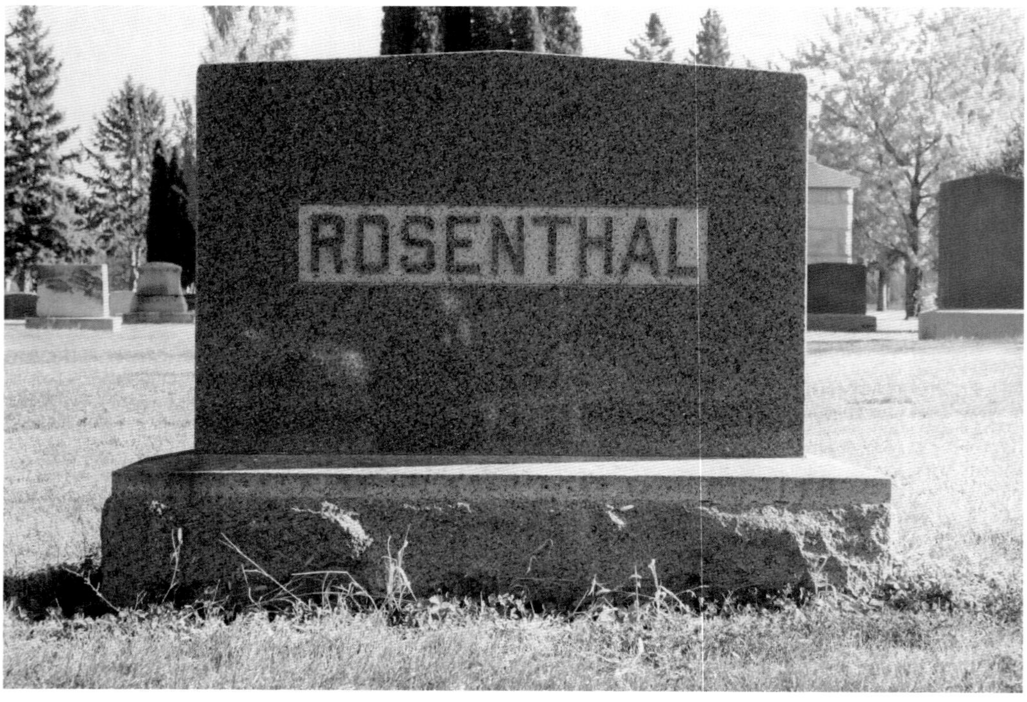

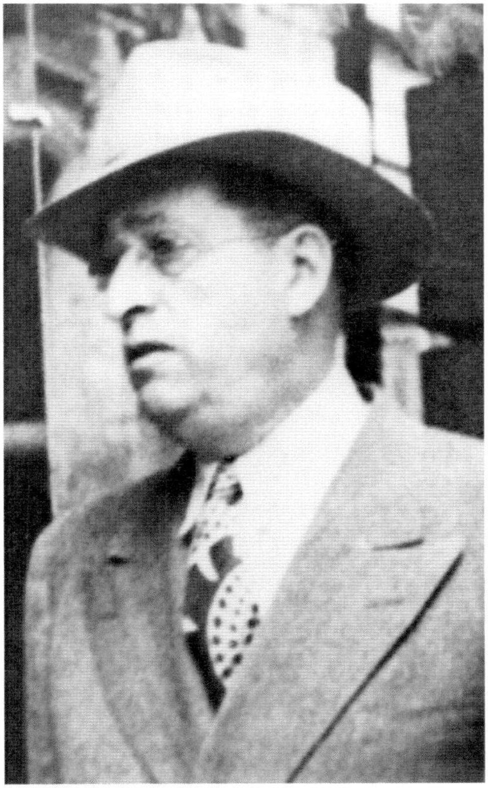

Maurice F. Rosenthal and the C.O.D. Store
Samuel Rosenthal Sr.'s son, Maurice F. Rosenthal, entered the service on May 8, 1918, and was stationed in Syracuse, France, from August 22, 1918, to August 17, 1919. When his father died in 1922, Maurice worked alongside his Uncle Harry in the family business. Maurice and his wife had one son, Samuel F. "Sammy" Rosenthal Jr. When the attic to the C.O.D. building was cleaned out, there were some artifacts left behind, such as a sled Sammy used and a fishing rod Mark Twain had brought as a stage prop when he came to perform in Crookston. Twain was entertained in the Rosenthals' beautiful home, which was featured in *Better Homes and Gardens* magazine in the 1950s.

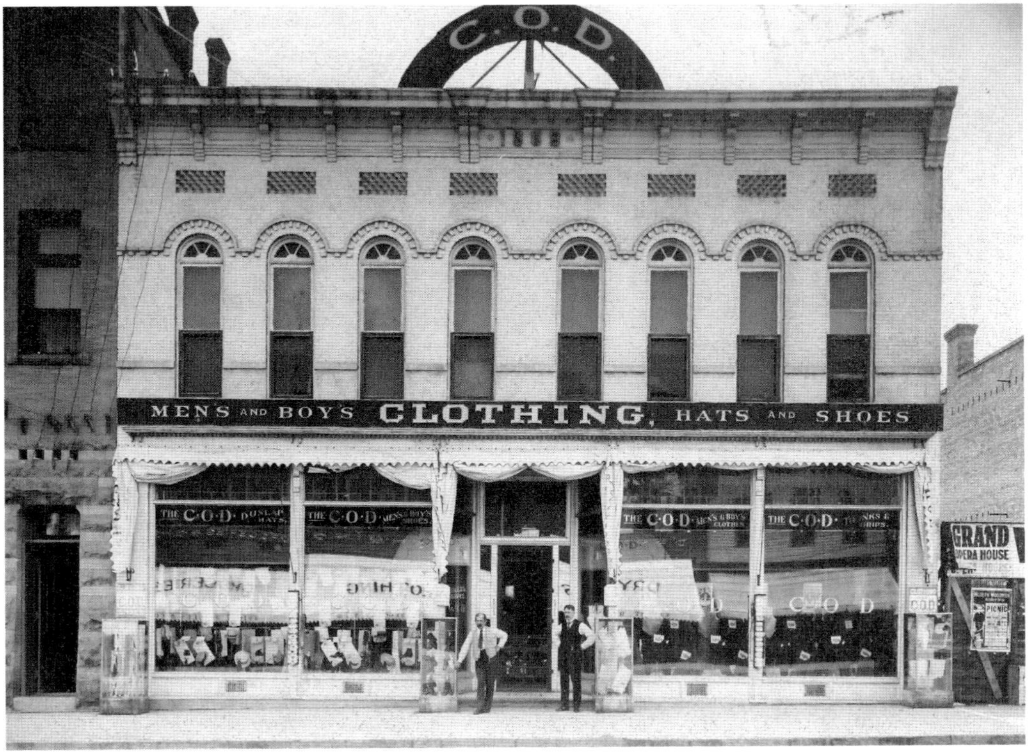

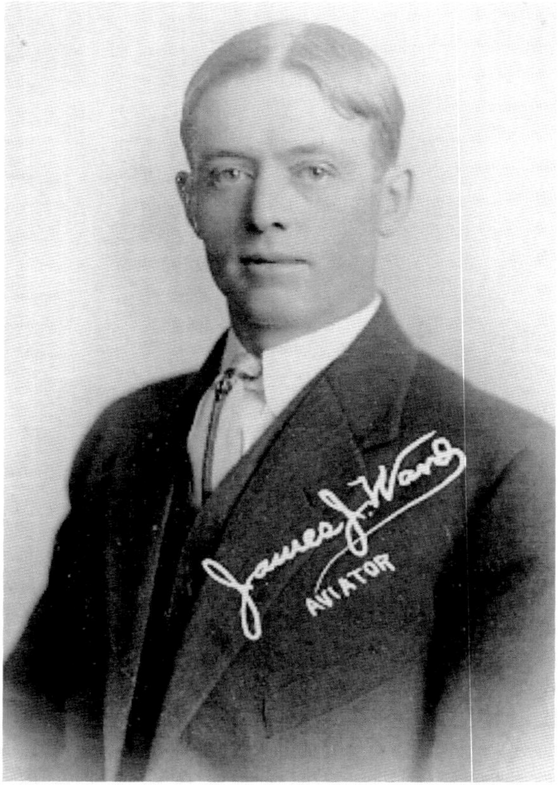

Jimmie Ward, Crookston's Bad Boy

Jens Peter Wilson, also known as Jimmie J. Ward, was born in April 1886, in Denmark, and immigrated with his family to Crookston in 1888. His father, Hans Wilson, was a well digger. Jens wanted nothing to do with manual labor, and by 1900, at age 14, he was already racing cars. Reportedly at odds with his father, Jens headed to the big city of Chicago, which he later claimed to the media to be his hometown. At some point, he also changed his name to Jimmie Ward; he later said that he changed his name because he had gotten so many speeding tickets under the old name. Small for his age (a reported 120 pounds), he was big in boldness. His weight served him well in his chosen career as a pioneer aeronaut. Ward's racing ability was noticed by wealthy aviation pioneer Glenn H. Curtiss. Curtiss saw that Jimmie was fearless flying the Curtiss Pusher airplane.

Originally self-taught as a pilot, as early as April 25, 1910, Jimmie sent postcards sporadically back to his sisters, Thomena and Christina Wilson. His family had moved to St. Hilaire, Minnesota, from Crookston. A portrait head shot on one of the postcards showed Jimmie among an elite group of early daredevil flyers like Whipple Hall, Eugene Ely, J.A.D. McCurdy, Charles F. Willard, and J.C. "Bud" Mars. Jimmie set flight records around the country. He got other awards and trophies that he sent back to his Minnesota family.

Researcher Steven R. Hoffbeck begins his 1995 Minnesota Historical Society journal article about Jimmie with the following quote: "Crookston has no monuments to honor hometown boy James J. Ward, Minnesota's first aviator hero who in 1911 and 1912 made headlines across the nation." According to a January 25, 1912, issue of the *Crookston Daily Times,* Ward made a visit to Crookston, in which he "wore $2,000 worth of diamonds when here and spent the evening with boyhood friends in the new Elks Club room."

Ironically, this man who faced danger weekly while flying early planes died in Florida on December 3, 1923, at the age of 37 from a cerebral hemorrhage. His remains are in an unmarked grave in Chattahoochee, Florida.

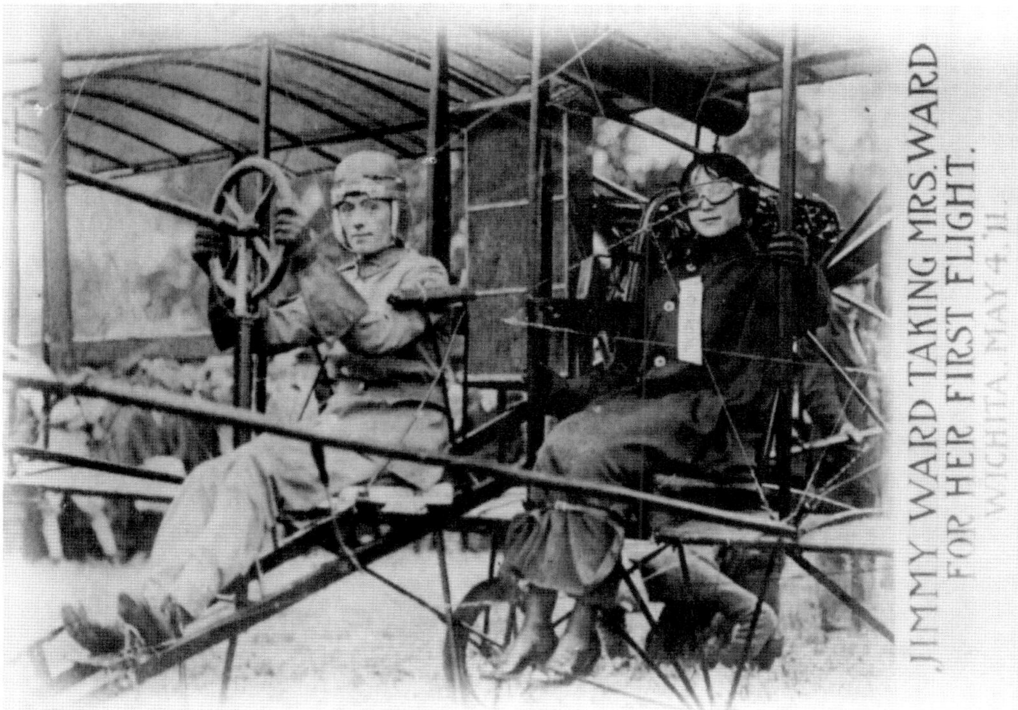

"Jimmie Ward with Mrs. Ward"
Newspapers were sensationalizing Jimmie Ward's story when his lies finally caught up with him. His first wife, Margaret Warner, filed for divorce on bigamy charges. The above photograph, taken on May 4, 1911, shows Jimmie Ward with most likely his second wife, Maud Mauger. There is an April 20, 1919, photograph where Jimmie is with his third wife at San Leon field in Houston, Texas; his third wife may have been the actress who died in a hotel fire in Kansas City, Missouri. At right is a 1917 photograph of Jimmie Ward next to a Curtiss Jenny OX5, an open cockpit biplane, when he was training military fighter pilots in World War I at Kelly Field in Texas. By this time, he did serve his country honorably, if not in obscurity.

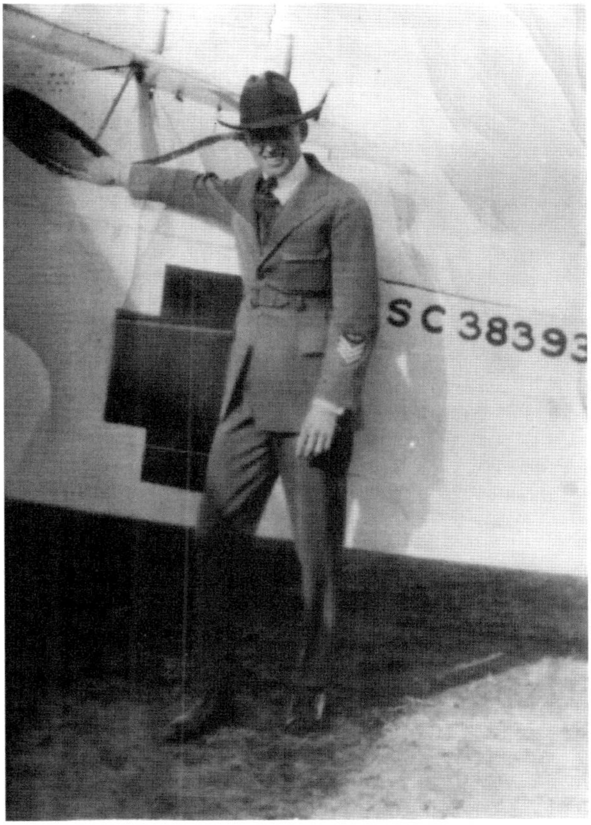

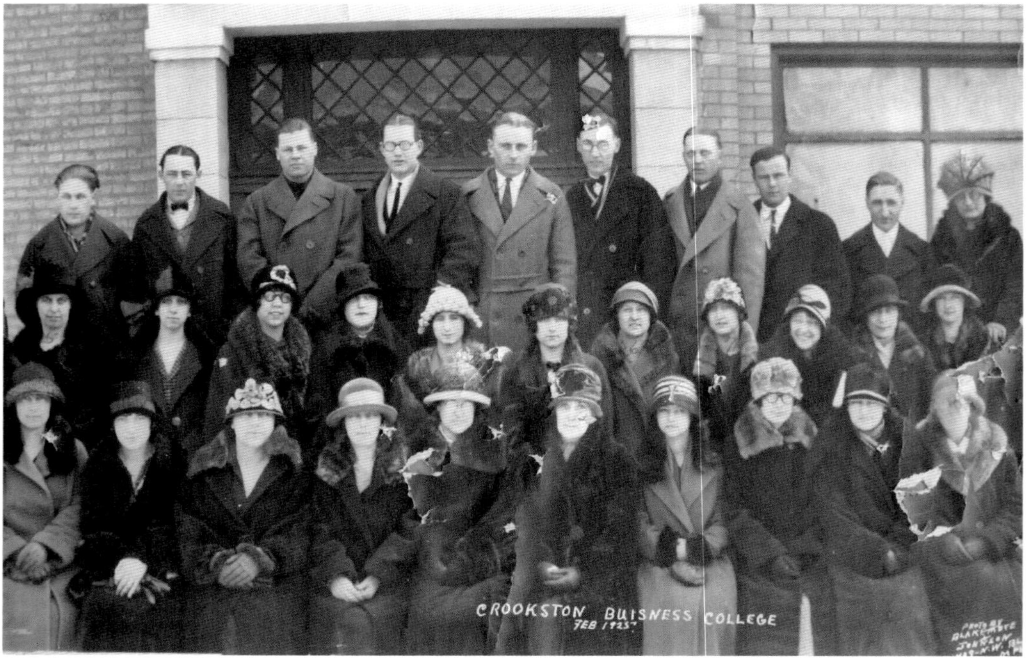

Jacob C. Sathre's Crookston Business College

Note the misspelling of business in "Buisness College"; the Minneapolis photographer must have made the spelling mistake on this February 1925 photograph. The Crookston Business College opened in the fall of 1894. By December 17, 1910, the Crookston College Block was being enlarged. The hats worn by these ladies were typical in the Roaring Twenties. Most of the women are unidentified; however, the first five women in the first row, from left to right, are Cora Miller, unidentified, Mrs. W.H. Kellogg, Karen Sathre, and Othilda (Tillie) Sathre. Behind Cora Miller is Louise Rasmussen; behind Mrs. W.H. Kellogg is Emma Sylvester Lee. Two others in second row are identified as Gertrude Jacobson and Nellie Peterson Oppegaard. The photograph below is of the Crookston College with the Robert Street Bridge on the far left. (Below, courtesy of Margaret Childs Rose.)

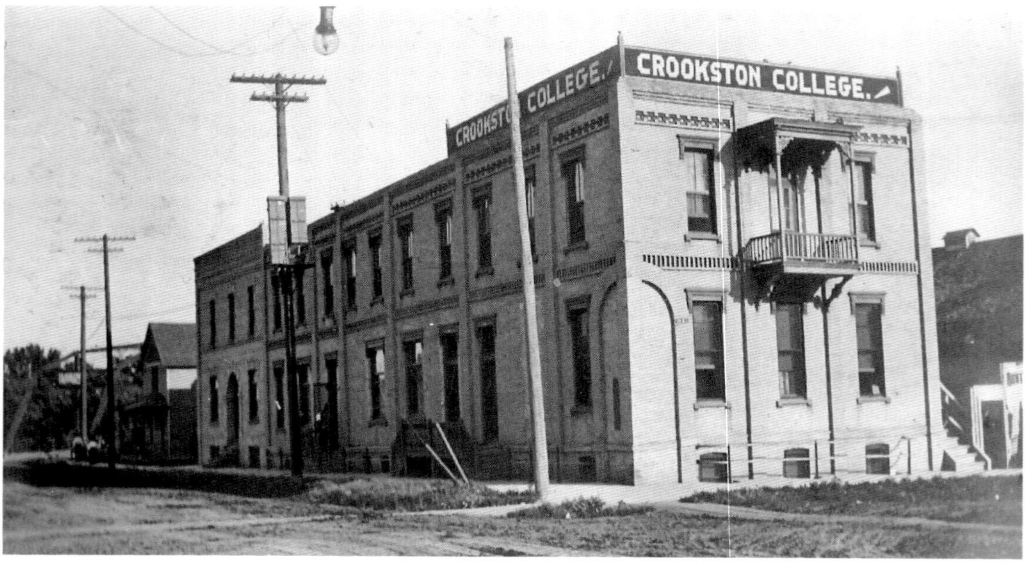

CHAPTER TWO

Exemplary Military

Crookston has always had a patriotic spirit. Through the years, many of our finest men and women have served in foreign wars. Once they returned, they led by example in their professions in civilian life. Some of those war heroes are represented wearing uniforms in photographs throughout the pages of this book.

On July 6, 2002, at the dedication of a veterans memorial east of Crookston on Fairfax Avenue, KROX radio announcer Don Mulvaney read a poignant poem over the KROX airwaves. The following poem, "It is the Soldier," was written by Charles Michael Province, US Army:

> It is the Soldier, not the minister, who has given us freedom of religion. / It is the Soldier, not the reporter, who has given us freedom of the press. / It is the Soldier, not the poet, who has given us freedom of speech. / It is the Soldier, not the campus organizer, who has given us freedom to protest. It is the Soldier, not the lawyer, who has given us the right to a fair trial. / It is the Soldier, not the politician, who has given us the right to vote. / It is the Soldier who salutes the flag, who serves beneath the flag, and whose coffin is draped by the flag, who allows the protester to burn the flag.

After a two-year campaign to raise $90,000, the Crookston Veterans Memorial Walkway leads to the polished black granite piece that is the veterans memorial. Etched in stone is "Poor is the community / which has no heroes, / poorer still / is the community / which has them, / but forgets." Crookston has American flags all along the path that leads to the memorial on display during Memorial Day and Fourth of July week. May the people from the city of Crookston never forget the ultimate sacrifice made by those soldiers who did not return and also by those who did. They are heroes.

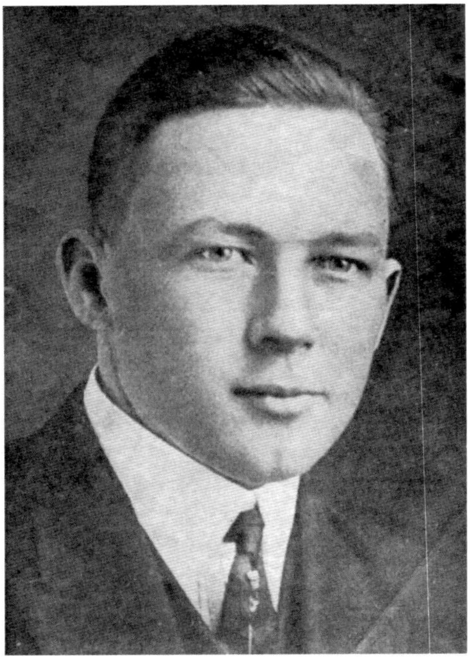

Nels T. Wold, Congressional Medal of Honor Recipient

Crookston's American Legion Post No. 20 is named for Congressional Medal of Honor recipient Nels T. Wold. In 1895, Nels was born to Tidemand and Klara Wold in Winger, Minnesota, the eighth of ten children. By age 17, he was orphaned and had taken over his dad's farming and blacksmith work. On April 12, 1918, he reported in Crookston and was sent off to France to fight in World War I. Nels died on September 26, 1918, only a few months after he left home and just a few weeks before the war ended.

Before he died, he wrote to his sister Inga, "I am laying in the grass under a big shade tree and taking a good rest. It is very pleasant and beautiful around here now." Soon after, he was positioned at the spear point of the long Meuse-Argonne front; he was one of 400,000 American soldiers flanked across France by millions of British, French, and other Allied troops.

Military historian Clair Kenamore's 1919 book describes what happened the day Nels died—in a chapter titled, "Nels Wold's Glorious Death." The following is taken from that chapter:

> With the fog lifted and deep behind adversary lines, Nels' new mission was to destroy enemy positions. The team located a German machine gun nest in a clump of bushes and deemed it too dangerous to attack head-on. Wold volunteered and received permission to crawl to the position and investigate. The rest of his group took cover while Nels crept to the rear of the emplacement and killed two occupants and captured three. Private Nels Wold's combat group advanced on, clearing ambuscades, sniper posts and gun emplacements . . . Nels' success ran out when he met his demise by machine gun fire while penetrating a camouflage screen which concealed the fifth location.

Nels's acts of heroism were read to troops to embolden them in the final weeks leading to the end of World War I. Nels's "superlative deeds of daring, for gallantry beyond the call of duty, were of such merit as to demand a conspicuous and special fame."

Two men carried Nels's body a mile from the front lines. Before he died, he reportedly told them, "Pray for me boys, and write my folks and tell them I love them all." He was initially buried near Cheppy, France, from which his remains were brought to rest in Winger. Congressional Medal of Honor holders are honored with a beautiful, huge monument in Indianapolis, Indiana. This Minnesota boy's name is there.

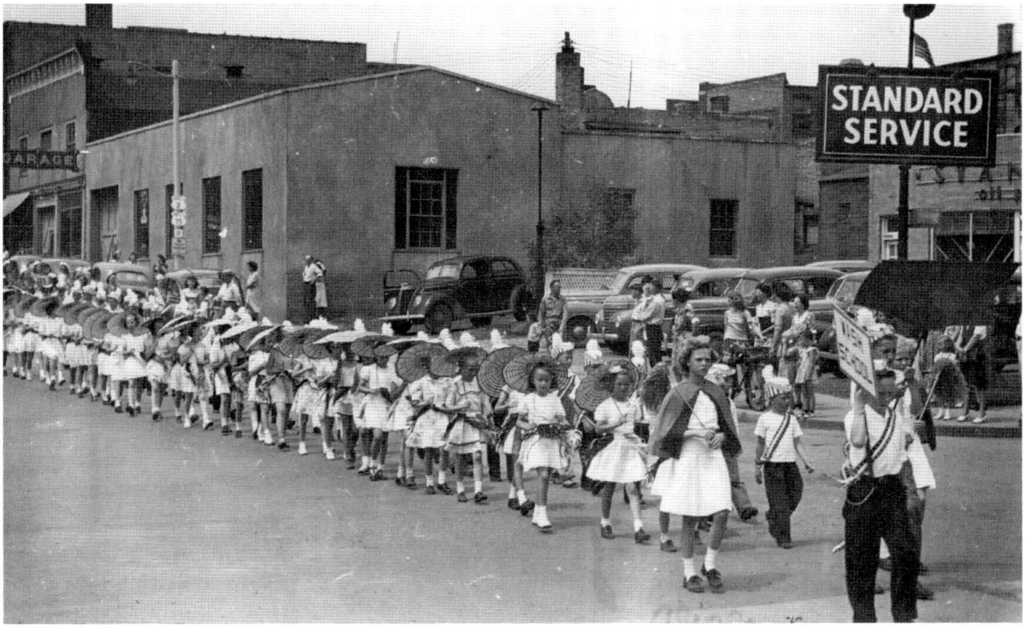

Nels T. Wold Honored 24 Years Later

In 1942, a group of Washington School students with parasols were at the beginning of this Memorial Day parade along East Robert Street. The parade shows a memorial banner honoring Nels T. Wold. Every November 11 at 11:11 a.m., college students with military experience go to the flagpole and hoist up the American flag—a University of Minnesota, Crookston (UMC) tradition. Afterwards, no matter how cold it gets, the assembly of people moves to the campus's war memorial, located near the entrance of the campus. The veterans of all foreign wars are honored with a wreath.

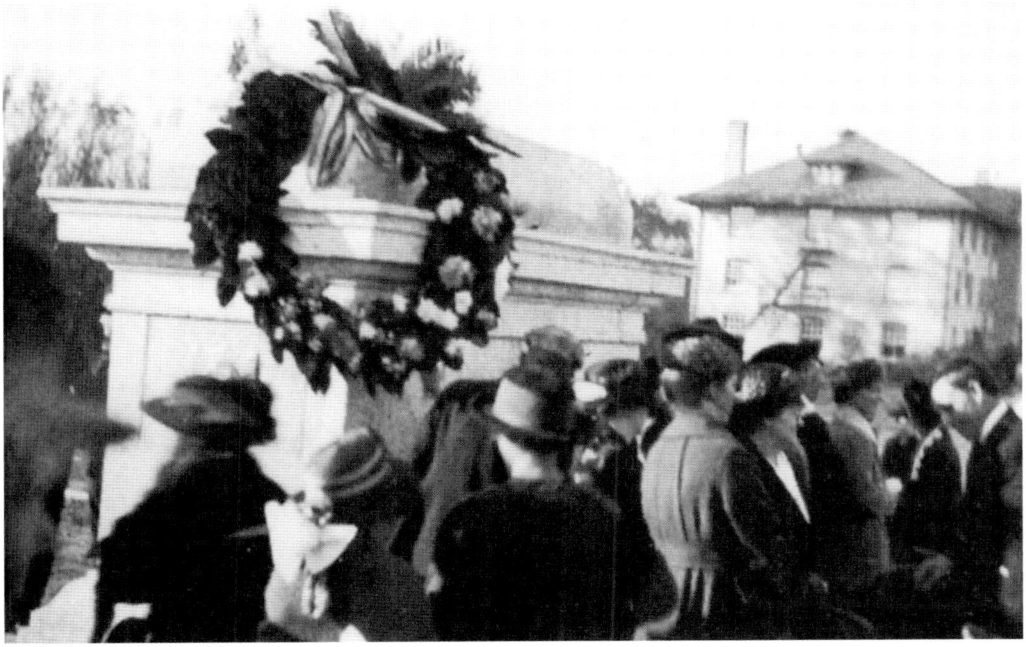

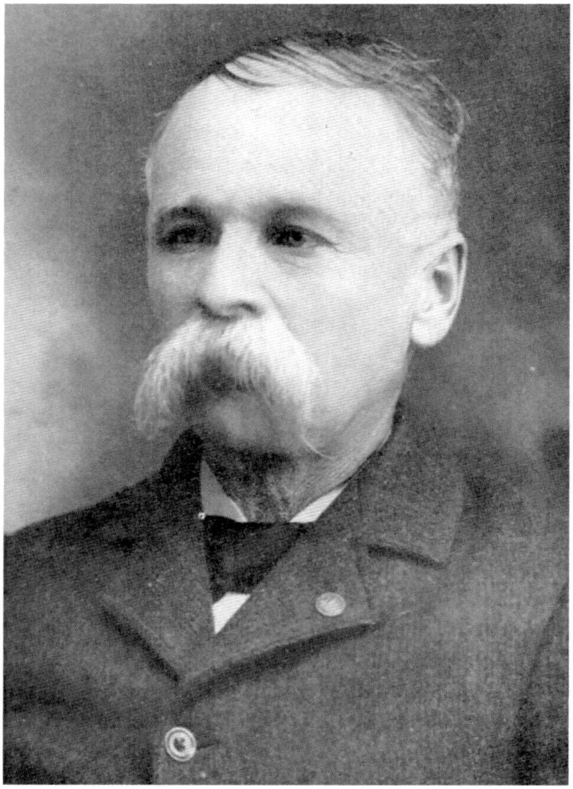

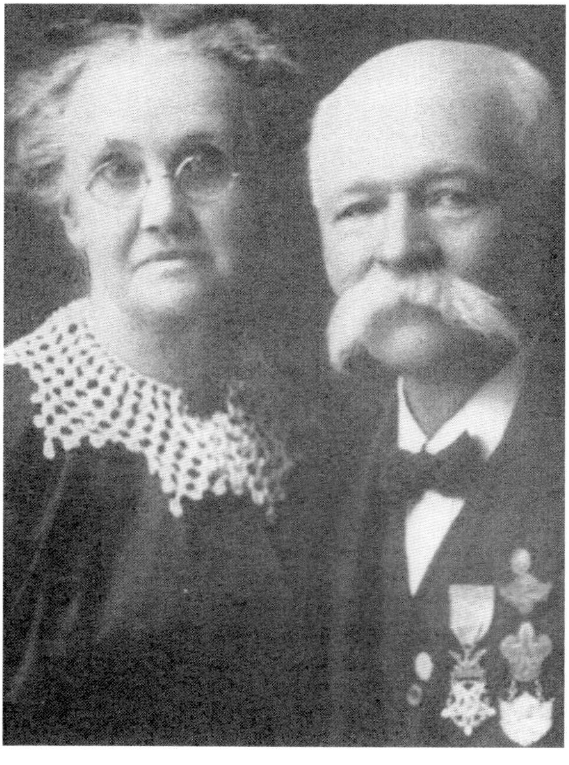

Andrew J. Kelley, Civil War Veteran
Andrew J. Kelley's Civil War Citation of Valor reads, "Mr. Kelley conducted himself with credit throughout the war, distinguishing himself at Knoxville, Tennessee where on November 20, 1863, he led a party of six in firing a stone mansion which was the key to the Confederate position. In recognition of this service, Congress voted him a Medal of Gallantry." He and his wife, Ella, had seven children, three boys and four girls.

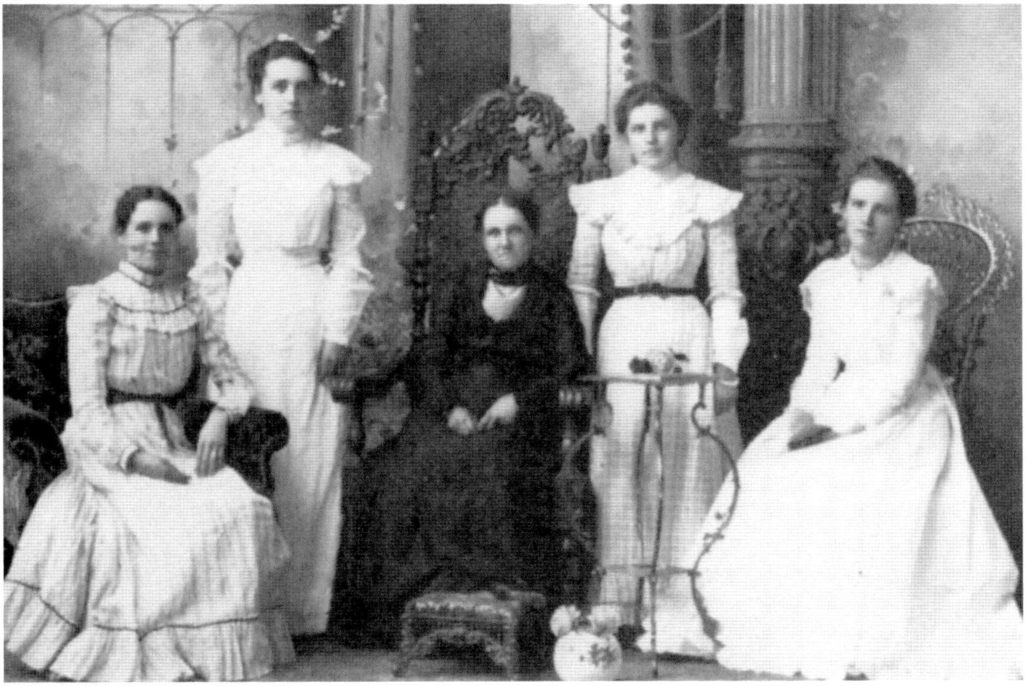

Andrew J. Kelley's Girls

Ella (Fleming) Kelley (seated center) was the daughter of a Presbyterian minister. The Kelley couple's four daughters were named Clara, Mabel, Maude, and Lulu. Supposedly, Clara was the first white child born in the Crookston area.

Andrew J. Kelley was born in Indiana on September 2, 1845, and later, his family moved to Michigan. In 1862, when A.J. Kelley was 17 years old, he enlisted to fight in the Civil War. Kelley came from a military family. His grandfather, also named Andrew Kelley, fought in the Revolutionary War under Gen. George Washington. His father, John Kelley, was a soldier in the War of 1812 and fought under Harrison at Tippecanoe. A.J. Kelley served as a sergeant in the Union army. He was awarded the Congressional Medal of Honor when he served as a private in Company E, 17th Michigan Infantry for action on November 20, 1863, at Knoxville, Tennessee. Another citation reads, "Having voluntarily accompanied a small party to destroy buildings within the enemy's lines whence sharpshooters had been firing, Kelley disregarded an order to retire, remained, and completed the firing of the buildings, thus insuring their total destruction; this at the imminent risk of his life from the fire of the advancing enemy."

Kelley engaged in and survived nearly 30 battles. After returning to his Michigan home, he read a description about the Red River Valley and eventually moved his family to a simple shack on his Crookston homestead in 1873. With his growing family, he eventually built a nice house, which was the only one on the prairie between Crookston and the Red Lake agency. Indians would often visit his place for food, and they were always civil. One time, the Native Americans "borrowed" Kelley's ax, but he went after them to retrieve his much-needed possession.

Kelley served as city clerk since the town of Crookston was organized. Kelley was the first Sunday school superintendent in Crookston, presiding over a Union Church Sunday school, which he started in 1874. He rejoiced to see Crookston go dry, perhaps because he saw the effects liquor had on some locals, including the day laborers who worked on the railroad and at the sawmill. A.J. Kelley died on June 4, 1918.

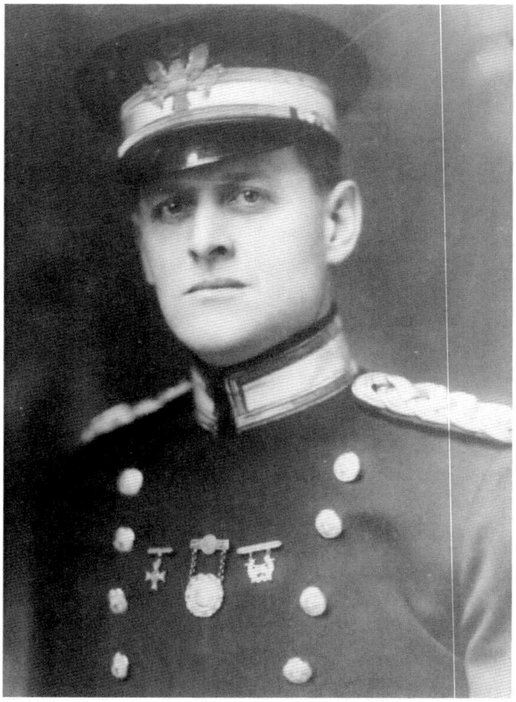

Peter J. Eide, World War I Hero
Peter J. Eide was born on October 7, 1878, in Polk County's Roome Township. An older officer, he wrote his wife, Erica Eide (née Danielson), from France during World War I. His April 13, 1918, letter was published in the *Crookston Daily Times* under the headline, "Local Man Writes from West Front." It reads:

> After one of our battles I stayed up all night and helped care for the wounded. During a battle and after it is over, all the slightly wounded make their way to the dressing station. Those totally disabled must wait until someone picks them up and carries them away. In this particular engagement, we gained our objective but had heavy casualties and the Boche lost more than we did. When the objective was gained, it was pitch dark and we had many helplessly wounded behind us in the woods we had gone through. I decided I was going to do what I could as I had gotten through without a scratch for which I thanked the good Lord. You have often heard said that the freedom of mankind is a costly and precious thing, well you bet it is. When you see stretcher upon stretcher come along with some gallant American boy all shot to pieces, maybe he has a chance for life, but even so only to be an invalid. Many die on the way to the dressing station. After being an eye witness to all this, I realize more than ever before the debt we owe those who fought for the freedom we have enjoyed so many years. Our American boys are gallant. These are not things to be frightened over—it is just the price that must be paid for freedom and let us hope that when this war is over all mankind may enjoy freedom and that they may never again be called to spill blood to maintain it.

The *Crookston Daily Times* reported that, upon Lt. Peter J. Eide's return to Crookston, he became an idol of the younger generation. He was given a rousing reception at the Northern Pacific depot. The Crookston Juvenile Band played while the crowd cheered. Inexplicably, the sun that had been blocked by clouds for two days appeared, throwing a distinct rainbow to the east. It was a good omen for a man returning home. Eide began and ended his Army career at Camp Dodge. He was the first commander of the Nels T. Wold Post No. 20. He owned a confectionery and raised a family in Crookston. He died on March 16, 1970.

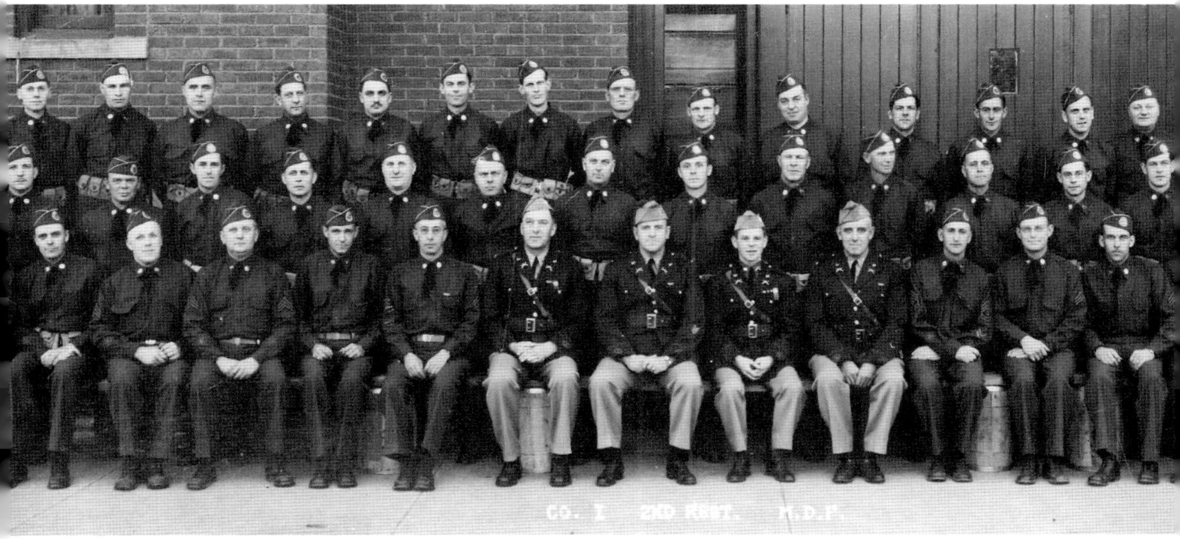

Peter J. Eide and the National Guard Armory

The above photograph taken by Benson Studio shows Company I, 2nd Regiment, sitting in front of the armory at 416 North Broadway. Peter J. Eide was elected captain of Company I on February 25, 1911. Three years later, Captain Eide proposed that Crookston should have an armory. He envisioned the armory as having many uses for conventions, shows, and dances. Later, the armory was used for Friday night dances or "sock hops." Below are Crookston representatives from different military branches, marching south in a summer parade on South Broadway. Wearing a white shirt is Dick Seddon; to the left of him is Harry McFarlane, and Robert Wilkins is to the left of Harry McFarlane. (Bottom photograph by Don Buness.)

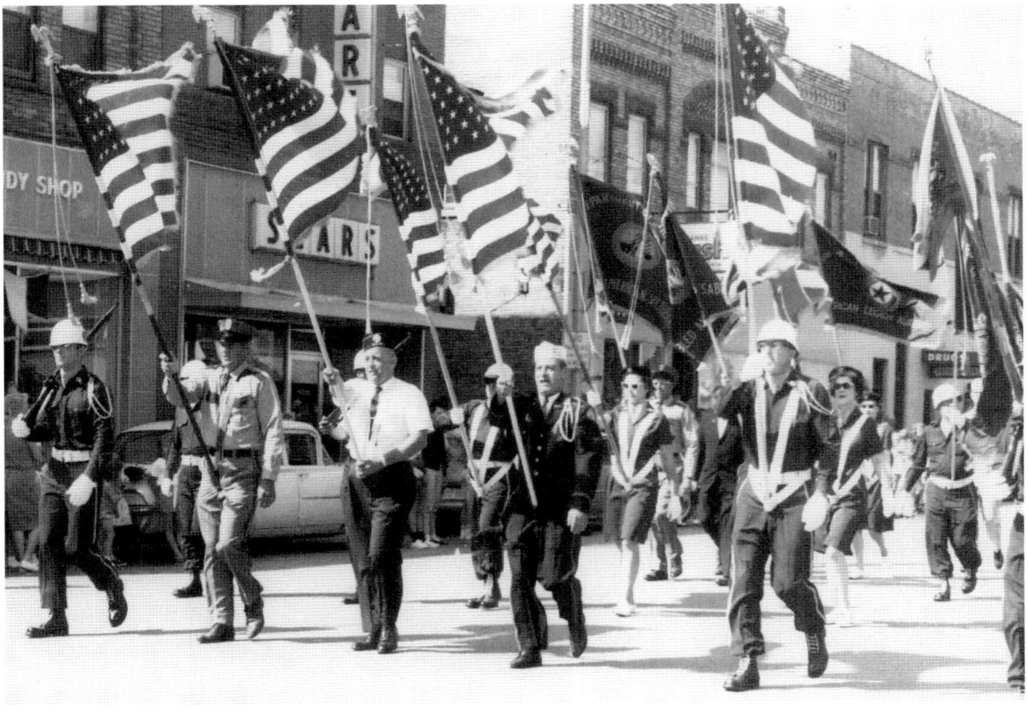

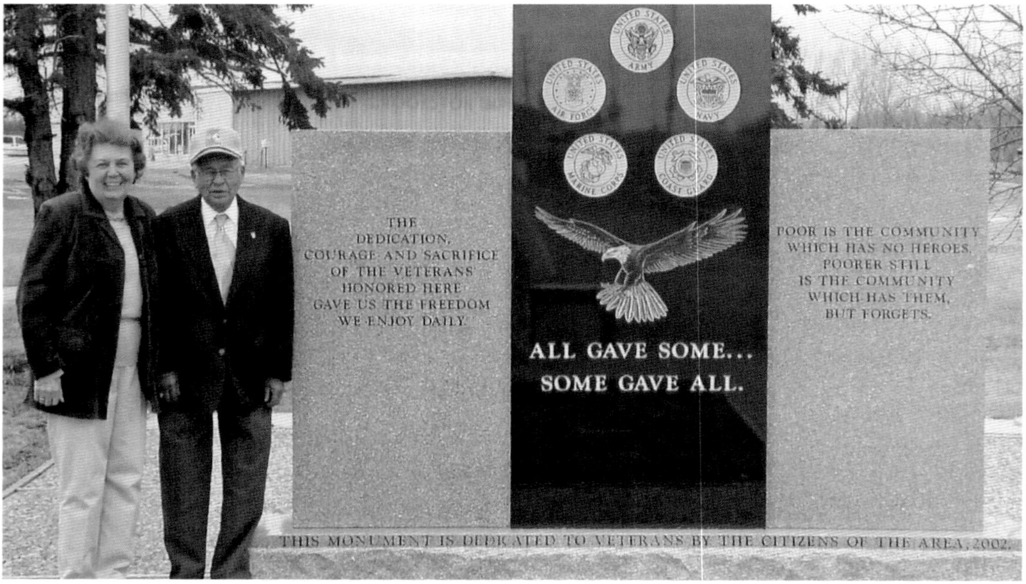

Murray and Darlene Warren

Murray Lee Warren, born on May 22, 1924, enlisted in the Army on December 3, 1942. He entered active service on April 2, 1943, and received basic medical and engineering training before being assigned to the signal corps, where he was instructed in telegraph and telephone installation, operation, and repair. He departed for the China-Burma-India (CBI) Theater of Operations on January 11, 1945, by transport ship through the South Pacific, by way of Australia. He arrived in India on February 20, 1945. He remained in India and Burma, mainly working to maintain communications along the Ledo Road, which was under construction as an overland supply route to China. On at least one occasion, he flew in a supply plane on a dangerous "over the hump" mission, meaning over the Eastern Himalayan Mountains from India to Burma and China.

By the time he left Burma on February 22, 1946, the Ledo Road was open, the war was officially over, and the world was returning to normal. However, as Murray recalls, tensions in China were noticeably increasing. Once the hostilities with Japan ended, the Chinese internal struggles resumed. Civil war broke out, which was destined to bring communism to China. As Murray was preparing to leave Burma, he witnessed efforts being made to evacuate any remaining Americans from China via routes that had only recently been used against Japan. Murray returned home to the United States on March 19, 1946, and was honorably discharged on March 25, 1946, with a rank of Tech-5 (Technician Fifth Grade).

Because of Murray's overseas experiences, a few phrases in foreign languages were used in the Warren home. One of his daughters wrote the following:

> I remember Dad telling me about his journey with other GIs "over the hump" sitting in the cargo hold of a supply plane. Dad says it was very dark, cold and very, very loud! They landed on a dirt runway somewhere in Burma, were given a compass and some general coordinates, and sent off into the jungle to hook up with their assigned unit. (Imagine that in today's world of GPS technology!) Dad also told me that day-to-day life wasn't what he would call "dangerous." Malaria and sniper fire were the two most common dangers. I asked Dad if he'd ever been shot at. He replied, "Not that I know of," then winked at me. Not sure what that meant!

The Warrens are pictured next to the Crookston Veterans Memorial on the east side of Crookston on East Fairfax Avenue. A man and woman saluting are etched into the stone and another quote reads, "The dedication, / courage and sacrifice / of the veterans / honored here / gave us the freedom / we enjoy daily." (Courtesy of Leah Warren Volker.)

CHAPTER THREE

Open for Business

In the early days, Crookston needed builders, brick manufacturers, architects, and engineers to construct the downtown district that ran alongside the main artery of railroad transportation. In the 1920s, the Chris Eickhof family started out by buying the Sash and Door Building off North Main Street. This north section of town, adjacent to the curve of the Red Lake River near Front Street, used to be the major hub of activity in the very early days.

Many people may have forgotten that not too long ago, Crookston was known as the "Little Mayo of the North." Pioneer Dr. Halvor and Henrietta Holte had much to do with that hard-earned reputation. Dr. and Mrs. Holte, alongside other angels of mercy, gave selflessly of their time and talents to make sure people experienced healing in the then new Bethesda Hospital along Woodland Avenue. A hundred years ago, people thought hospitals were a place to die, not to recover. Impassable, muddy roads or severe cold weather made it very arduous for a doctor to make house calls to the surrounding farms. It was better that patients came to a central, well-equipped place. The Holtes convinced the Crookston community to buy shares at $1 annually to be treated each year or pay $10 for a lifetime membership. Even today, RiverView Hospital remains a member association.

Old-time Crookstonites have fond memories of business proprietors. Some iconic places and people featured in this chapter are the Grand Theater before its remodeling, the outdoor municipal swimming pool, Widman's Candy store, Sundet's Hobby Shop, the Carnegie library, and the KROX Radio station. There may not be entirely fond memories of St. Vincent or Bethesda Hospitals or the Northwestern Clinic—but as a result of good medical care, Crookstonites have lived longer and more productive lives! Many physicians in the 1950s and 1960s came to serve the people of Crookston in their specific fields of expertise. Everyone has a story about their favorite doctor, such as one physician who was asked by a young mother how she could prevent her children from getting strep throat, one after the other. His answer for a quick remedy—"Burn the house down."

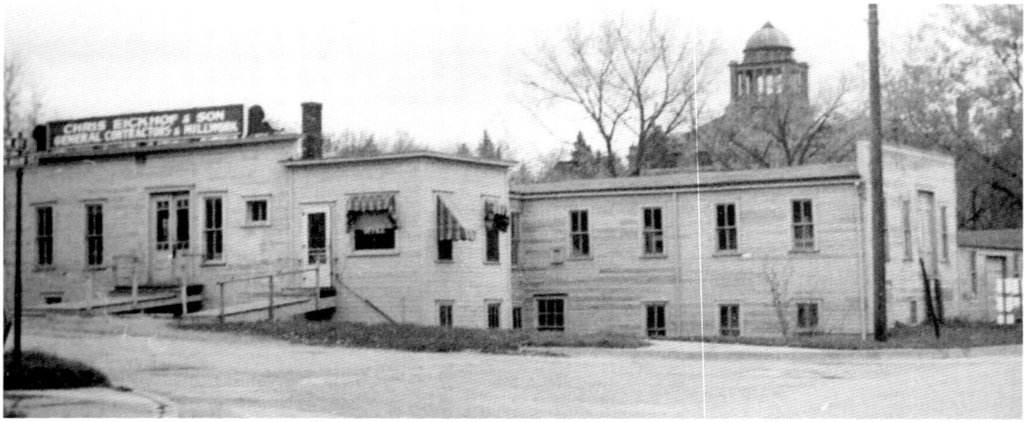

Chris Eickhof and Family

Pictured above is the original Sash and Door Company at 604–606 North Main Street. This business, purchased on April 20, 1923, was used exclusively by Chris Eickhof and Sons by 1926. By 1953, the Eickhofs were busy builders in Crookston and the outlying area. Close by their place of business was the original Eickhof home, located at 510 North Front, as seen below. Below, this 1907 wedding photograph of Dora Eickhof and Arthur Ziaser shows many relatives. Among those attending were the Bill McCaffery and Ziaser families, Ann Laughlin, Nettie Eickhof Wentzel, Lena Hoeft, Laura Risch, Edward Risch, Herman Eickhof, Gus Sommer, Presbyterian reverend Wilfred Ward, Hannah Eickhof Sommer, John Eickhof, Marguerite R. Kopp, Julia Bloom, Clara Eickhof, and Chris and Johanna Eickhof. The following is written on the back of the photograph: "Otto is standing behind his mother Johanna, maybe tickling her." Otto is second from the far right. (Both courtesy of Paul Eickhof.)

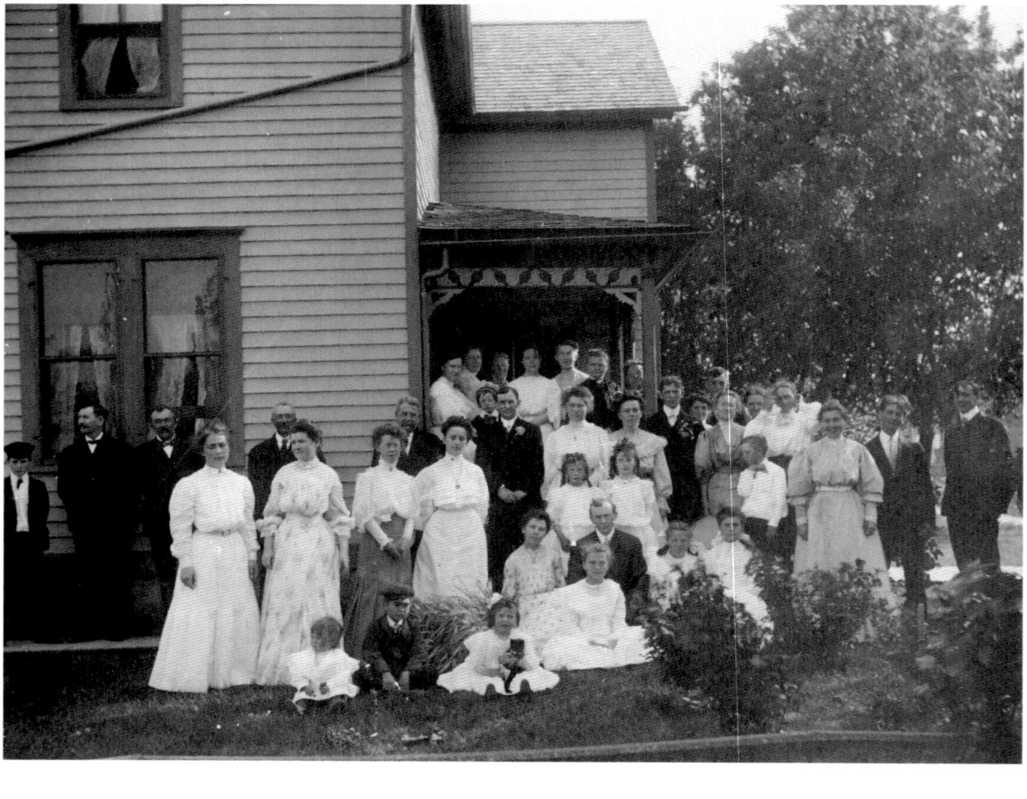

Otto Eickhof

Otto John Eickhof (right), born on October 13, 1887, is shaking hands with Herman Miller (left). (The other men are unidentified.) For years, Otto was a main source of information about early Crookston since his parents, Chris and Johanna, were some of the later pioneers in Crookston. He graduated from the Crookston Business College in 1906 and went on to Hughes Business College. Otto was a good businessman and built up Eickhof and Sons, Inc. There are many well-built structures that can be credited to the Eickhof construction firm. Today, sturdy structures erected by the Eickhofs used mainly for education or for business are the following: Polk County State Bank (Tri-Valley), Eagles Building, Bethesda Hospital (RiverView), Northwestern Bell Telephone Building, St. Francis Hospital (Summit/Villa), Highland Middle School, and Washington Elementary School. Buildings on the UMC campus include McCall, Hill, and Dowell Halls along with reconstruction of the Kiehle gym into the present Kiehle Auditorium. Some structures that no longer exist are the Ottertail Power Company Building, where the old lumber mill used to be, built in 1926, and the 1953 outdoor pool, which is where the new library now stands.

Otto was a charter member of the Crookston Rotary Club with the early motto "One profits most who serves best." That Rotary motto eventually changed to "Service above self." The Four-Way Test for Rotarians includes the following: "Is it the truth? Is it fair to all concerned? Will it bring goodwill and better friendships? Will it be beneficial to all concerned?" It was known that Otto would never miss a Rotary meeting, even when out of town. He would make sure to attend a meeting in order to have perfect attendance for 40 years.

Otto and Denora (Borsheim) Eickhof (1889–1976) celebrated their 50th wedding anniversary in 1968. They lived in their brick home on 549 Summit Avenue, which had been erected by Eickhof Construction. When the Benedictine sisters saw how well constructed the Summit Avenue house was, they awarded the contract to the Eickhof Construction to build St. Francis Hospital in the 1950s.

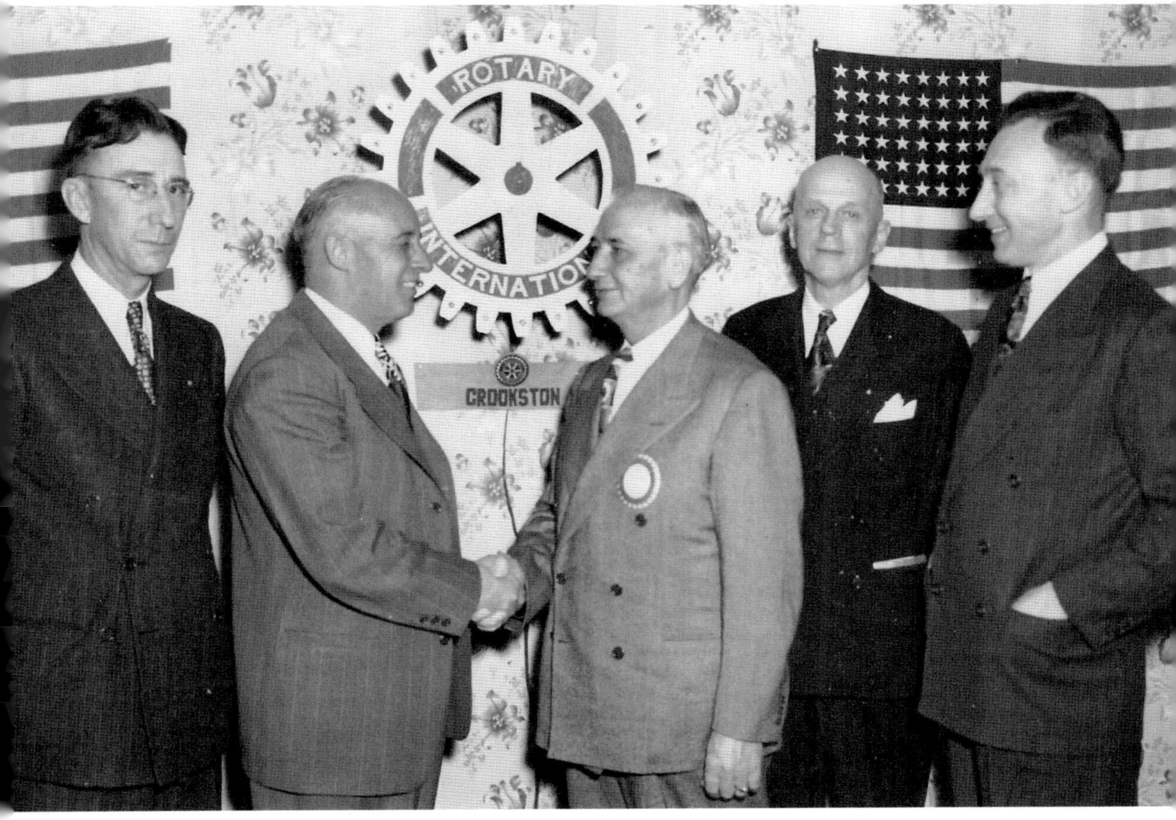

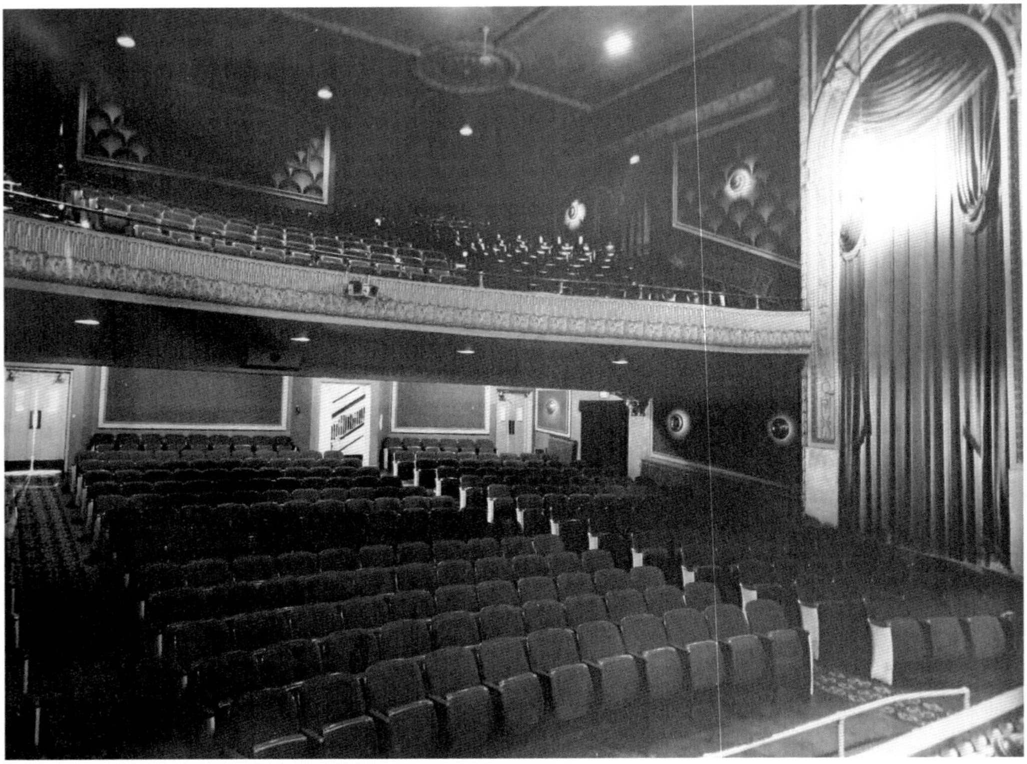

Charles Hiller and Sons

Three generations of Hillers ran the Grand Theater. According to a November 5, 1910, *Crookston Daily Times* article, the 1910 Grand Theater was built at a cost of $50,000, which included equipment, by investors from the Twin Cities and was located at 124 East Second Street. The Hiller family became operators of the Grand Theater after 1918, when Charles Hiller and a partner named Hays became co-managers. Sometime in the 1920s, Charles Hiller and Hays purchased the Grand Theater from the Minneapolis firm, and later, Charles Hiller bought out Hays's share.

This old Grand Theater building originally had a house capacity of 875 seats and Art Deco lighting fixtures. For the performers, there were nine dressing rooms, with hot and cold running water—an extravagance at the time. The stage had a proscenium opening more than 30 feet wide and a depth of 28 feet between the curtain line and the rear wall. The height to the rigging loft was 42 feet. The Grand hosted some of the best vaudeville and stage players in the early part of the century.

According to Crookston historian Russ Sundet, magician Harry Blackstone (and his identical twin) would disappear in one spot but show up elsewhere! Maude Adams and James O'Neill as well as Boris Karloff, of monster-movie fame, made their appearances. Sunday nights were really the big nights for the Grand because of the blue laws in North Dakota forbidding business on Sunday, which brought show-goers from there to Crookston.

Charles "Duckie" Hiller was a vaudeville performer, musician, and soloist. (For more information see page 105.) He was a world-ranked saxophonist and also played the drums and violin. If the orchestra was missing a musician, Hiller would jump down to the orchestra pit and play whatever instrument was needed. In April 1929, he began to measure the demand for talking films, and in October 1929, he contracted for Warner Bros. films. Hiller had the Grand extensively remodeled in 1933 to accommodate movies, cutting back the seating capacity to 670 seats and making room for a projection booth.

Ernotte Hiller, Charles's son, was the second generation of Hillers to manage the theater. He took over after he returned from serving in World War II. Ernotte Hiller died in 1973, which was the same year his son Jeff Hiller, a member of the third generation, took over. (Photograph taken by Wayne Anderson.)

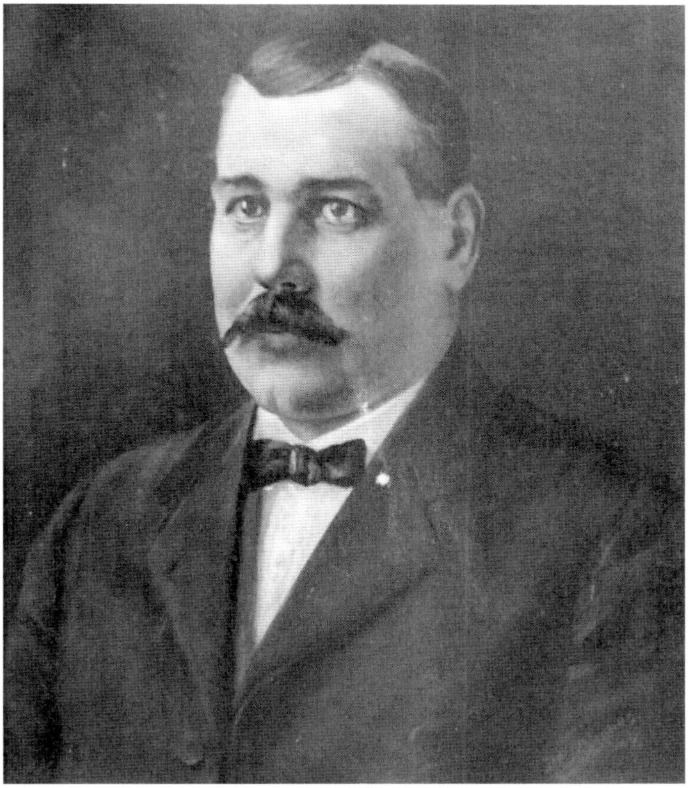

Peter H. Gramer

P.H. "Pete" Gramer came to Crookston in the late 1890s and was financially successful in Crookston's concrete and culvert business. Pete had grown up on a large farm right next door to the famous car manufacturer Henry Ford and his family farm, in what is now known as Dearborn, Michigan. Henry Ford, Pete and Joseph Gramer, and the other siblings were all best friends growing up. They all attended the same one-room schoolhouse together back in the 1870s. There is documentation of this in the Henry Ford Museum and also in a Gramer history book put together by a Michigan relative, Laura Gramer Haldane, published in 2012. Naturally, Pete was one of the first to own a Ford car in Crookston after traveling as a salesman in the earlier days by train or horse and buggy.

Also, Pete Gramer had been an entrepreneur when it came to working with farm machinery. He started a large custom steam-powered threshing business and worked the wheat harvests from Kansas up to the Dalrymple Bonanza Farms of North Dakota. Once Pete started a family, they settled in the Fargo, North Dakota, area where he worked with the culvert industry before he moved his family to Crookston. Pete was good with languages and mixed well as a salesman with Germans and Scandinavians.

By August 1906, Crookstonites knew they needed a public bath. The *Crookston Daily Times* reported that there had been too many river drownings. Unfortunately, Pete's eight-year-old son Bobby drowned one hot July day in the Red Lake River near where Mount St. Benedict is located. Pete grieved and did not want any other Crookston family to suffer such a loss, so he started a fund drive to erect a public swimming pool in Crookston.

Pete did very well in his business as a traveling salesman. He and his wife, Mary, lived on 717 North Broadway. Another bad year for the Gramers was 1915 when on January 30 their home was partially burned. Also, according to the *Crookston Daily Times*, the Gramer home was burglarized on July 31. This portrait was an actual oil painting done of him that remains in the family to this day. (Courtesy of Ron Gramer.)

Dr. Halvor Holte and Bethesda Hospital

Halvor Holte was born on July 11, 1857, on a farm in Selland, Stavanger, Norway. As a thoroughgoing Norwegian man, he did not have an easy life. Yet it would seem that his life mission was to take away the pain from others who suffered. He and his parents came to the United States in 1873. They settled in Fillmore County, Minnesota, when he was 16. He went with other Norwegian immigrants to the Thief River Falls area and claimed a homestead, building his own 14-by-16-foot cabin, close by a village named after him, called Holt. The first winter there, he had little human contact and only three books in his possession: the New Testament, a hymn book, and a *Farmer's Almanac*. He memorized most of what he read for his solitary entertainment.

Halvor set out for St. Olaf College with very little money, graduated from there, and then received his medical doctor's degree from the University of Minnesota Medical School in June 1893. He returned to Crookston the following month to set up his medical practice, understanding that physicians were in very short supply in this young, burgeoning town. Dr. Holte knew intimately the privations of those people who lived outside the city limits because he had survived in that environment himself. He knew the Crookston area needed a hospital where people could come to stay, instead of his traveling out in the cruel winters or sloppy roads in spring. At the rate horses traveled, it meant that someone could die in the amount of time he took to arrive to aid the sick.

By 1896, Dr. Holte felt the need for a clean, well-equipped central place where proper medical attention could be given. He named the two-story building he purchased in the Sampson's Addition, Bethesda or "Pool of Healing." He was a kind and gentle doctor, and yet it was a tough sell for people to go to the hospital for preventive reasons. Most preferred a country doctor who made house calls because a hospital was thought of as a place where people went to die.

Dr. Holte's first wife and their daughter died of consumption, or tuberculosis, in 1899. So Dr. Holte helped to start the tuberculosis sanatorium on College Avenue in Sampson's Addition for patients who needed cure and rest. His second wife, Henrietta Lunde, who was born in 1871, was a suitable helpmate for him. They were married in 1902 and had two of their own children. When Dr. Holte's days of transporting himself by horse, sleigh, or train were over, his wife, Henrietta, would drive him to distant calls while he slept in the car. Once there, Henrietta would sleep in the car while he saw his patients. Dr. Holte practiced medicine in Crookston from 1893 until his death in 1937.

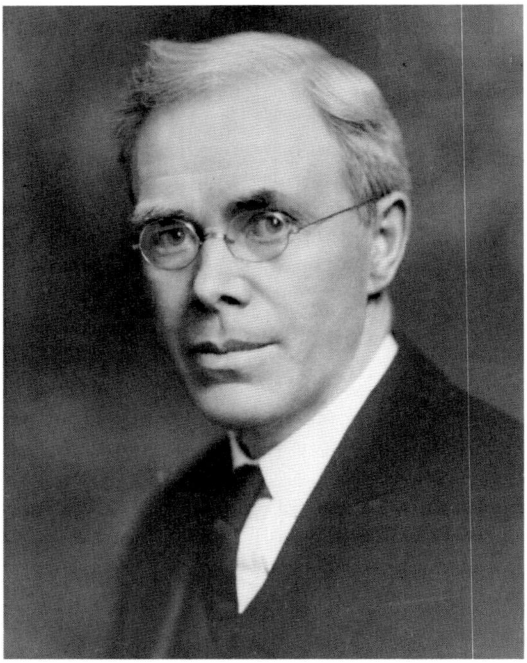

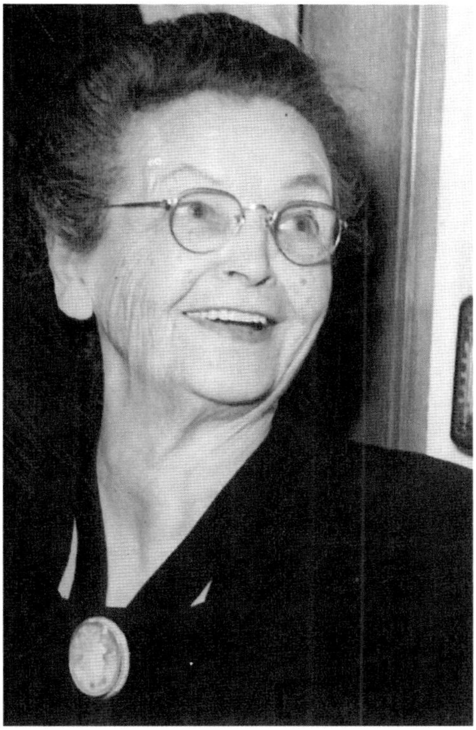

Henrietta Holte and Other Angels of Mercy

Henrietta Holte was 14 years younger than Dr. Halvor Holte, her compassionate husband. She was energetic to help where she could as an angel of mercy. The Bethesda Hospital Association was formed in March 31, 1898. The association sold stock certificates for $25. The shares did not earn dividends, but they could be used toward payment of hospital bills. In 1906, a fine, new hospital was built for $11,000. Henrietta set up the first Bethesda Hospital Guild in 1910.

Another angel of mercy was Sr. Anna Forlie, who was the superintendent of the Bethesda Hospital from 1911 to 1925. Sister Anna lived in the hospital and worked and filled in for every department; she kept books, made hospital rounds, even cooked and baked, and fired the furnace. Every morning at 6:50, she led the nurses in devotions and singing, and the patients could hear the voices of their nurses singing.

Another woman who came to Dr. Holte's aid was Ruby Gregerson. She began her hospital work at Bethesda in 1932 as supervisor of the second floor. Ruby became the administrator of the hospital in 1937 and continued until 1950. She was largely responsible for getting plans started for the new Bethesda Hospital and was instrumental in starting the first drive for funds.

A more familiar name of a woman who helped at Bethesda was Mernie Gredvig. In 1943, she graduated from St. Luke's School of Nursing in Fargo with a three-year registered nurse degree. Mernie worked many days a week for $85 a month. Sometimes she worked from 7:00 a.m. to 7:00 p.m. She was a surgical nurse and would often have to get up at night to help with emergency surgery. The surgical nurses had to sterilize everything including the gloves. During World War II, they had to patch gloves because rubber products were at such a premium. In 1953, the new Bethesda hospital was built. Mernie retired in 1984.

In an interview in May 24, 1953, Henrietta said, "One of the hardest jobs of all was to get sick people to put their trust in a hospital. In those days, people thought that once in a hospital all hope was gone for saving their life." The idea of going to a hospital with the real intention of getting well had to be promoted and worked on by Dr. Holte and the others who used the hospital. Henrietta Holte died on March 24, 1964, in a Washington, DC, hospital. She was 92 years old. (See page 116 for more on Henrietta Holte.)

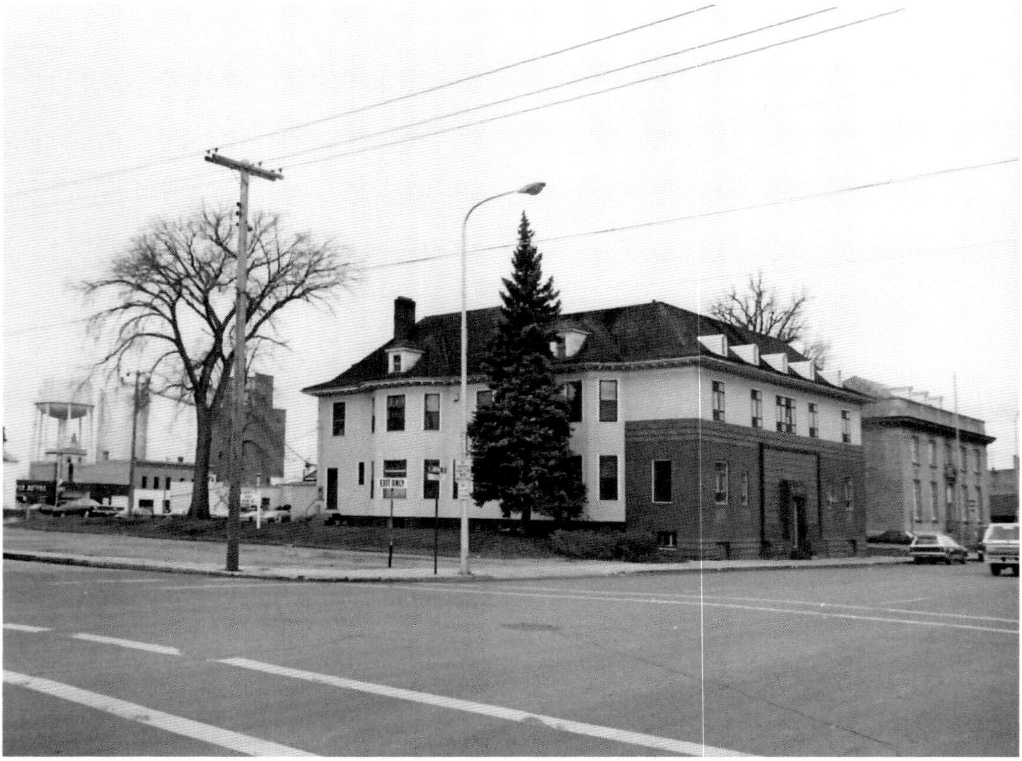

Dr. Russell Sather and the "Little Mayo of the North"

In 1920, Dr. Halvor and Henrietta Holte sold their home on 220 South Broadway to Dr. Locken, who turned it into the Northwest Clinic. This structure was enlarged from the Holtes' home to what was known by some in the area as the "Little Mayo of the North." This clinic, just south of the post office, was demolished on September 10, 1981, and replaced by Leever's Super Valu. Below, Dr. Russell Sather is pictured enjoying a Memorial Day parade with his wife, Inez, a registered nurse at the hospital, along with family and friends. Dr. Sather was a physician in Crookston for 38 years. In 1937, Dr. Sather joined the other doctors on the staff of Northwest Clinic. Sather said, "Those were the days when infectious diseases, scarlet fever, pneumonia and TB were some of the biggest problems in this area."

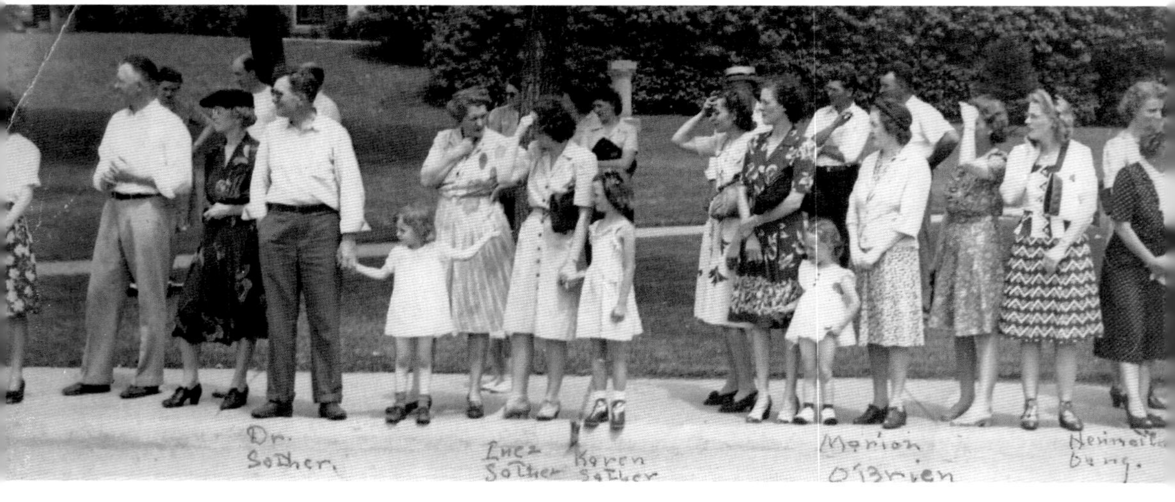

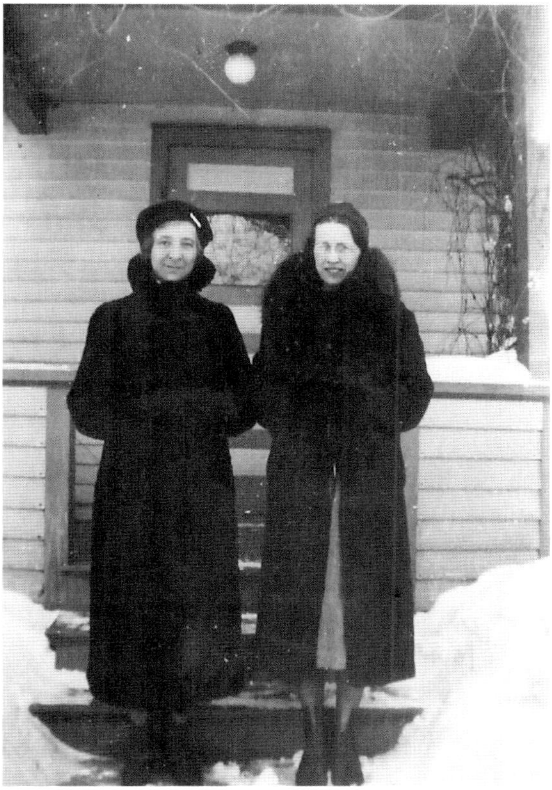

Mae Rideout, Manager Extraordinaire

There were many stories about Mary Mae Rideout (left), particularly how Mae's mother and her sister Edna escaped from Texas during the Civil War. Mae was born on a farm near Kennedy, Minnesota, on August 7, 1889. She was born prematurely, and her mother claimed that Mae's first bed was made out of a cigar box. Her mother's wedding ring served as the baby's bracelet. She was so tiny that Mae's father could hold her in the palm of his hand. Miraculously, she grew and lived to be 95 years old, having enjoyed a long, fruitful life. Mae died in 1985.

After Mae finished the eighth grade, her first job was as a clerk at the Golden Rule Store in Crookston. Evenings were spent at night school to further her business education. Mae was the business administrator of the Northwestern Clinic from 1932 until retiring in 1954. As more doctors came with their specialties to help people from all over the Red River Valley, she oversaw the growth of the Northwest Clinic. Upon retirement, Mae's managerial duties at the Northwest Clinic were taken over by June Shaver in 1954 until it closed in the early 1980s.

At age 15, Mae started to serve as superintendent of the primary department of the Methodist church's Sunday school program. She also was the choir director at the Methodist church for almost three decades. Mae had a boyfriend, but apparently, she broke off her relationship with him because he preferred being at the lake on Sundays instead of going to church. She remained single all her life.

Mae was director of the Crookston Civic Music League for many years and was an active member of the Garden Club. Her own yard was a showplace for local residents. Mae also loved to square dance. She was instrumental in starting Crookston's Business and Professional Women's Club (BPWC) in 1921. Mae served as president from 1922 to 1924 and again from 1948 to 1949. She also reignited the flame for Camp Fire Girls activity where there were once 10 groups of 15 girls in each club.

Mae Rideout and Wilma Coss are pictured in 1937 in front of Mae's house on 514 Elm Street. (Courtesy of Jessie Brolsma.)

Five Generations of George Widmans

Former residents who return to Crookston make a requisite stop at Widman's Candy Shop to visit with George Widman III and his wife, Lois. The original George Widman opened his candy business on South Broadway in 1911. It is one of the oldest family-owned businesses in the state. The founder, George H. Widman was followed by George William Widman II, brother of Margaret Widman and father of the current George F. Widman III. George and Lois have a son named George Mark Widman IV and a grandson, George Parker Widman V! The Widman family has branched out with stores located in Fargo and Grand Forks, North Dakota.

Most people who enter Widman's Candy Shop leave with their famous Chippers, a Widman's specialty since its invention in the early 1980s. Chippers are made of potato chips covered with chocolate, which preserves the freshness. The chips come from Red River Valley–grown potatoes. The Widmans are a family of innovators; William Widman, the patriarch and pioneering candy maker in St. Paul invented the "7-Up bar." It involved seven individual squares with different fillings fused together with a chocolate coating. Widmans ceased to make this candy bar in 1979 when the 7-Up soft drink company got the trademark.

Many of the same pieces of equipment are still in use in the spotless back room today that the first George Widman used in 1911. Donning an apron and baker's hat, old Mr. Widman used to mix his batch of "tingaling" candy on the baker's stove. The marble slab is still used, which was bought by the first George Widman for cooling candy, along with the copper kettles where every piece of Widman candy is dipped and handmade, the good old-fashioned way. The customers from a century ago would order nougats, caramels, and crèmes along with fudge, ribbon candy, and other Christmas treats. Even today, a whole array of candy is displayed in the front windows. Not too long ago, paperbacks, favorite comic books, and daily newspapers would draw people in. Today, the Images of America: *Crookston* book is on sale there, sitting on the back counter. (Photograph taken by Steve Hannah.)

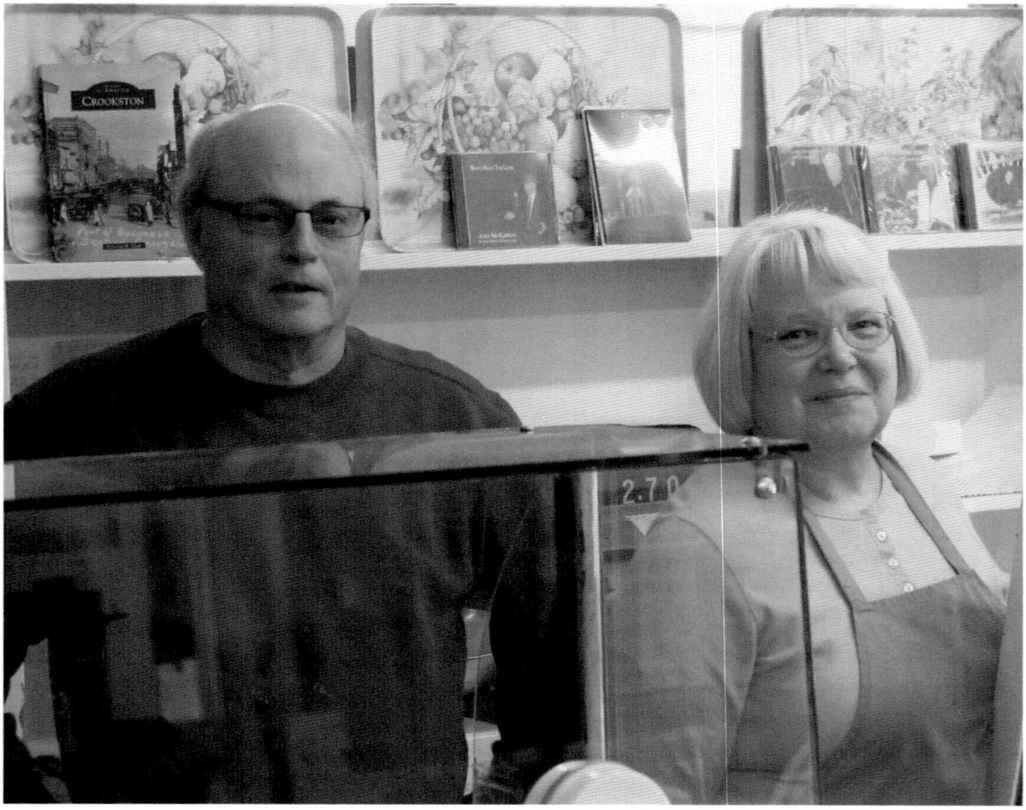

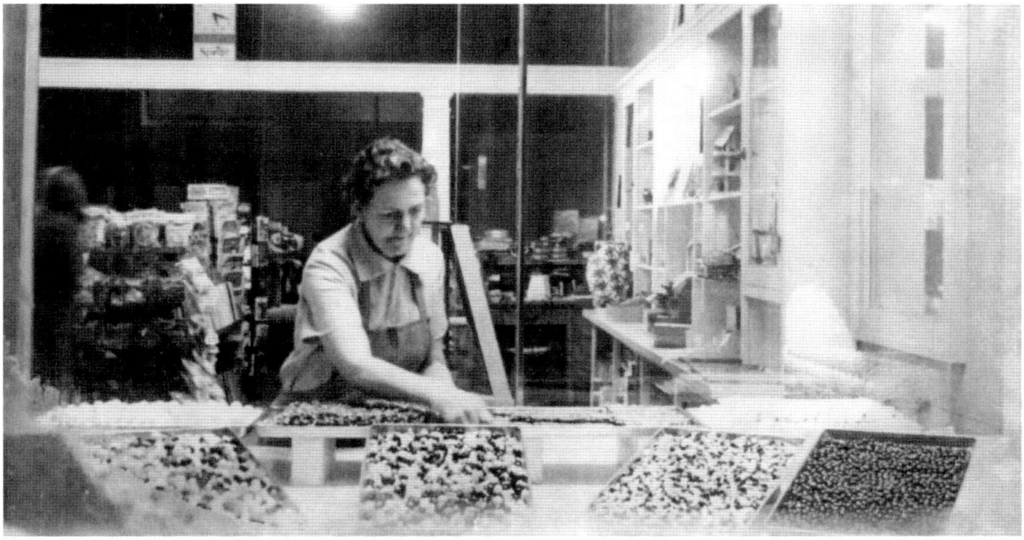

Margaret Widman

Margaret Widman recalled when her dad bought the first Frigidaire cooler back in 1929. Their original icebox, wood with metal compartments, was packed with ice to store ice cream. Margaret did not know how her Dad survived the Great Depression with five kids, but he did it. Coming in for ice cream after the movies was a special treat for Crookstonites. Some of the fountain specials were called Scotch Lassie, Three Graces, Gold Dust Twins, Nancy Brown, and Black-Eyed Susan. (Courtesy of George F. Widman.)

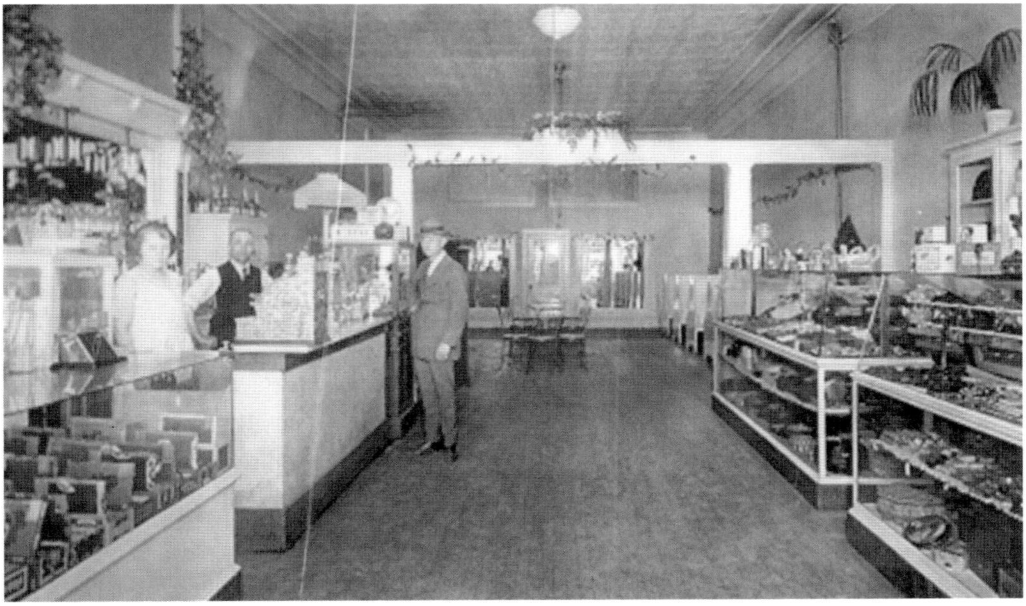

George H. Widman Sr.

In the 1920s, this little store was an ice cream parlor where the big affair was Saturday night when farmers and their families came into town with money to spend. Even today, this iconic hangout has the ambience of an old-fashioned soda fountain establishment. Here, Alice Sundet and George Widman Sr. are ready to serve the man in front of the counter. George Widman Sr. bought the present building in 1919, and the Widman Candy tradition has continued there ever since. (Courtesy of George F. Widman.)

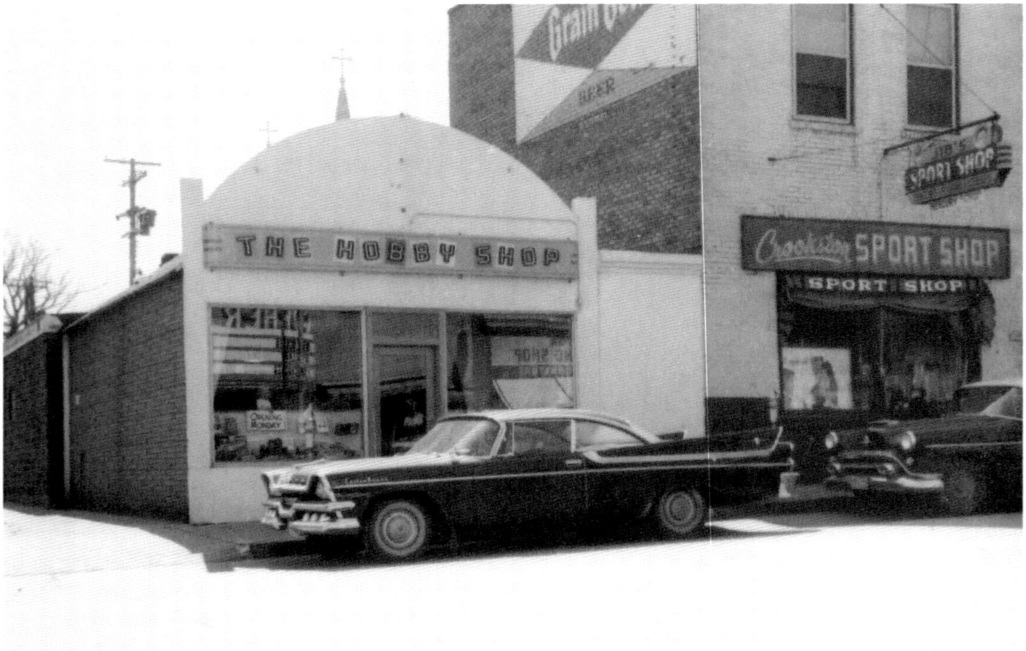

Russell Sundet's Toy and Hobby Shop

In September 1958, Russell Sundet opened a business in Crookston called Sundet's Toy and Hobby Shop at 214 North Broadway. Russ happily promoted stamp and coin collecting and building fuel-powered model airplanes. He constructed wood models of airplanes and boats from kits. In the 1960s, over a two-year span, he constructed, from a wooden kit, the USS *Missouri*, which was about three feet long and capable of operating by a fuel-powered engine with remote control. The Sundets sold their shop in 1980, retiring from business but not from keeping busy. (Both courtesy of Richard Sundet.)

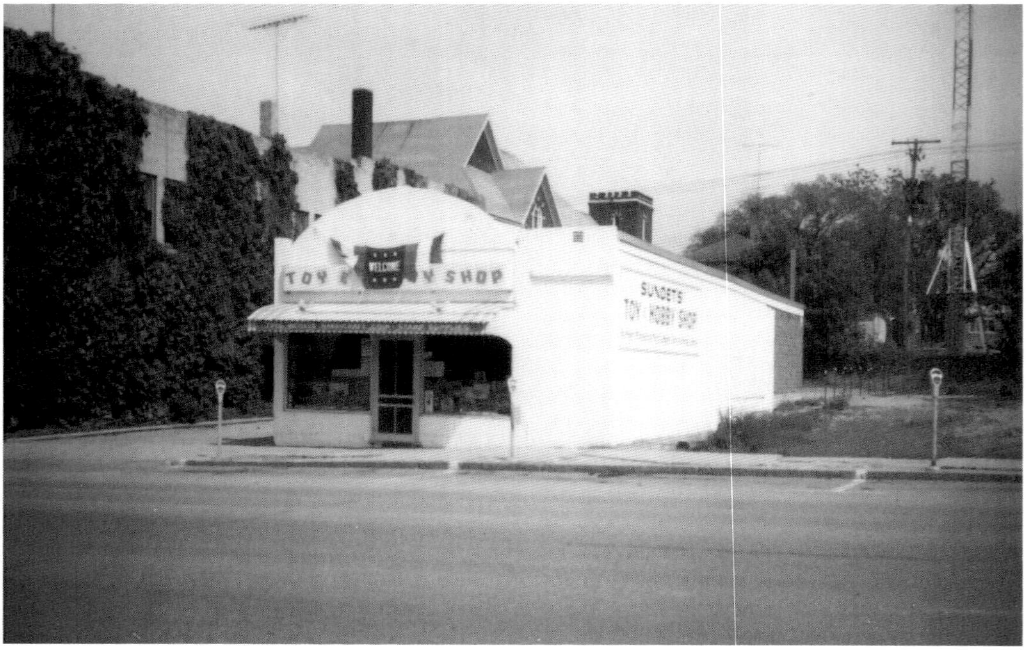

Russ Sundet and Helen (Schmidt) Sundet

Russell Stanford Sundet was born in Crookston on July 28, 1917, to Ole and Bertha Sundet (see page 25). Just out of high school, Russ applied and was nominated by a local congressman to West Point. However, he was denied acceptance because of bad teeth due to a mild case of rickets when he was a child. He volunteered for the Army on August 29, 1942. Russ was in the 1891st Aviation Engineer Battalion as a first sergeant. He saw some of the same action in China, Burma, and India that Murray Warren saw (see page 30). In 1945, he was shipped back to the United States.

In September 1943, Helen Mae Schmidt enlisted in the Navy WAVES (Women Accepted for Volunteer Emergency Service) and served as a yeoman 2nd class in the transportation department of the Navy Annex in Virginia near Arlington Cemetery in Washington, DC. She was discharged on February 16, 1946.

On June 21, 1949, Russ Sundet married Helen Schmidt (February 22, 1923–November 22, 1998), who was also born in Crookston. They had met on a blind date arranged by mutual friends. From 1937 until Russ went into the Army and then again from February 1946 to September 1958, he worked as the manager of the Lyric, Gopher, and Grand theaters in Crookston. In September 1958, Russ opened a new business in Crookston, called Sundet's Toy and Hobby Shop, at 214 South Broadway. Russ had faithful customers who came to buy school supplies and candy; others were in to model trains and some had enough money to purchase the expensive brass models.

Russ has been considered a local historian of Crookston and the Red River Valley area. Between 1987 and 1995, he wrote articles for the monthly newspaper, published by the Golden Link in Crookston. Russ's interest in history included writing articles about Crookston's early life, titled "Reminiscing with Russ," for a local news publication. (Courtesy of Richard Sundet.)

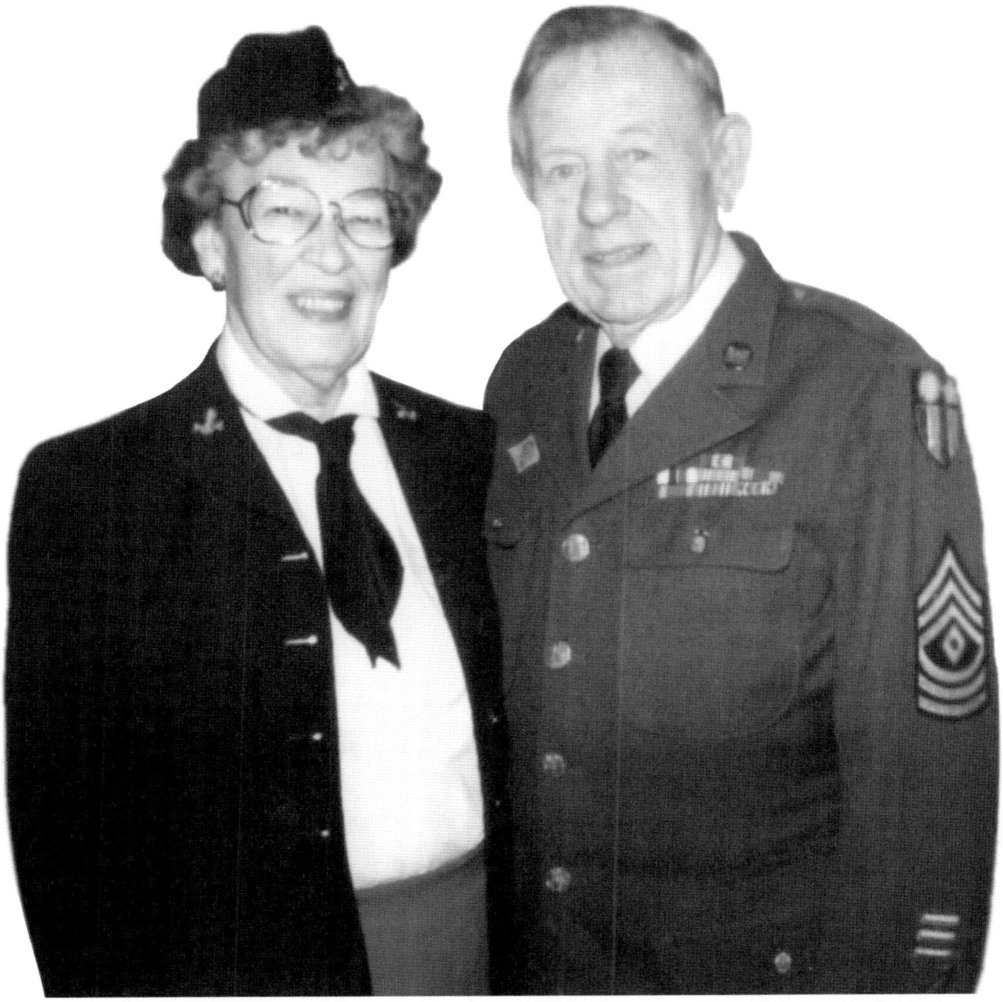

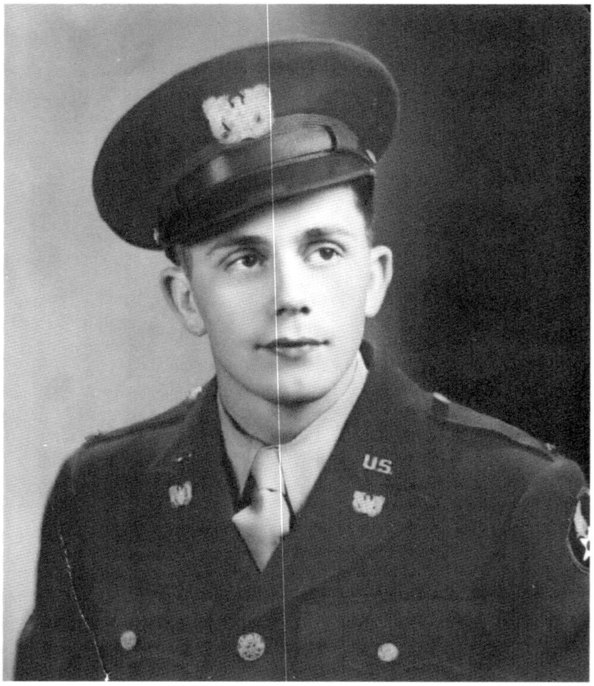

Bill Kiewel, the Radio Guy
A *Crookston Daily Times* article reported on April 25, 1948, that "Bill Kiewel had founded and went on the air with KROX." According to one of Bill's daughters, "He built his first radio as a kid from parts collected from the dump. He was truly self-made and talented. He literally built the radio station's transmitter from the ground up as a self-taught engineer." Bill admitted that he and his buddies "were just kids out of the service" when they put KROX on the air in Crookston. (Courtesy of Kathy Kiewel Romuld.)

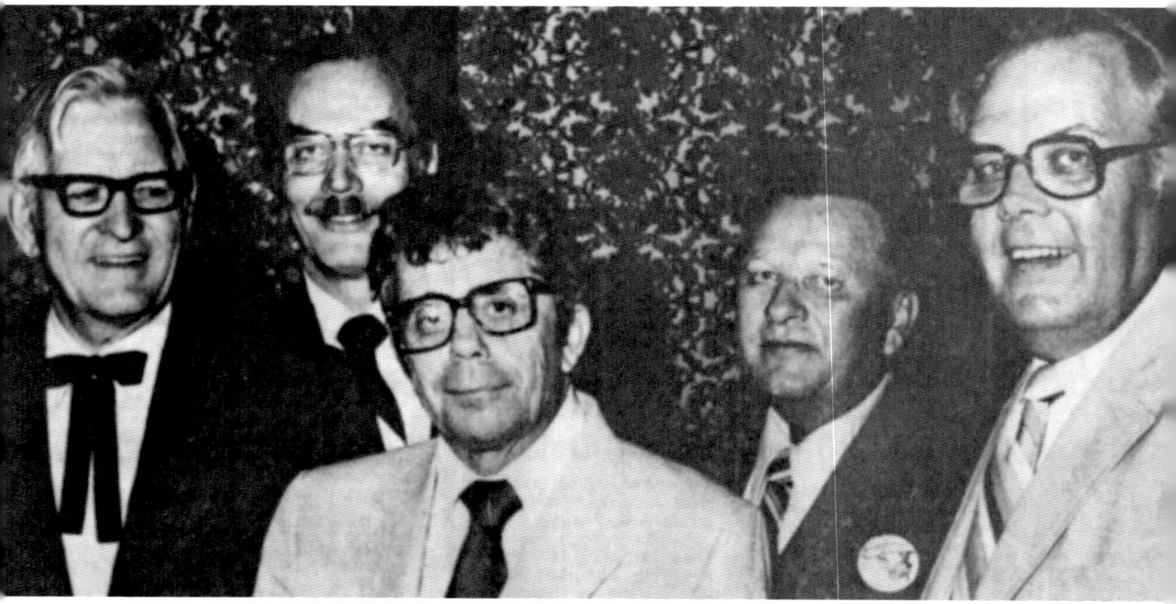

The KROX Radio Crew
The radio station was, and still is, 1260 on the AM dial. Actually, the KROX Radio studio involved other men besides Bill Kiewel. They were, from left to right, Don Broden, Don Mulvaney, Butch Melbye, and cofounder Jerry Dahlberg. Wearing a white suit, Bill Kiewel is in the middle. Others on the KROX team, not pictured, were Earl Handyside and Ed Boh. A headline, dated January 3, 1952, read, "William Kiewel new manager at KROX." The Crookston banks took a chance on these young men trying something new. (Courtesy of Junice Mulvaney.)

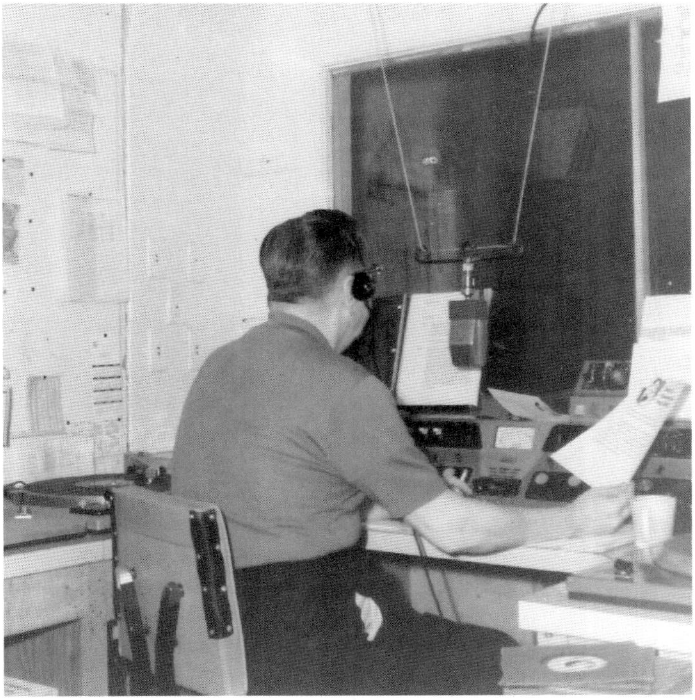

Edward J. Boh
Ed Boh was behind the scenes of the new KROX Radio venture. However, Jerry Dahlberg was co-owner with Bill Kiewel. Jerry was KROX's on-air manager. If people could not attend a sporting event, they could count on Jerry Dahlberg and other sportscasters giving commentary of the football, basketball, or hockey games they were missing.

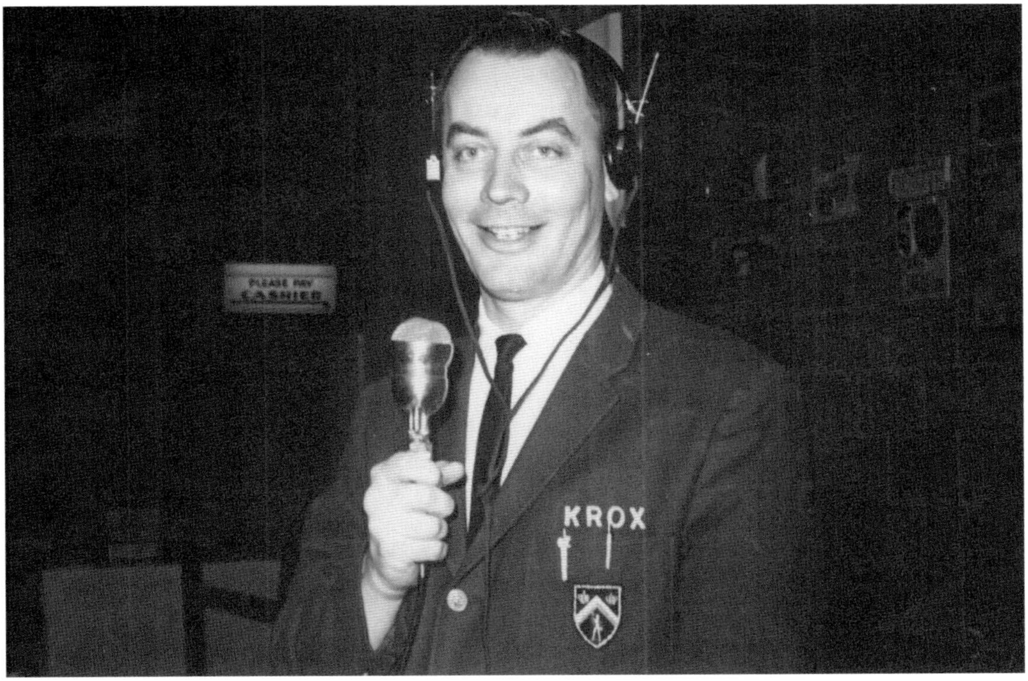

Don Mulvaney, Chief Announcer
According to Bill Kiewel, "10,000 people woke up every morning to Don Mulvaney's voice." Don—"the voice of Crookston"—was steady and dependable when reading the news or reporting the weather. Note the KROX crest on the Mulvaney's suit coat. No more listening to stations like WCCO, when Crookston had its own radio station reporting local news. (Courtesy of Junice Mulvaney.)

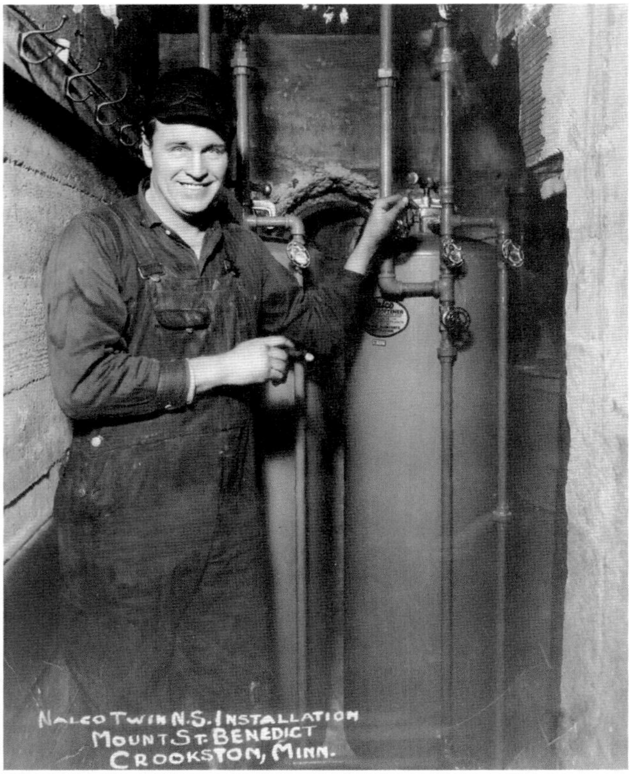

Anton Ellingson, the Sisters' Big Brother

Anton Ellingson (1900–1960) was considered an indispensable handyman by many women, especially the Benedictine Sisters in Crookston. He married a St. Vincent nurse, Blanche LeBlanc, and converted to Catholicism at age 24. A tribute about his life stated, "Officially he was chief engineer, first at St. Vincent Hospital, then at Mount St. Benedict, and finally at both the Mount and St. Francis Hospitals, covering a period of 42 years. Unofficially he was the community's most selfless and militant champion, and the 'big brother' of every sister invested at the Mount." (Courtesy of Bette Ellingson Talbert.)

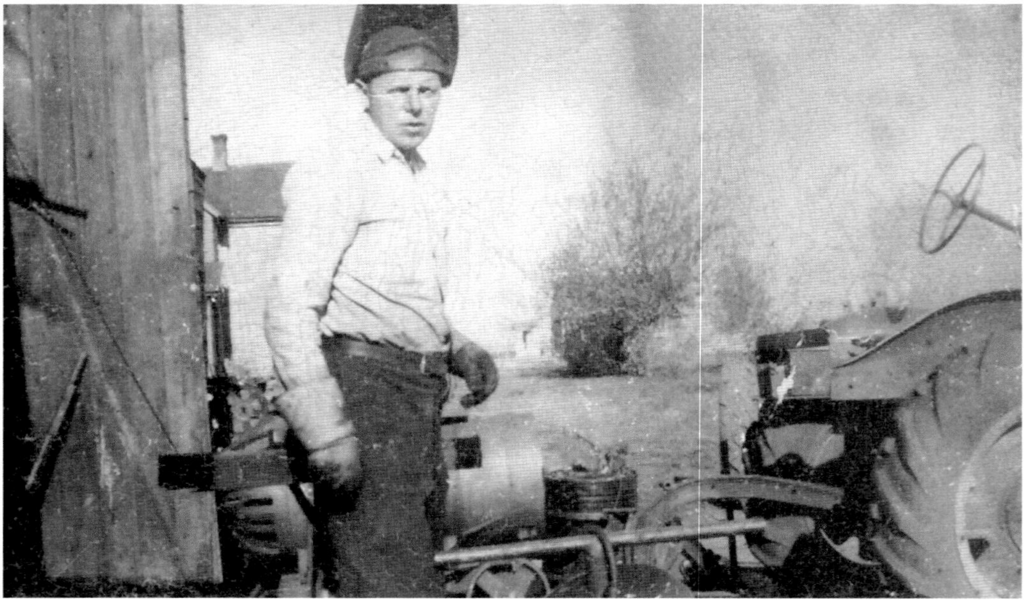

Gust Swenson, the Farmers' Welder

All Crookston-area farmers wanted the latest model tractor or tool from Crookston's implement dealers. However, when the equipment for planting or harvest broke down, there was one man who was valued above all others: Gust Swenson. One farm wife claimed, "No farmer could survive without the help of Gust Swenson." (Courtesy of Kenny and Bob Swenson.)

CHAPTER FOUR

Inventors and Tillers of the Soil

Old-timer Sheldon Roningen knows much about farming. He graduated at the top of his class at the Northwest School of Agriculture in 1952. Sheldon has an addendum to a quip that most people have heard before, "Necessity is the mother of invention." He asks, "Who is the father then?" Sheldon's answer is, "Mr. Pat Pending."

E.C. Davis, the McKinnon brothers, A.O. Espe, Lyle Kiel, and many others in the surrounding area garnered patents on their inventions. They all tried to make life easier for the farmer who dealt with the often water-saturated and sticky soil. It was difficult to sow and reap a crop in the Red River Valley's short growing season. In the limited time available, repair tasks often got the verbal trademark that it was "good enough for now." A Red River Valley farmer had to be a "jack-of-all-trades." Most farmers and their hired labor had to be handy with their machines in order to survive with equipment and technology. To be labeled a "good mechanic" was considered high praise among practical men who were tillers of the soil.

In the Southern states, where the growing season is much longer, farmers have the luxury of time to talk over their trade with other farmers. They swap stories about how they can improve their techniques or farming methods. But shooting the breeze with a Crookston-area farmer, especially in the summertime, is not too likely. Red River Valley farmers commonly learned from people like Carl Ash, the county extension agent, or they attended the annual Red River Valley Winter Shows when farm tasks were not too pressing.

The tradition of hard work with the pressure to save the farm from always-pending disaster was instilled in every farmer at an early age. These days you have to be born into the Crookston farming culture, apprenticed by a father or grandfather, and to develop at an early age a love for the land and endurance for the challenge of long hours of hard work. Being a tiller of the soil meant that the farmer had to be on good terms with the implement dealer and know a good welder. A farmer distressed by tractor or implement breakdown sometimes meant a 3:00 a.m. phone call to a repair establishment. Another difficulty now, but especially then, was draining land that was as flat as a pancake. Faced with many problems, every farmer had to have an optimistic, positive attitude in order to survive crop seasons with too little rain or too much snow melt and spring runoff. Local inventors created reason for optimism.

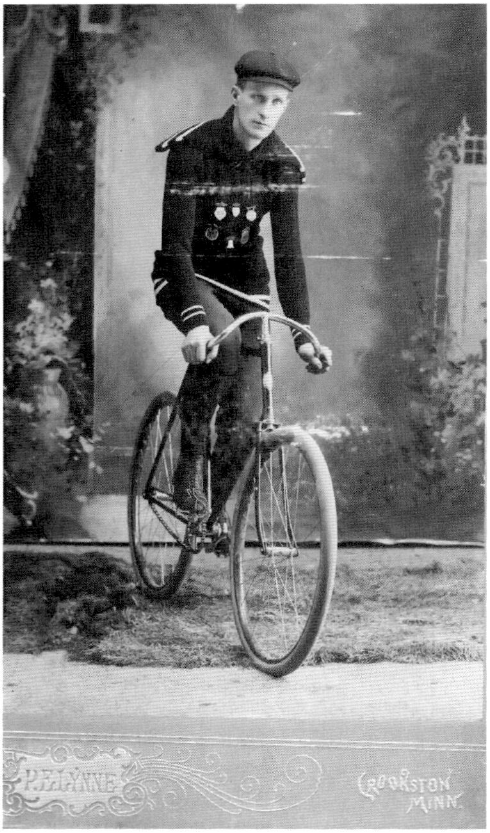

William Olds, Bicycle Dealer
William Olds had a bike shop for 12 years before he invested several decades into building cars. His garage was located on 208 North Main Street. After William Olds had been in the bike business, which had been all the rage in the early 1900s, he invented something that resembled a horseless carriage. According to the April 2, 1910, *Crookston Daily Times*, "Bert Keck constructs elegant garage for William Olds," and by February 1, 1913, "Olds made improvements to his garage." A bike dealer became the car inventor of Crookston's "Olds' mobile."

William Olds, Crookston's Inventor of Cars
Here inside William Olds's garage, he and other mechanics are tinkering with the newest and latest possibilities. Crookston residents were moving more in the direction of cars to get where they needed to go, faster. This was far from the days of racetracks and racehorses. A well-established fact was that William Olds was Crookston's first car owner. Second was Dr. G.A. Morley, who had to make house calls to his ailing patients. Farmers were also some of the first to own cars in order to shorten the time on their weekly trek to town.

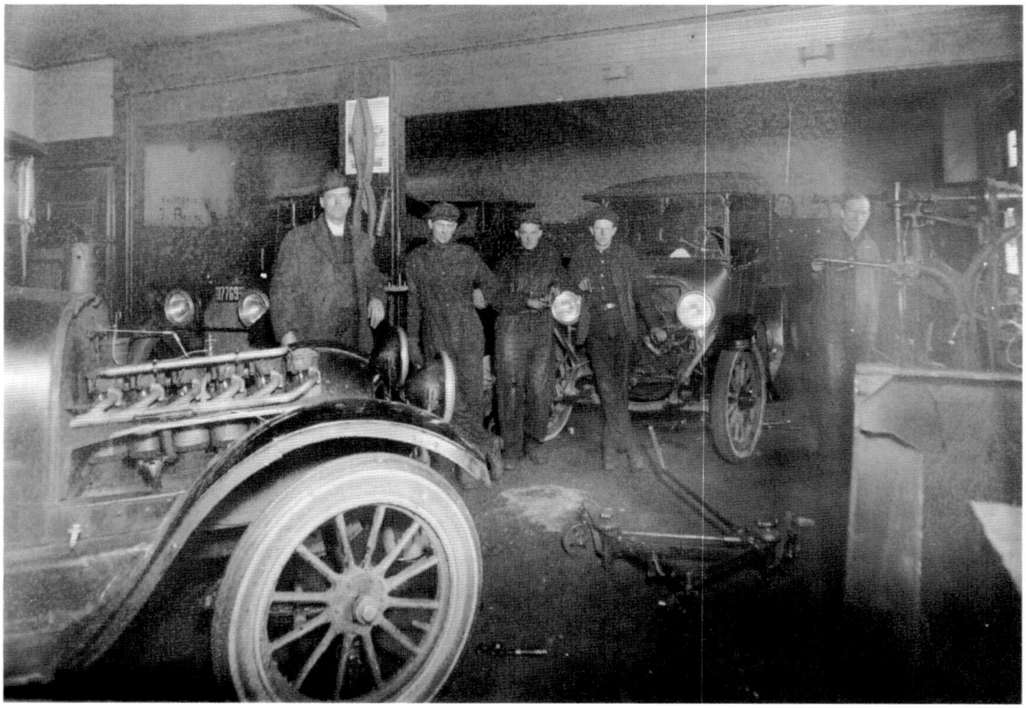

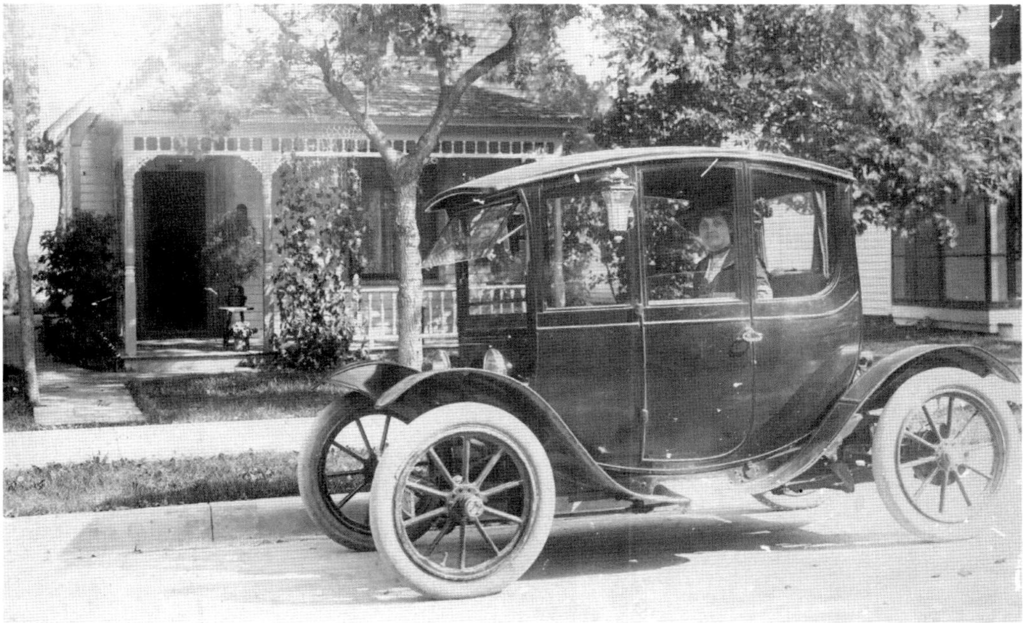

Nellie Olds

Mrs. William Olds (Nellie) lived on 413 South Ash Street and was her husband's intrepid test driver. In the photograph above, she is in a "two passenger, one cylinder gas affair capable of going 12–15 miles an hour." The photograph below shows a later model that Nellie Olds is driving in her neighborhood. Margaret Widman, confectionery businesswoman on South Broadway, remembers Nellie driving an electric automobile all over town. She recalls how Nellie drove it without a steering wheel, just steered it with a straight stick. It was reported in the *Crookston Daily Times* on February 19, 1924, that William Olds's horseless carriage drew a special ordinance.

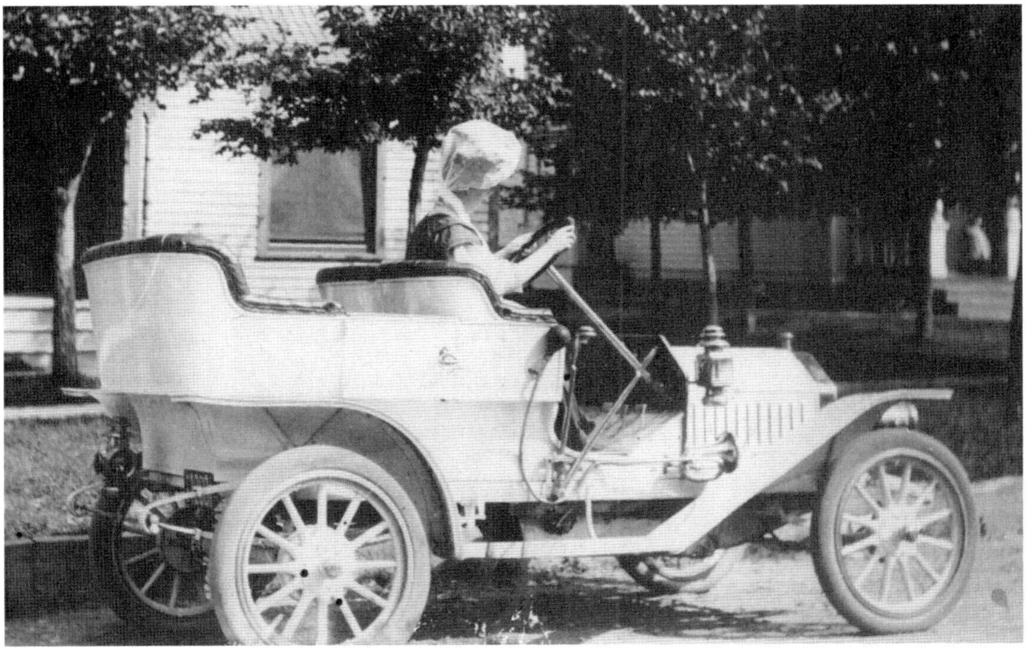

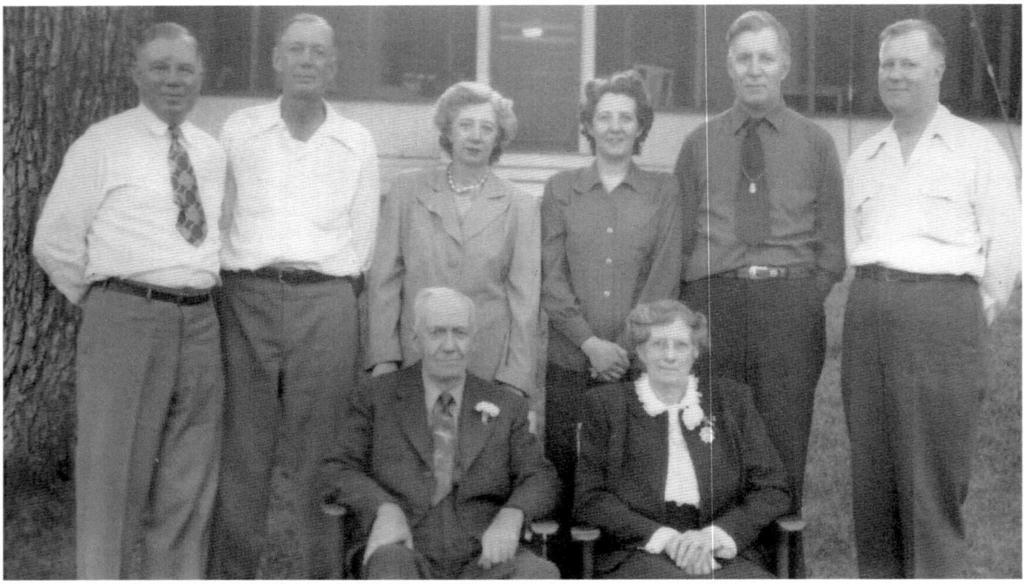

A.O. Espe and Family

Seated is Albert O. Espe with his wife, Mathilda "Tilla"; they married in 1896. Their children, from left to right, are Henry, Clarence, Glenda, Selma "Sally," Mylan, and Roy. William is not pictured; he died in 1931. When A.O. Espe retired in 1943, he turned over his business to his sons Henry and Mylan and daughter Glenda. A.O. Espe died in September 1952, a month short of his 80th birthday. His family continued to carry on the family manufacturing business until 1969.

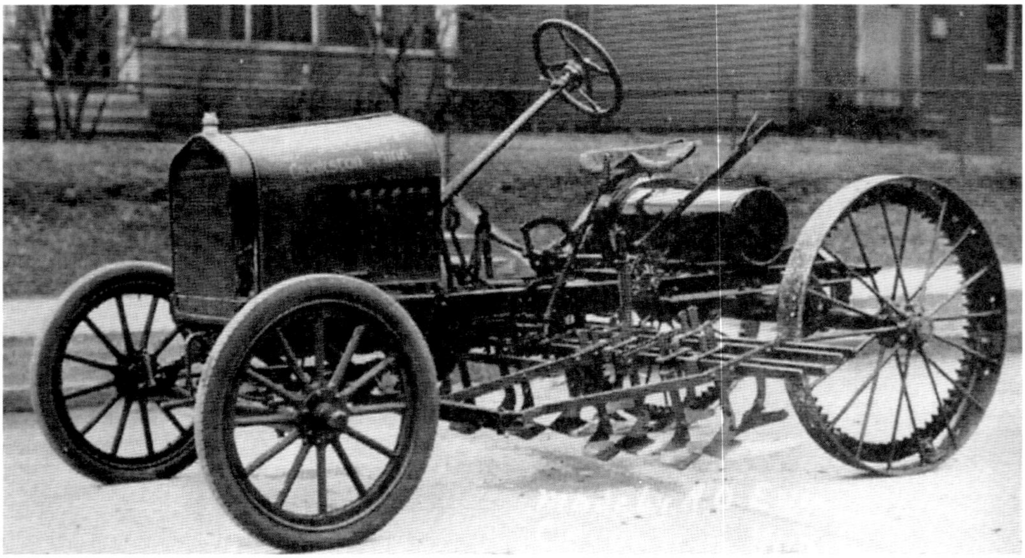

A.O. Espe's Inventions

By 1907, automobiles and tractors were introduced in Crookston. A.O. Espe applied his mechanical know-how to create a two-plow gas tractor that he used to plow his own land in Jerome's Addition. Note that the hood of this Model T turned tractor reads, "Crookston, Minnesota." Not many of these were made. Later, in 1949, Espe was still tinkering and invented a "snow ditcher," which successfully helped plow 125 miles of ditches for easier runoff in the spring thaws.

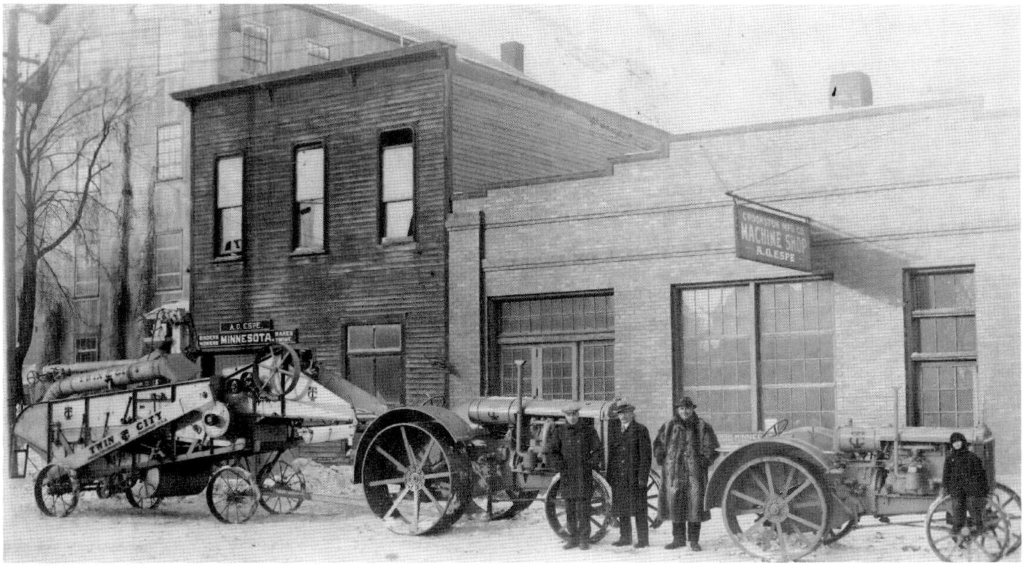

Espe's Manufacturing Foundry

A.O. Espe established a machine shop and implement business in Crookston in 1899. Perhaps his best known invention was the Espe Tractor, in the transition from steam engines to gas engines. In 1907, his first gasoline tractor was built in the Espe Foundry. In 1909, a four-plow tractor was made, and the Crookston Manufacturing Company was formed to produce them. The photograph above was taken at 411 Main Street North in the spring of 1927; the photograph below was taken on December 28, 1926. Both show off some of A.O. Espe's implements. By then, Espe had sold many of his patents to Minneapolis-Moline Tractor and Farm Machinery Company. The Avery Company bought Espe's other patent rights and manufactured on a larger scale. In 1938, Espe received a patent on a wide tractor disc harrow. In 1940 and 1941, he experimented with beet lifters, which helped save growers backbreaking work.

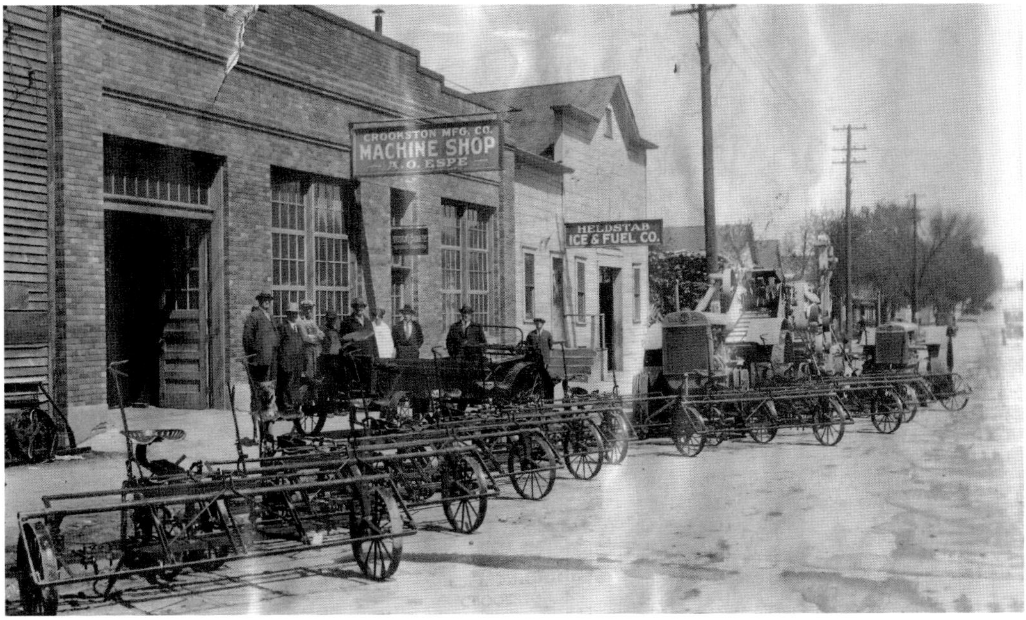

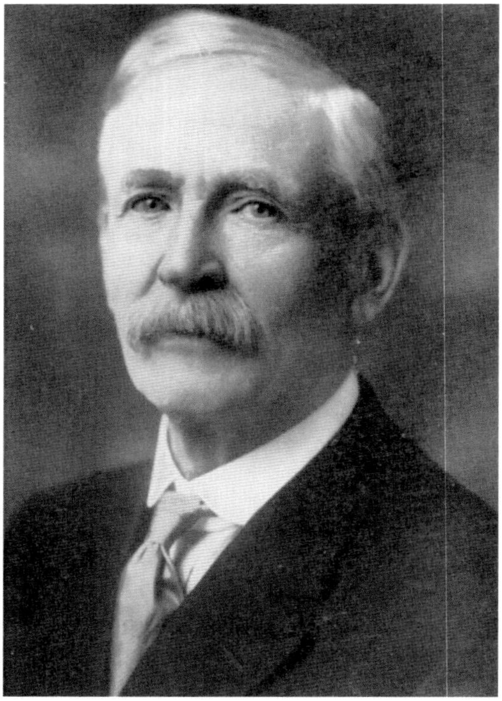

N.P. Stone's Implement Dealership

Nathan Perry (N.P.) Stone was on born January 21, 1838, in Massachusetts. He started his implement business in the Carman area in 1879 and, later, settled across the river in Crookston. N.P. Stone was the Polk County Old Settlers' Association's historian, and by the mid-1910s, he wrote the Red River Valley's true story. He had a high respect for the old settlers who had prevailed in settling the prairies. As an implement dealer, he was well aware of farmers' needs for good machinery to work the land.

In 1888, the N.P. Stone business was located at 302 North Main. By 1890, it was well established in the Red River Valley. William Stone, the oldest son, played a part in developing the swather pickup attachment, which is on every combine today. Prior to this development, nearly all combining was done straight. The Stones started out selling the horse-drawn McCormick Imperial reaper and mower and then the McCormick No. 141 Harvester-Thresher. In 75 years' time, the Stone dealership had seen a lot of progress in machinery.

N.P. and his wife, Ada, were members of the Congregational church located across from Central High School and the Methodist church on Ash Street. Since their home was on 620 North Broadway when he was well into his 80s, he would often walk to the church on Sunday afternoons to play the organ. N.P. died on October 30, 1926, at age 88.

Honesty was something N.P. Stone inculcated in his family. Both of his sons—William, born in 1875, and Walter, born in 1877—were also active in Crookston baseball. In fact, Will organized the Crookston Pirates of the first Northern League baseball setup. The following story was told about Walter Stone, the father of Merle Miller, set in rhyme in a *Crookston Daily Times* article on April 24, 1916.

> Two Crookston teams were pitted against each other with a tie game in the ninth inning. Marcus Stephen hit out to left field where Walter Stone made a bee-line for the ball running into tall grass. He fell and quick got up with the ball in hand. A big cheer for Stone's team resulted but when the umpire went out to ask Walter if he had caught it, he truthfully admitted he had not caught it for the final out. "Walter wanted victory but he didn't want it at the cost of his self respect and that's why I say he is an uncommon fellow, the kind whose names go into history or ought to.

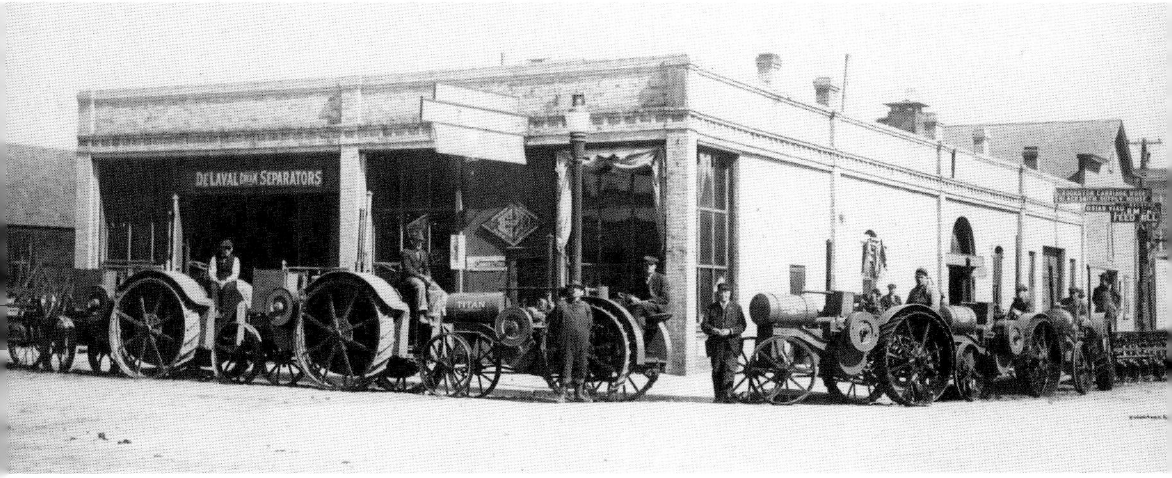

N.P. Stone's Business and Employees

N.P. Stone's business building at 302–304 North Main Street still stands today. Not only did it sell farm machinery, but by 1915, N.P. Stone added automobiles to keep up with the demand for cars. By the 75th anniversary of N.P. Stone's business in February 1954, the following people, pictured below, were associated with the business: Russel Johnson, Dave Altepeter, Cecil Sewill, Gerald Altepeter, James Duckworth, Charles Reitmeier, Linda Becker, O.C. Lee, William Stone, Melvin Peterson, Martin Knutson, Cornelius Wilkens, Lloyd Johnson, and Buster Tiedeman. Martin Knutson had set up and serviced Stone's machinery for 42 years, starting in 1912; Dave Altepeter was the shop foreman for 26 years, starting in 1928. N.P.'s son Will Stone was a pioneer in the beet industry. In the 1930s, N.P. Stone company sold the first beet loader and the first beet harvester and helped in the development of the first beet planter.

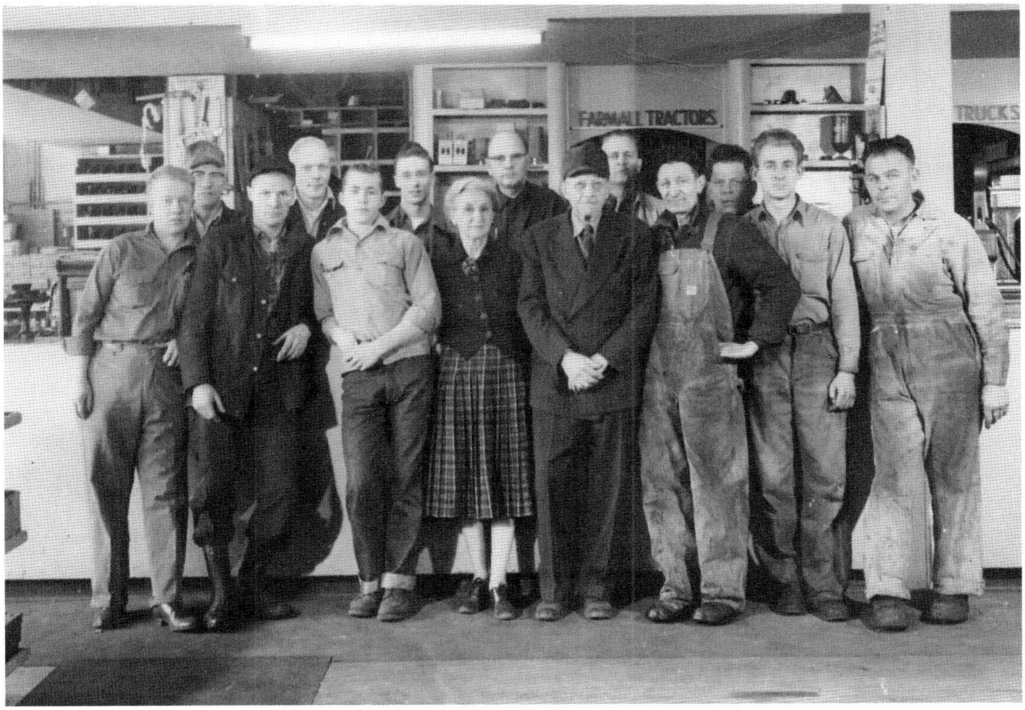

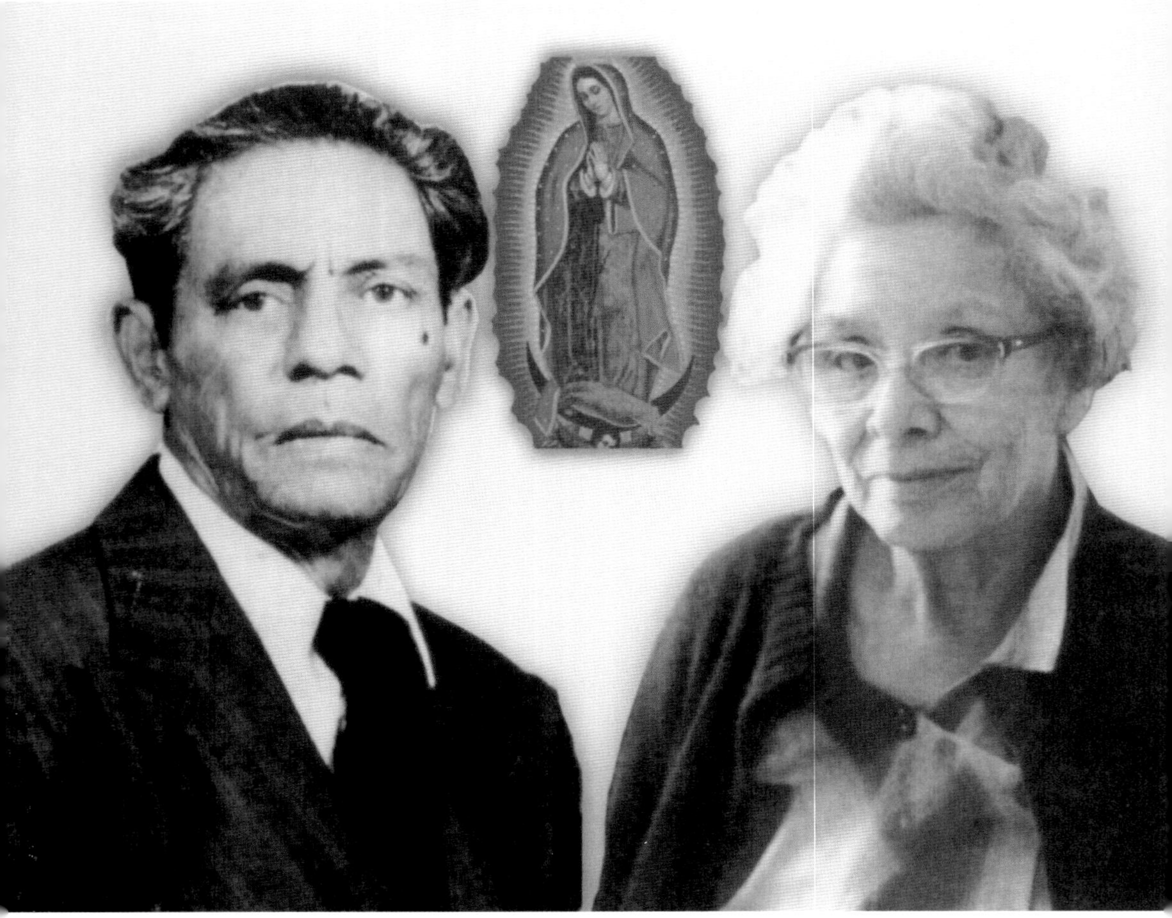

First Hispanic Migrant Workers, 1942

Among the first Hispanic migrant workers who came in 1942 were members of the Catarino and Angela Dominguez family. They lived amid great political and economic turmoil. They found a permanent home in Crookston in the early 1940s and raised nine children here. Catarino was born in a border town, Piedras Negras, Coahila, Mexico, on Christmas Day, 1891. He came to Texas at age 21 at the beginning of the 1910–1917 Mexican Revolution. His wife-to-be, Angela Lozano, was born on March 1, 1904, at Cerralvo, Nuevo Leon, Mexico, near Monterrey. She immigrated to Texas at about the same time as Catarino did.

Catarino was a lignite coal miner in the East Texas town of Malakoff but lost his job after the mine shut down when the power plants it served switched to natural gas in 1942. Catarino was enticed by recruiters from the Red River Valley in Minnesota to move north to work in the sugar beet industry. He was 51 years old when a formal registration document showed him to be employed in July 1942 by field man for American Crystal Alfred L. Kiel, the father of Lyle Kiel. Some of Catarino and Angela's children also worked in the beet fields. Catarino found a job in the winter, and then year round, with the City of Crookston. The family is reputedly the first permanent Hispanic family to settle in Crookston.

Some things in life do come full circle. Finding a job with the same Kiel family that brought his grandfather to Crookston, grandson Gerry Moreno drives a beet truck for the grandson of Alfred Kiel, Lonn Kiel, during the demanding harvest season each year. (Courtesy of Gerry Moreno.)

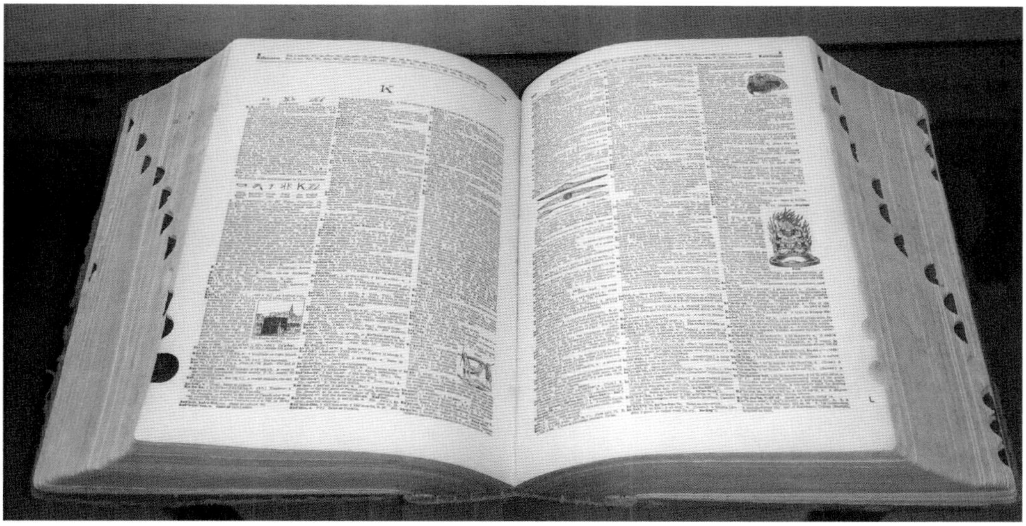

Dominquez Family Learned English

Former Crookston police detective Gerry Moreno, grandson of Catarino, tells the story of his grandfather's purchase of the 1913 leather-bound Funk & Wagnalls dictionary. He required his children to learn one new English word each day and use it correctly in a sentence. This 20-pound volume had almost 3,000 pages with illustrations next to some of the words. This showed Catarino's intent that his family make a successful go of it in Minnesota. (Photograph taken by Tony Torkelson)

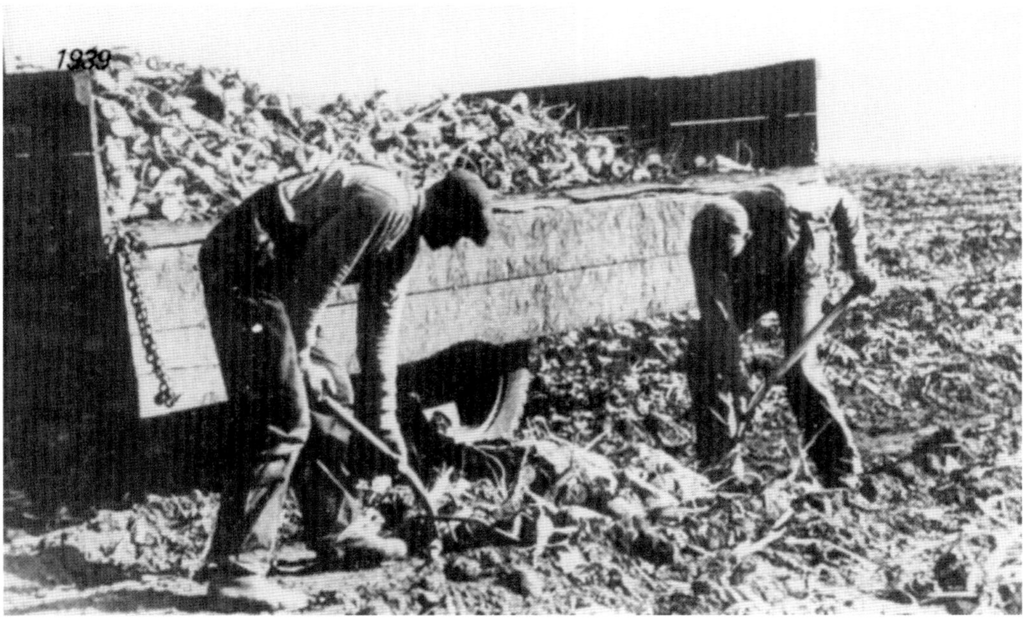

Migrant Laborers

First, laborers in the springtime went through the beets to thin them and hoe out weeds. By late September and October, there was more backbreaking work to be done with lifting sugar beets onto the truck with the side gate open. Up and down the Red River Valley, farmers and laborers loaded beets with beet forks in 1939. That changed with the advent of Espe's inventions and Lyle Kiel's improvements to make raising and harvesting beets easier.

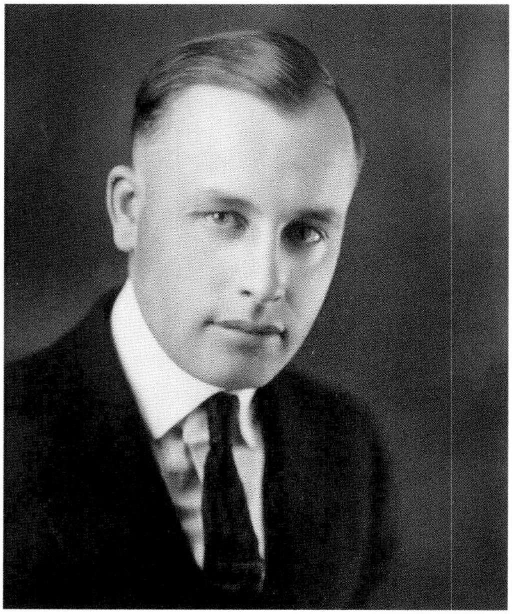

Gus Heldstab, Crookston's Young Entrepreneur

Gus was born in 1894 and died on February 2, 1980, at 86 years old. Gus's father came from Switzerland; his mother was from Germany. His father started a dray company. According to Gus, "He had done farm work, saved a few dollars, bought a team of horses, got started. He was conscientious, no question about it." The dray company turned into an ice and fuel business. All of Crookston knew its advertising jingle, "We keep you warm; we keep you cool, Heldstab Ice and Fuel." However, when the electric fridges arrived, they put the Heldstab ice business out of business.

Gus's life illustrates that area farming was a continuum into the town of Crookston. When he turned 80, Gus Heldstab did an oral interview. He told how he started raising fighting cocks at 12 years old. He explained, "Every farmer back then had their own chickens. Our backyard had 100 feet, lots of room. I got the idea to build a chicken house." Gus continued:

> There was a feed mill close by where they were unloading 10–15 cars a day. I got remnants of about a bushel after sweeping out each car. It didn't cost me nothing to feed my chickens. There was a municipal judge nearby who was 85 years old. He heard that I had chickens, "Say Gus would you mind hatching me some separate eggs for game chickens?" It was against the law to fight cocks, but you could raise them. People were fighting cocks on the sly . . . Every Saturday the judge would put a chicken or so in his sack and they would fight for blood. There would be betting money, like on a horse or dog race.

Eventually, the judge gave Gus all his cock fighting stuff. Gus claimed he was too busy to ever have his cocks fight, he just raised them for others.

Gus ran an advertisement in the *Grit and Steel* magazine. "I got letters from every state of the U.S. . . . every state, from people wanting to buy my cocks. $4.50 for eggs. Some birds would go for $7.50 or even $10," Gus said. He would build crates, crate the birds up, and send them express to places like North Carolina or Tennessee.

Gus was an entrepreneur when it came to raising rabbits as well. "At the grocery store, I got the old lettuce they would have hauled off to the dump, left over vegetables from the grocers and fed that to the rabbits. I would go down with my cart on Saturday and get enough vegetables for the rabbits to last a week." Such an entrepreneurial youngster had many stories of Crookston's past. (Courtesy of Betty Heldstab.)

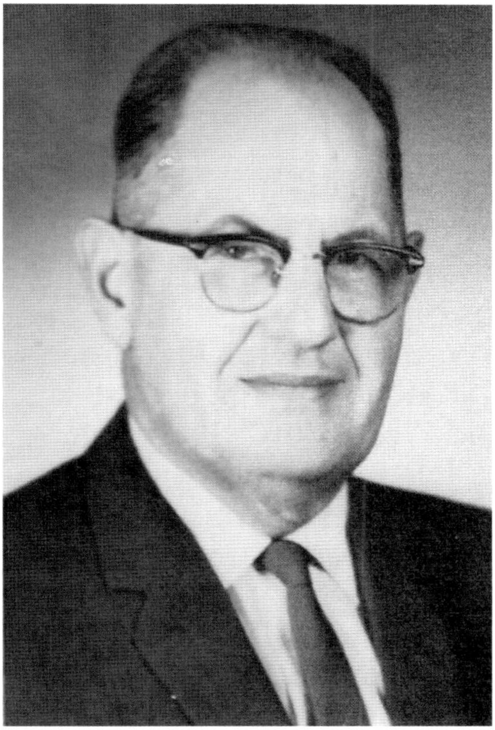

Carl Ash, County Extension Agent

Carl George Ash was born on May 26, 1903, on a farm outside St. Vincent, Minnesota, in Kittson County. He was the second of six children. When he finished the eighth grade, he attended high school in Humboldt, Minnesota, a distance of 3.5 miles, usually riding horseback. He graduated as class salutatorian in 1922. The first car he owned was a Ford Model A coupe, which he bought around 1930.

On June 17, 1931, he married his high school sweetheart, Marge Sylvestre. In March 1932, they moved to Crookston, where he started his new job as county agent of West Polk County. He served in this position for 35 years, from March 15, 1932, to his death on October 18, 1967. He was known in the county and even the state for his outstanding work in crop production, livestock production, and farm management in the Red River Valley.

A plaque was dedicated in Carl's honor after his death. It reads, "Hardly an African violet or a milk cow or a clod of dirt or a human being has passed through Polk County without having been affected in some way by the life of this man. He was more than a man, he was an institution in a plaid shirt. Because he lived among us, our life is so much more abundant. He taught us that it was not enough to raise a crop, we must also raise a family, values and standards."

As county agent, in 1943, Carl Ash helped avert a crisis due to impending labor shortage for the fall harvest because able-bodied men were serving in World War II. He contacted the 7th Army in Omaha, and it sent German POWs from Montgomery, Minnesota, to help with potato and beet harvests near Crookston. They arrived on Saturday, October 6, in a convoy of Army trucks. They were quartered for a month in the old sports arena. Residents were requested to stay away from the area during this time. The prisoners were paid the same as any workers. Three hundred and sixty-five prisoners came to help, and they reportedly worked hard and did a good job.

For many years, Carl was active in the Red River Valley Winter Shows. He first went to Crookston's Winter Shows as a 4-H exhibitor showing animals. Years later, he was a member of both the board of managers and the executive board. At the time of his death in 1967, he was one of six county agents in Minnesota to hold the rank of full professor at the University of Minnesota. He received the rank of assistant professor in 1946, associate professor in 1953, and professor in 1962.

Lyle Kiel, Inventor

Back in 1918, Crookston area farmers shipped their beets to Chaska for processing via trains. Lyle Kiel was born on July 17, 1918. His father, Alfred, obtained his first beet contract in 1933. On August 28, 1954, American Crystal dedicated a new processing plant for sugar beets in Crookston, the third in the Red River Valley. However, something had to be done to make sugar beet harvesting easier for farmers. That is what happened with Lyle Kiel's sugar beet row-finder, introduced and patented on August 24, 1961. The patent was No. 2,993,548 for this invention, which kept a sugar beet harvester on the row. Kiel and his son later experimented with a down-the-row rotovator so that farmers could plant sugar beets into bare stubble. The stubble could catch snow and also eliminate soil erosion from high winds.

By December 6, 1961, Lyle Kiel was head of the Valley Beet Growers Association. In an interview done in 1989, Kiel looked back to the World War II days when he said that no farmer wanted to raise beets. He said, "They had a tough time getting growers because the price of wheat was $5 a bushel; it was tough to recruit labor. We had to get 'nationals' or prisoners of war. It was tough to get farm labor, period. Beet farming during the war was atrocious. It was a tough time all around."

Kiel answered the question about wet seasons and dry seasons, something always on farmers' minds, as follows:

> Well, I'll tell you, beets take moisture. And who is going to determine what's a dry season or not? Like this year, started out beautiful. And these beets could still recover. Once you get them emerged and get them on their way, they are a tough crop. They'll stand a drought as good as anything. Maybe not as good as sunflowers, from what I understand, but year in and year out you look back in the history of sugar beet production in the Valley and—with the cultural practices we have—they are an excellent crop.
>
> We used to plant them [sugar beets] on summer fallow. That was number one. At first, we couldn't plant them on stubble ground. Or you could plant on corn ground or potato ground. But on summer fallow, you'd always have a few inches of moisture stored up there for you. But [with better tillage] we raised a lot better crop as we went to stubble, than we ever raised on summer fallow. (Courtesy of Deb Kiel.)

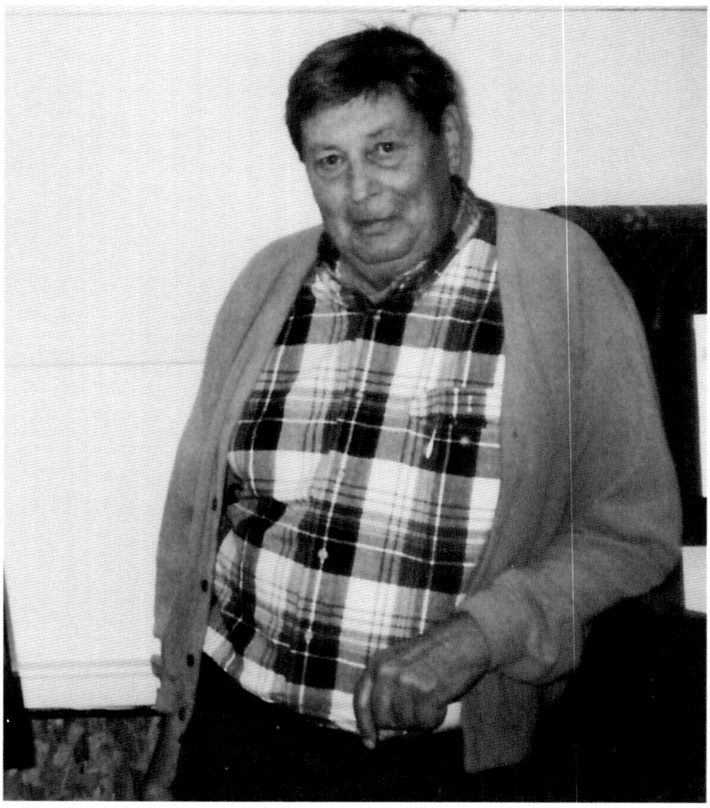

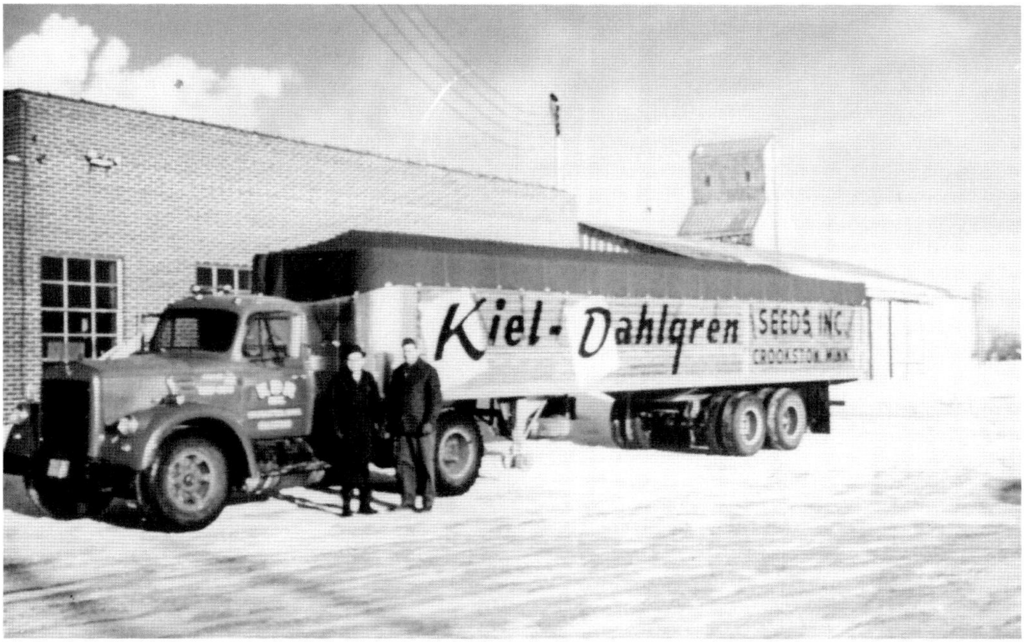

Cofounders Kiel and Dahlgren
Kiel-Dahlgren Seeds, Inc., was started with Lyle Kiel (right) and Clark Dahlgren (left) as partners. The company was founded in the late 1950s to buy and sell sunflower seeds produced in the Crookston area. By 1962, Kiel got out of the business to focus on sugar beets. Dahlgren took the company steadily to the next level in the Midwest, then nationally, and eventually Dahlgren Company became known internationally. Many Crookston jobs were created for those working under Dahlgren by the time he retired and moved to Florida. (Courtesy of Deb Kiel.)

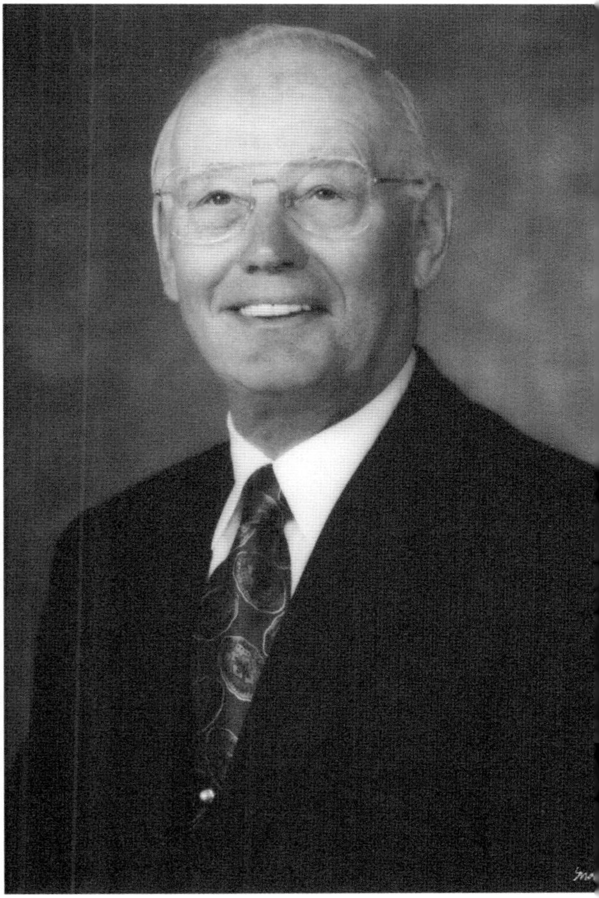

Clark Edson Dahlgren
Clark Edson Dahlgren was born in Cambridge, Minnesota, on July 27, 1923, and died in Florida in 2006. He served in the Coast Guard, based on Catalina Island, California, from 1943 to 1946. Clark returned to Minnesota in 1955 and, with Lyle Kiel, cofounded Kiel-Dahlgren Seeds, Inc. Dahlgren expanded the business to numerous cities in the upper Midwest until 1972, when he sold to Beatrice Food of Chicago, now called SunOpta. (Courtesy of Sally Dahlgren.)

Gary Wagner

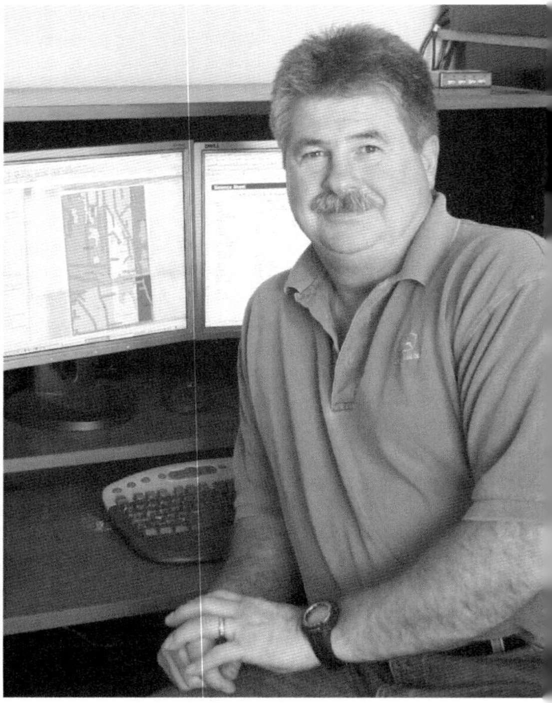

With two brothers and his son-in-law, Gary Wagner operates a third-generation family farm in the Crookston area. In 1993, the Wagner farm pioneered in precision farming. Precision agriculture is a system of crop-farming based on measuring and responding to differences, mainly yield and soil conditions, between and within fields. Precise mapping allows inputs to be efficiently varied, to optimize the returns on them and enlarge profits.

Wagner's farm now has 20 years of data and a long series of maps over time. With computer resources now available, this has allowed setting up a decision support system for whole farm management. Any farmer gains intimate knowledge of his fields, but Gary says, "Farmers through the years had no good way to transfer the 'land knowledge' from one generation to the next. But with this technology the next generation of farmers can continue where we left off, instead of starting all over again." (Both courtesy of Amber Wagner Bailey.)

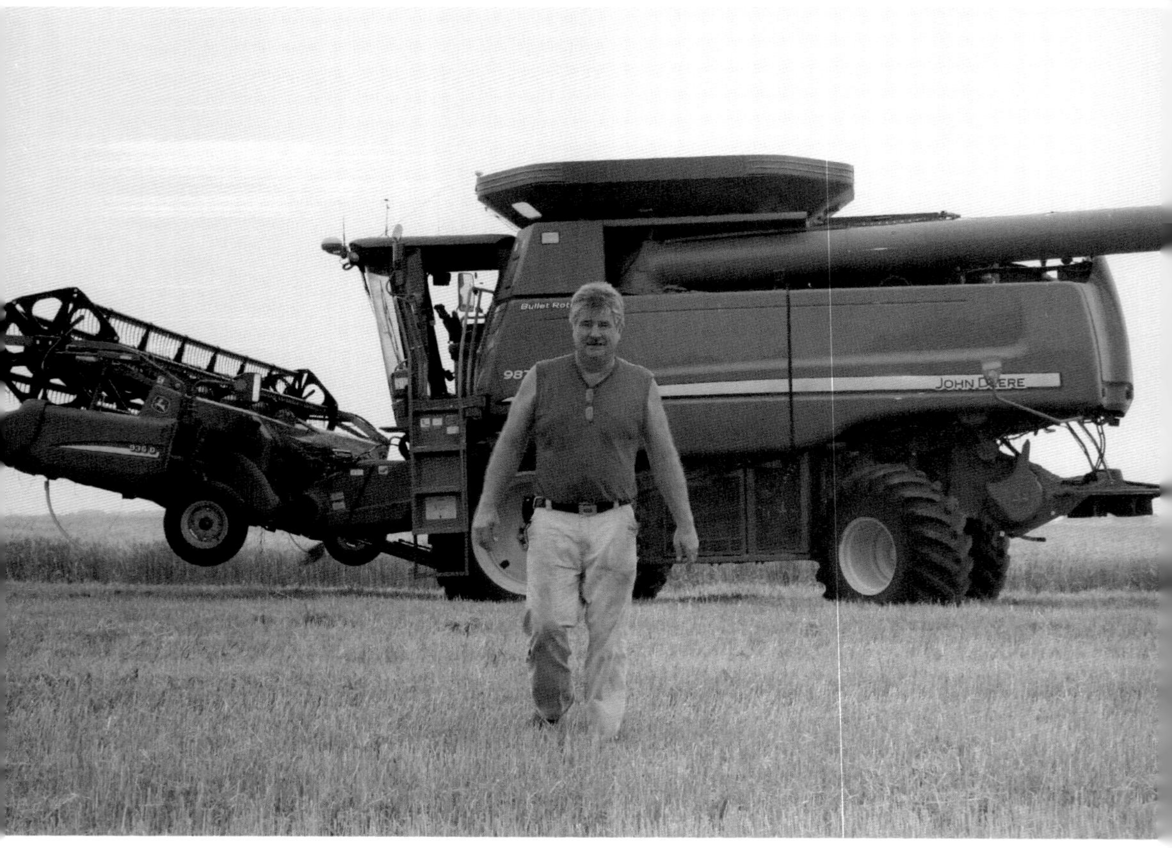

CHAPTER FIVE

Classrooms and Boardrooms

Starting in 1896, classrooms in the Crookston Business College filled a need of those new immigrant arrivals who wanted to improve their English or better themselves in professional jobs. Pres. Jacob C. Sathre hired several professors to teach stenography, bookkeeping, shorthand skills, and so on. Railroad baron James J. Hill is often credited for donating the land to what is now the UMC campus, but few people know that it was Sen. A.D. Stephens, for whom the NWSA's Stephens Hall was named, who strongly encouraged Hill to donate. There was a groundswell of Red River Valley farmers who had earlier answered the call to embrace diversified farming in this challenging environment. These farmers did not need a liberal arts education. Using the curriculum that Minnesota's superintendent of education Dr. David Kiehle (Kiehle Auditorium) recommended, the NWSA gave farm kids a practical education during the winter months while having the other months free to do farm chores.

Thus, while classrooms were required, the requisite boardrooms were necessary to make decisions on how to effectively further everyone's education. UMC has had several of its key administrators also serve as regents to the University of Minnesota. Herman Skyberg, Stan Sahlstrom, and Dr. Charles Casey, UMC's most recent chancellor who retired in 2012, have had oversight over all of the University of Minnesota campuses. Crookston has benefitted from all the professors and administrators who came to the small campus that now has a "big degree" aligned with the University of Minnesota in the Twin Cities. Many of the halls or dormitories are named after those who invested their time and energy into solving problems that involved hands-on practicality.

Currently, UMC's much-touted and long-established laptop campus is bringing in online pedagogy, which serves well in the winter months when the blizzards and abundance of snow makes for dangerous or impassable roads. Taking technology several steps further, the campus touts precision agriculture, which helps farmers know what nutrients to use and apply them in defined locations of their fields. Technology is here to stay, and UMC's prowess attracts international students from all over the world.

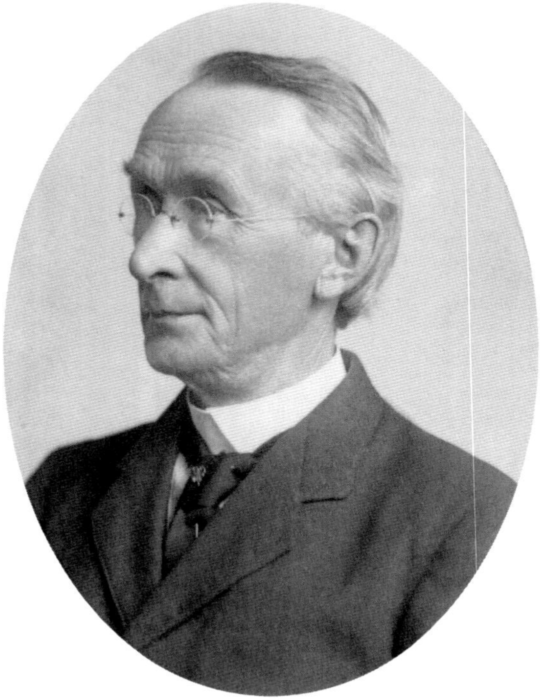

Dr. David Kiehle

Dr. David L. Kiehle, of Minnesota, a state superintendent of public instruction, regent, and university professor, came up with an exceptional plan for farm boys: the experimental farm. Young boys would have hands-on, practical experience to take back home with them. In the curriculum, Dr. Kiehle proposed to university president Cyrus Northrop in 1888 that, instead of farm boys being educated for a "learned, liberal and intellectual pursuit," they should be given one term of studies in six of the winter months. Then with the remaining months, they would have study projects while they were needed back home to do farm work, practicing what they had learned at school. Kiehle's scheme seemed to be embraced by the university president and regents alike. It became the order of the day that farm kids learned to farm smart by "doing" in a boarding school setting.

Mrs. Arthur Miller (Alice) came with her husband to Crookston in 1889. When chronicling Crookston's history in April 1922, Alice specifically wrote the following about UMC's early start:

> While not within the city limits yet so closely allied with the city that I cannot omit mentioning it as belonging to Crookston, is the Northwest School of Agriculture and Experiment Station. No more fitting recognition of this school in its relation to Polk County and the Red River Valley could have been given than when Mr. J.J. Hill offered 499 acres of land as a site for this school. By the passage of a bill through the legislature of Minnesota, the School of Agriculture was established in Crookston. This school has become a dominant feature in practical husbandry and is of untold benefit to the farmers and the young people from the farms of northwest Minnesota.

In 1894, plans had been outlined for this farming school. Miller continued, "In 1895 work was begun at this school and has steadily advanced until now we have a station we are proud of. Crookston is filled and surrounded with possibilities and there is no reason why she should not become the Queen City of the Northwest."

The fifth NWSA building was constructed in honor of Dr. Kiehle. It was considered the largest and most useful on campus. At first, it contained a well-equipped gymnasium, but then in the 1930s, it was changed to Kiehle Auditorium, which seats about 500. (Courtesy of Minnesota Historical Society, St. Paul.)

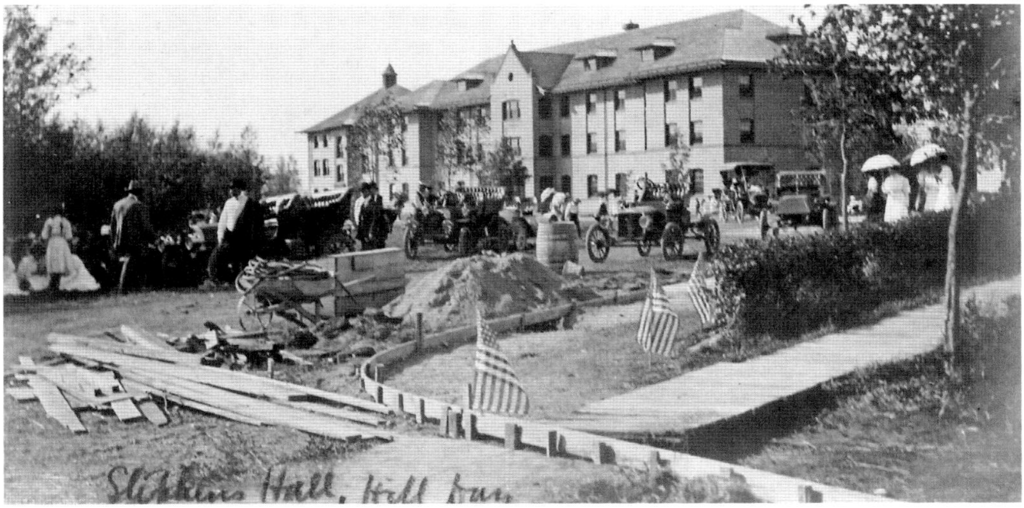

Stephen's Hall and Hill Day

On September 17, 1908, James J. Hill, the Great Northern Railroad baron and legend, came to Crookston to dedicate Stephens Hall at the Northwest School of Agriculture. He gave a speech about farming to a crowd of farmers. Hill honored Senator Stephens, who talked him into giving up the wetlands he owned for a campus while the Crookstonites honored Hill for showing up again. Not to be outdone, the city folks of Crookston declared September 17 to be "James J. Hill Day." Back in the 1880s and 1890s, Hill had a large presence in Crookston. He understood the importance of drainage and subsidized a four-county drainage conference in Crookston. The 1904 photograph below shows a ditching machine, with John Ruhberg in the foreground. He and John McKinnon had a patent for this steam shovel, which dug ditches to help move standing water. (Above, courtesy of Margaret Childs Rose.)

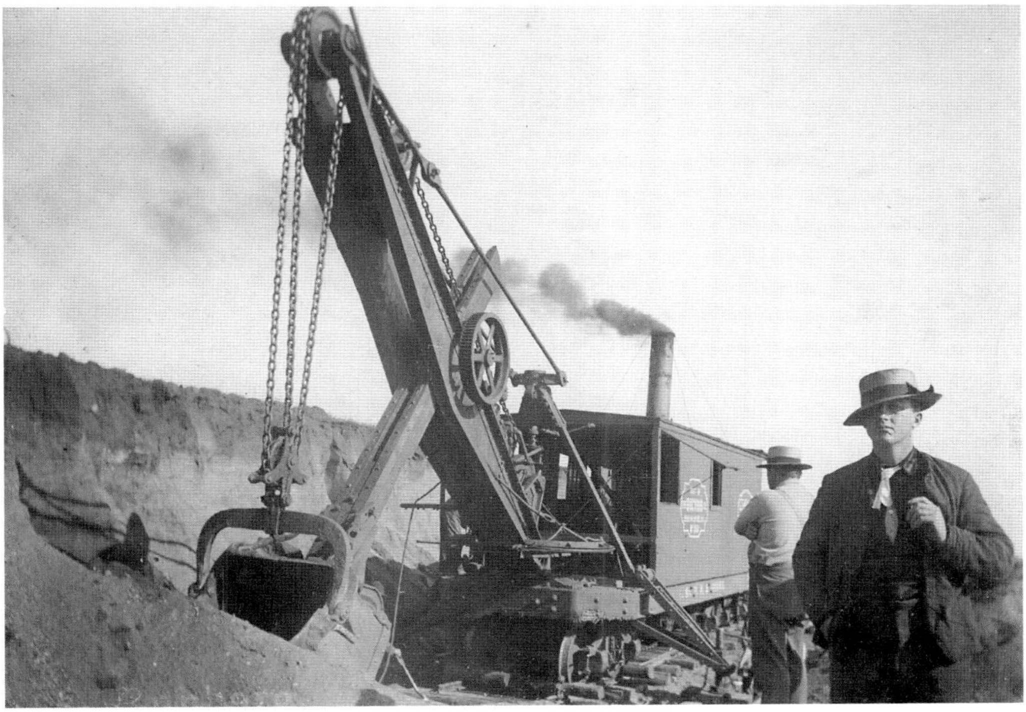

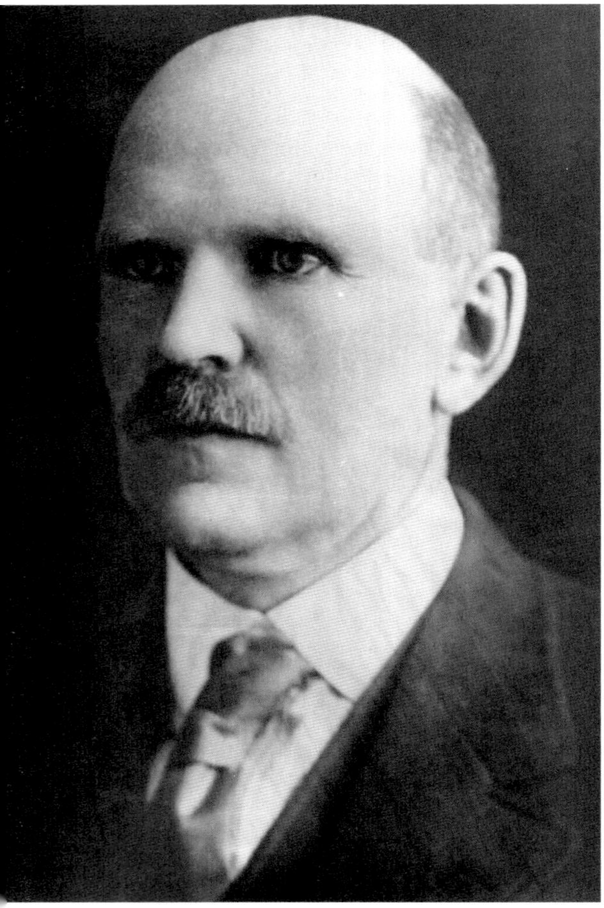

Supt. William Robertson

On August 5, 1905, Prof. William Robertson was named superintendent of the Northwest School of Agriculture and Experiment Station, after Toger Hoverstad left. Robertson was ambitious to make NWSA a model farm, but drainage of water was a problem every spring. By October 10, 1907, Superintendent Robertson erected four houses for the on-campus faculty. People on campus grieved greatly when their dearly loved superintendent died unexpectedly in 1910. (NWROC.)

Former Superintendents of the Northwest School of Agriculture

The 40th anniversary of NWSA featured a reunion of living superintendents. They are, from left to right, (sitting) the first superintendent of the Experiment Station, Toger Hoverstad; Supt. Conrad Selvig, and Sen. A.D. Stephens; (standing) Dean Walter C. Coffey from the Twin Cities campus and Supt. Austin A. Dowell, who filled Selvig's vacancy in 1926 when Selvig was elected to Congress. (NWROC.)

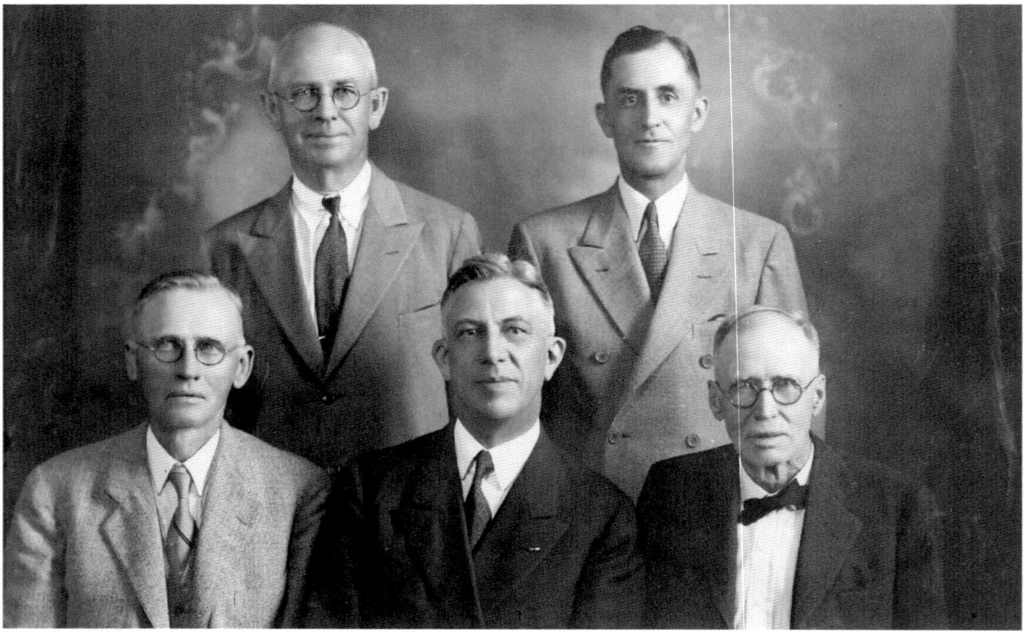

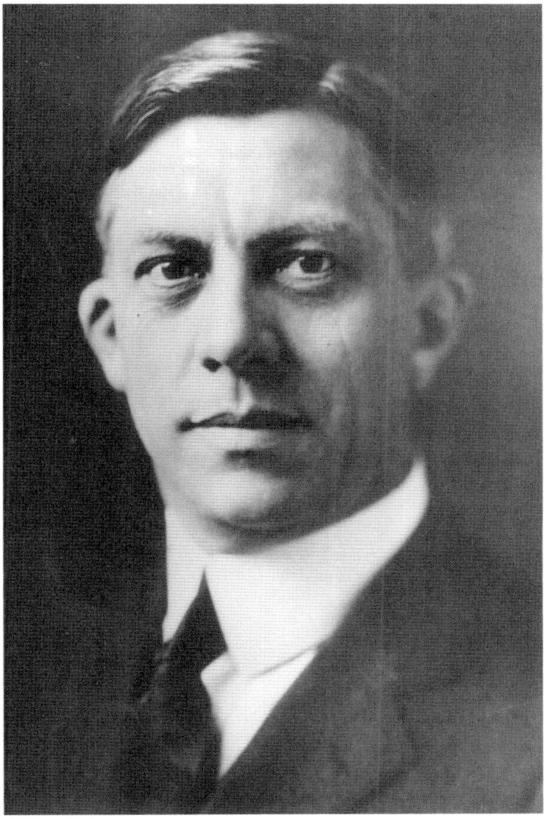

Representative Conrad George Selvig

Conrad George Selvig was born in Rushford, Minnesota, on October 11, 1877. His parents had emigrated from Stavanger, Norway, in 1871. He served in the US Army during the Spanish-American War. While at the University of Minnesota in Minneapolis, Selvig became interested in practical education as a method to prepare students who were not college-bound for vocations after school. Selvig lobbied the legislature to authorize state aid for agricultural and manual and domestic training in the state's high schools. By July 1910, Selvig's high profile had gotten the attention of the University of Minnesota Board of Regents, and he was appointed superintendent of the Northwest School of Agriculture to fill Superintendent Robertson's shoes.

Superintendent Selvig remained in Crookston for nearly 17 years and earned a reputation as an expert on agricultural education and farming issues. Over those years, Selvig served as president of the Red River Valley Dairymen's Association, the Red River Valley Livestock Association, the Red River Valley Development Association, and the Minnesota Export League, as well as being closely involved with the popular Red River Valley Winter Livestock and Farm Crops Shows. In 1910, the shows were inaugurated, largely through the efforts of C.G. Selvig. There was a five-day short course that was held at the Northwest School of Agriculture during the winter of 1910. When it got too big to handle on campus, the meetings and shows were transferred to downtown Crookston in 1914.

In 1926, Selvig decided to campaign for the 9th District seat in the US House of Representatives. He was elected and, subsequently, served three consecutive terms in Congress and was a member of committees on flood control, roads, census, and labor. Even with all his expertise at the Experiment Station, he was never appointed to the committee on agriculture.

Congressman Selvig died in California on August 2, 1953, after writing his autobiography, *The Tale of Two Valleys*. He compared the valley of his birthplace in southern Minnesota to that of the Red River Valley. He was 75 years old. He and his wife are interred in Oakdale Cemetery in Crookston. (NWROC.)

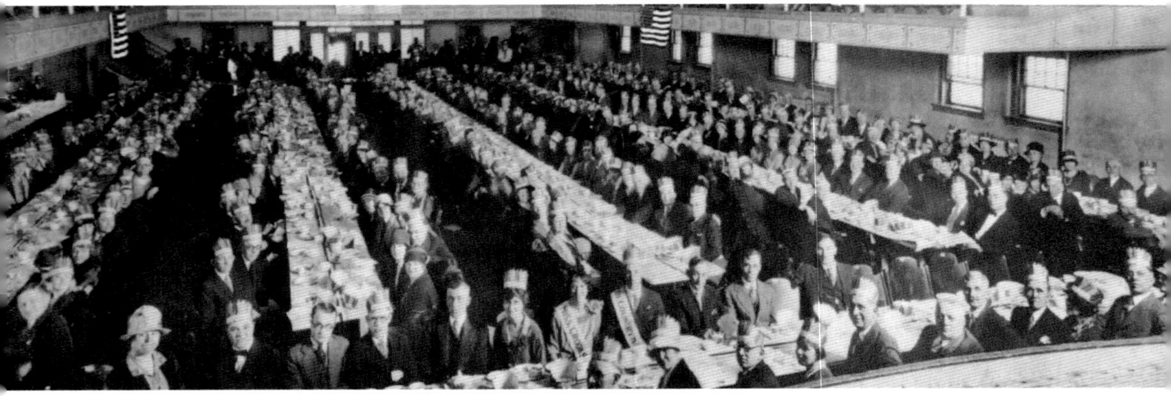

Miss Crookston and Mr. Countryman

A lavish banquet was hosted in the armory on North Broadway during Crookston's annual community dinner. The photograph was taken by Benson Studio around 1925. The head table closest to the stage shows a woman wearing a "Miss Crookston" sash. She is Mae Rideout. The man next to her wearing "Mr. Countryman" is Leo Anderson. Superintendent Selvig is off to the right, third in, looking directly at the camera. More than 600 businessmen and farmers and their wives attended the annual community dinner, given under the auspices of the Crookston Association of Public Affairs. The 1938 postcard below, looking north on Broadway, shows the abundance of cars in Crookston.

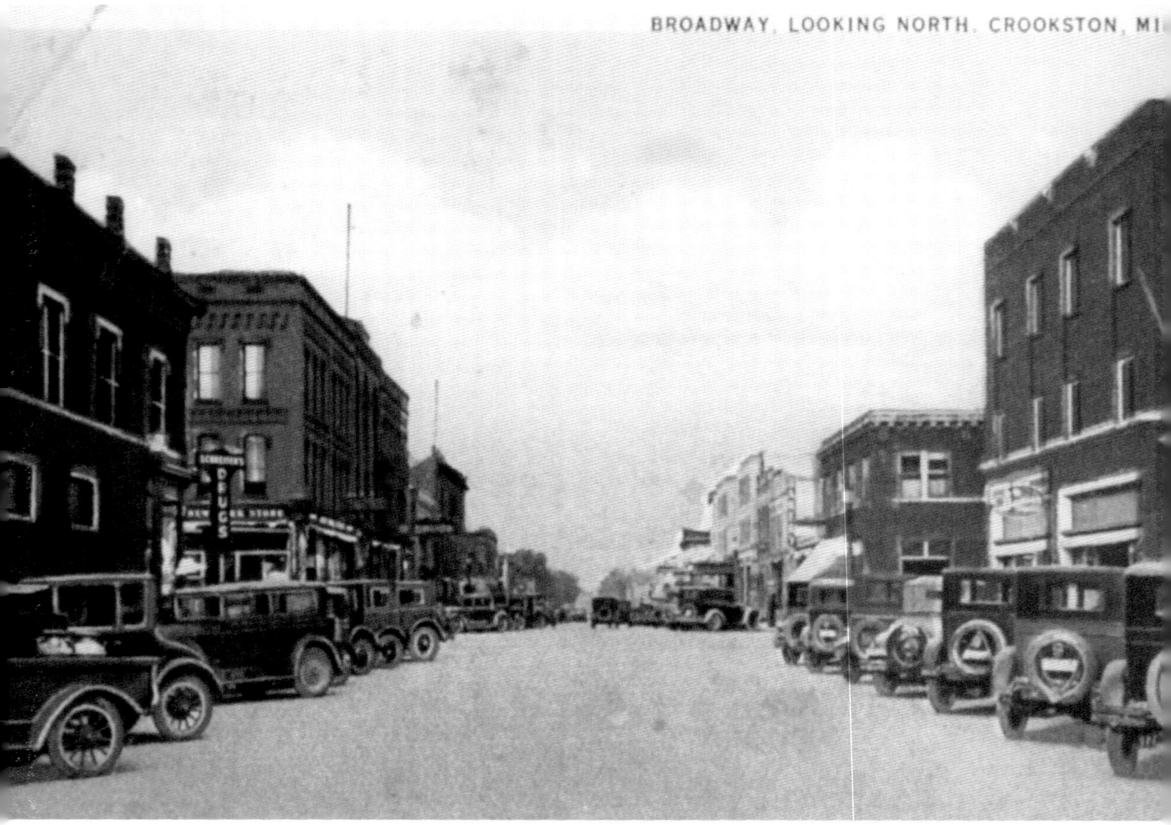

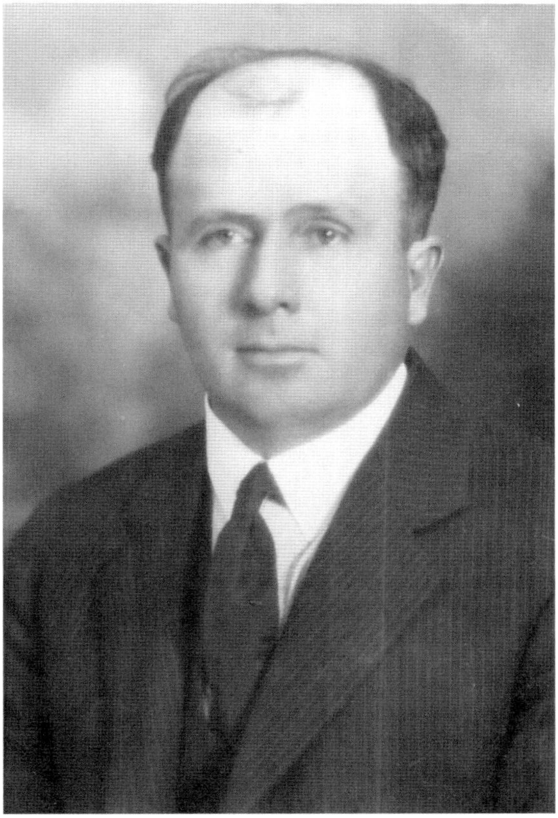

Supt. Thomas McCall

When NWSA superintendent Austin Dowell resigned in 1937, he was succeeded by Thomas McCall. According to T.H. Fersle, "McCall's name has literally become synonymous with agricultural progress in the Valley and rightly so, because he has carved a special niche as a leader, advisor and teacher since 1911. His 45 years of service to the area is a record of which we are all justly proud." Correspondence with McCall's daughter Barbara McCall Hughes reveals that though her father was a quiet man, he had a way of inciting people to action.

He was the superintendent throughout the Depression years, when it was very difficult for some farm families to afford the tuition and board for those six months of on-campus study. One family lived five miles away, and the children were needed to do the chores in the predawn morning and after school, in order to not end up on the poor farm, as their parents intoned.

One of the daughters would read the old Sears, Roebuck & Co. catalogs, daydreaming about life anywhere else but cold, northern Minnesota. It was in the last semester of her senior year that the family funds just would not stretch, and she was not going to graduate with the rest of her classmates in 1931. When Superintendent McCall got wind of this, he called the mother and said that the daughter would graduate and that he would find a way for her to get work study on campus. She worked in the kitchen her last semester, and she did graduate. This young woman with the secretarial skills she learned at NWSA ended up in warm Southern California after marrying a young man who had graduated from Central High School. For decades, she was secretary to the dean of liberal arts for one of the colleges in the University of California system. That one act of kindness among many of Tom McCall's affected many lives.

At UMC, the McCall Hall dormitory to the south of Selvig Hall is a tribute to this humble man who also wrote about *The Centennial History of Polk County.* McCall loved the NWSA campus, and the trees he planted are straight and tall, nearly 100 years later.

Supt. Bernie Youngquist

Dr. Bernie Youngquist came on board as NWSA superintendent in 1956 when Thomas McCall ended his tenure as leader of the campus. In 1958, Youngquist had done his very thorough doctoral dissertation on how, with the evolution of farming, the farming high schools were becoming obsolete throughout the nation and most particularly in Minnesota. The Board of Regents of the University of Minnesota decided to phase out Crookston's farm high school to become a two-year technical institute. The way Youngquist put it, "the technical college concept makes it [the high school] as old-fashioned as a butter churn." The board of regents decided that Youngquist would be the sole director of the Experiment Station. Instead, Dr. Stan Sahlstrom was tasked to head the new University of Minnesota Technical Institute (UMTI) or what Crookstonites called "the Tech." Agriculture was retained, but other technical studies were infused.

Dr. Youngquist became more involved with the annual Winter Shows. By 1962, Dr. Youngquist was part of the auspicious dedication of the new Winter Shows Building, which was an area of 2.5 acres under one roof. The Winter Shows in downtown Crookston had outgrown its facilities there. Youngquist drew on the strengths and expertise of many people in the 14-county area. He knew he could not take on the load of having the new building erected without the financial help of many others from the Crookston community and surrounding area.

What was spawned from Youngquist's heavy involvement with the Winter Shows was the increased visibility of Crookston throughout the Northwest region, bringing potential students to be recruited for the two-year technical institute. The Winter Shows also was home for several decades to the Great Midwest and Winter Horse Shows that brought in much talent from the Dakotas, Canada, and Minnesota. (NWROC.)

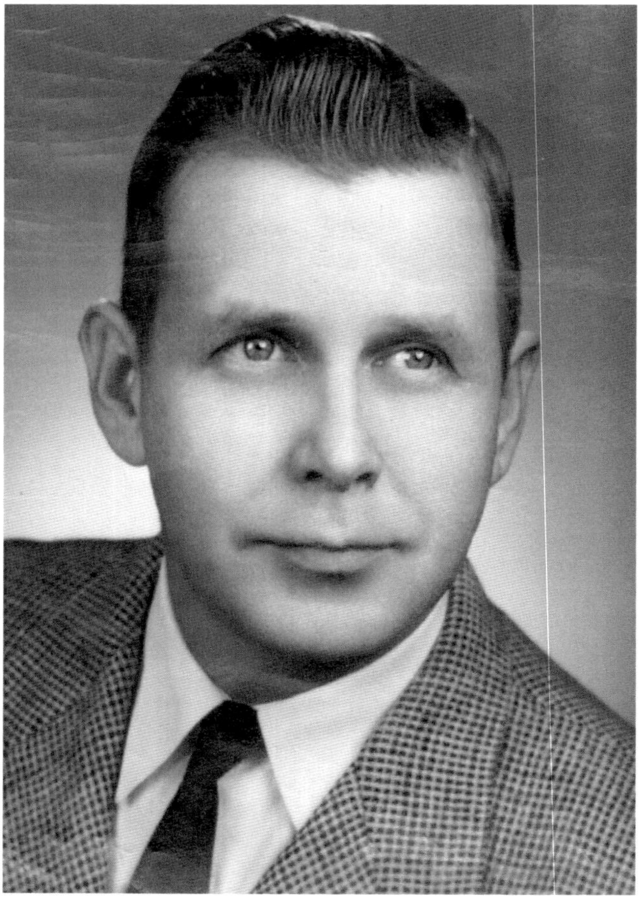

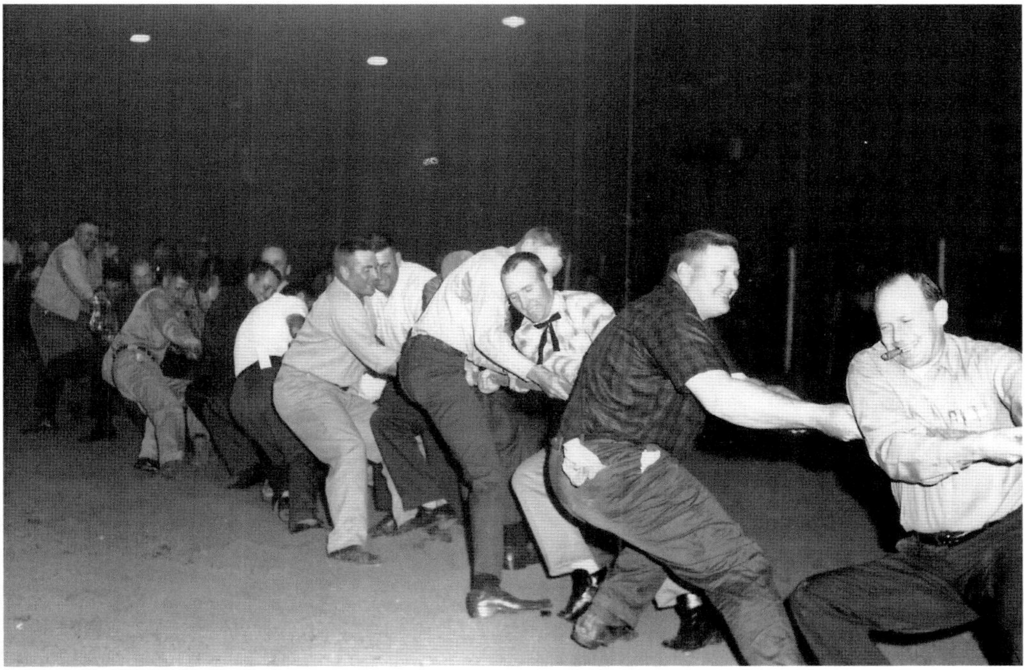

Merchants vs. Farmers Tug of War

In any farming community, there was always some antagonism in school between farm kids and city kids. For example, a Lincoln Elementary School farm boy always had his big overcoat brought down to the basement by a kind janitor; this was because he was teased about the smell of manure left on his jacket after doing early morning chores in the barn. The "friendly" tug-of-war at the horse show between merchants and farmers in November 1964 was a match between the two interests. Bill Briden on the far right was the anchor man for the farmers.

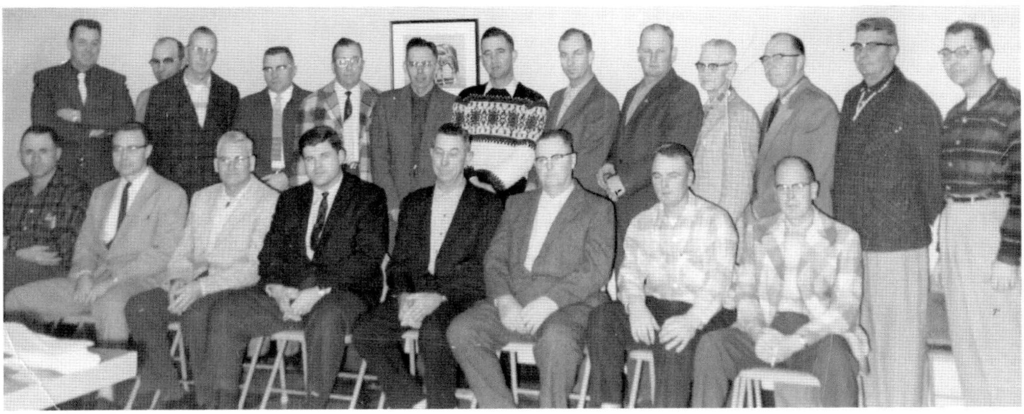

Crookston Area's Fundraiser for the Winter Shows Building

This 1960 group photograph is of the West Polk County Committee responsible for the fundraiser for the Red River Valley Winter Shows Building. Both town and country men are represented, from left to right, (sitting) Lloyd Hughes, Ken Erie, Ben Strickler, Bob Stone, Walter Ross, Helmer Peterson, Herman Skyberg Jr., and unidentified; (standing) Lyle Kiel, Ray Eggert, Paul Brekken, Gil Hanson, John Romuld, Brekken, Dale Peterson, Alvin Wagner, Ralph Eickof, Herb Hanson, Oscar Thureen, Einer Queren, Jesse Filipi, and Gerhard Ross.

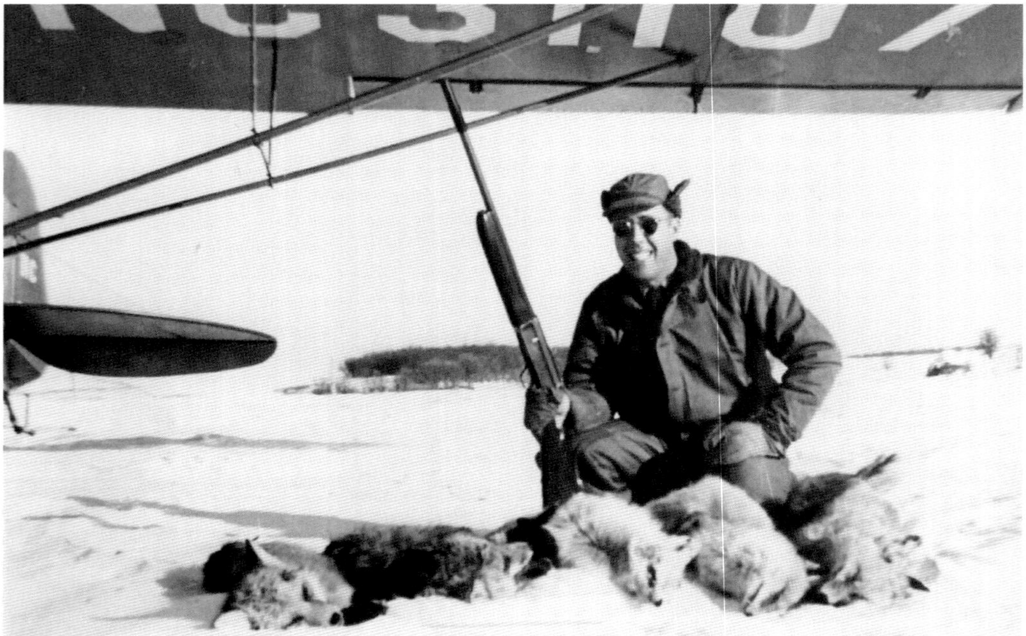

E.C. Miller

E.C. "Gene" Miller was a hunter, pilot, photographer, engineer, teacher, cowboy, and writer. In this 1949 photograph, he is next to his Red Piper Cub NC 31107, showing off five foxes he shot near Starbuck, Minnesota. Gene Miller was Dr. Youngquist's right-hand man at the Northwest School of Agriculture and the Winter Shows. Miller helped the Agassiz Riders run the horse shows in the 1960s and 1970s and organized the Canadian Flag Run, promoting Canadian participation. Miller also wrote an extensive book about Red River Valley pilots.

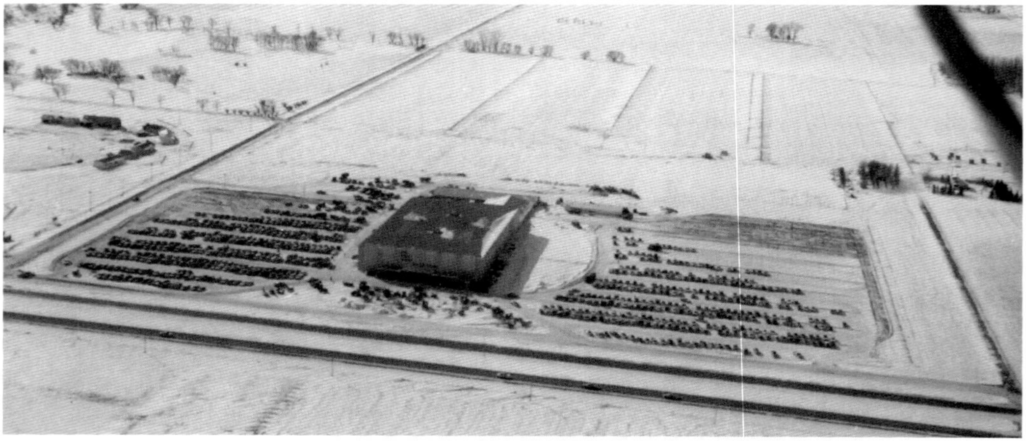

Red River Valley Winter Shows from the Air

An aerial view of the Winter Shows Building shows the area to the south, the Minakwa golf course without trees. Also, it shows the area to the east of the Winter Shows Building, which is now part of the commercial section along Highway 2. Hard as it is to believe, the Winter Shows had been housed downtown in the armory on North Broadway and other adjacent buildings. Soon after, a new armory was built to the north of the Winter Shows Building, a kind of symbiotic relationship. (Photograph taken by Gene Miller.)

 70

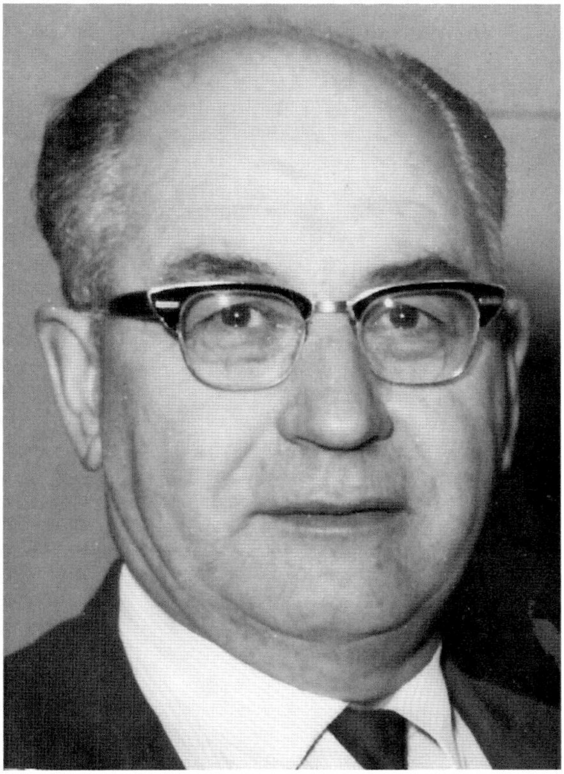

Mayor Harold Thomforde
In July 1968, Crookston mayor Harold Thomforde got a telegram requesting his presence on very short notice at Vice Pres. Hubert Humphrey's home in Minneapolis. Hubert H. Humphrey had been a mayor of Minneapolis, and Mayor Thomforde dropped everything and said yes. He was glad he did because he met 85 other mayors from all over the United States with 12 being from Minnesota.

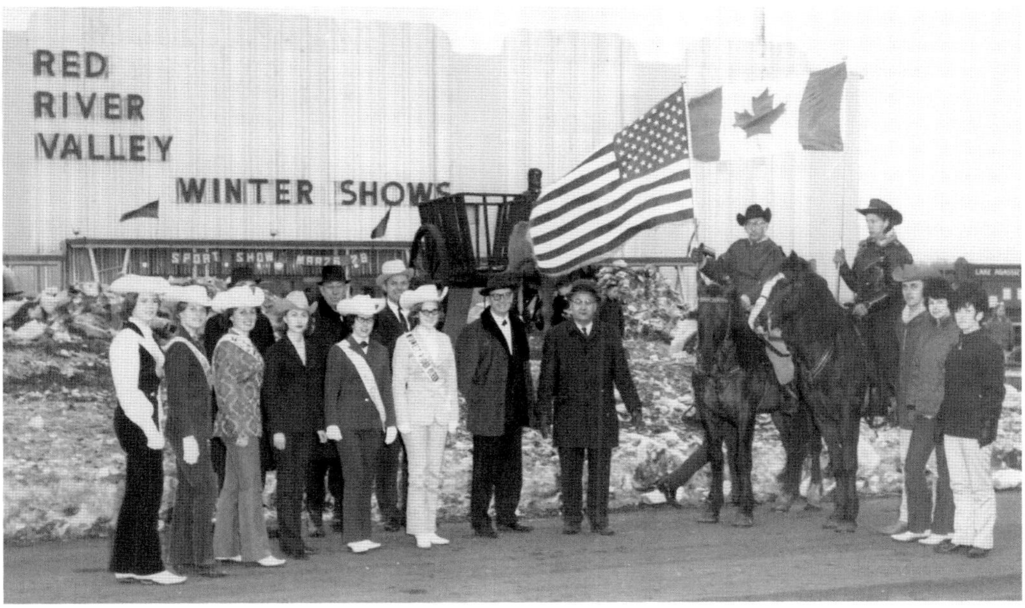

Mayor Thomforde and Winter Shows Saddle Club Queens
Harold Thomforde served as Crookston's mayor in the busy years from 1952 into the 1960s. He is standing below the American flag, closest to the horse. The flag was carried more than 100 miles, down from Canada along Highway 75. As part of the horse show, it was an emblem of solidarity between the two countries. (Photograph taken by Don Buness.)

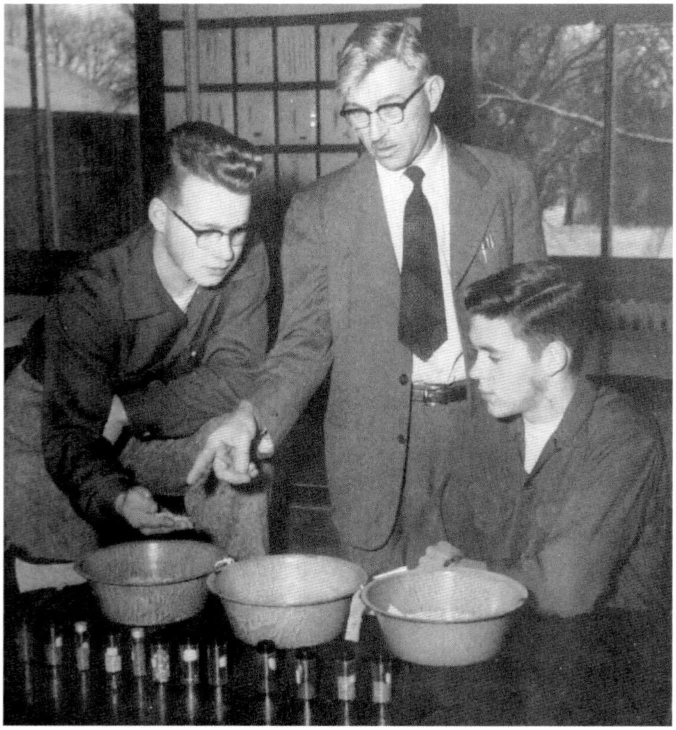

Dr. Olaf Soine, the Weather Man Agronomist

On September 14, 1945, Dr. Olaf Soine came to teach at the NWSA. As any good agronomist would do, every day, he recorded the precipitation and temperatures, hot and cold. He faithfully did that for almost three decades, daily recording what started back in 1895. The booklet put together by James Cameron titled "105 Years of Weather Reporting in Northwest Minnesota" shows much weather data that was collected. When asked by the Winter Shows committee which month in the winter had the least frequency of blizzards, Dr. Soine settled on the last 10 days of February.

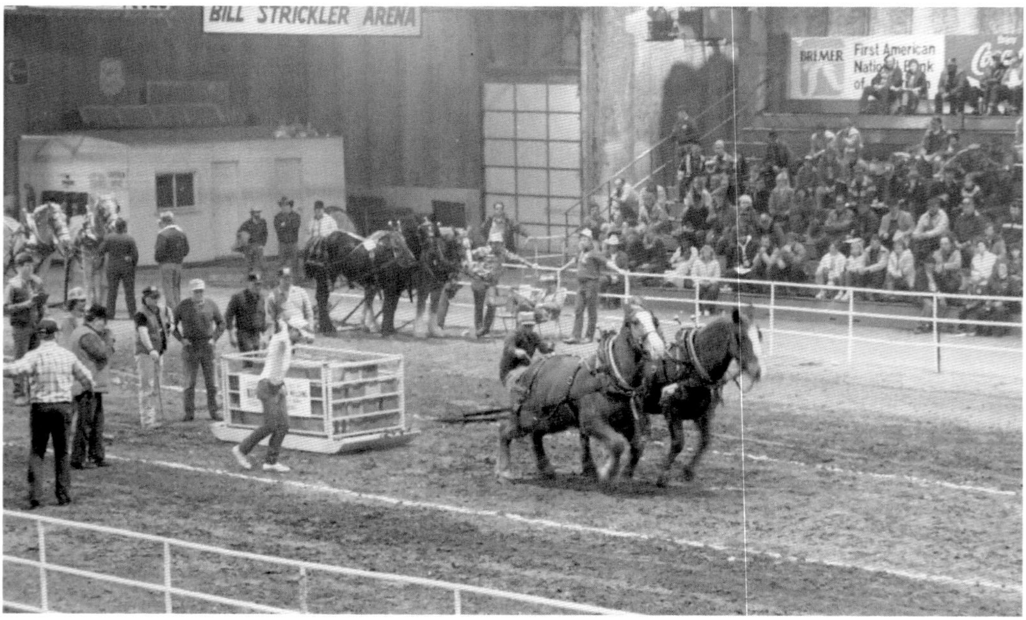

Bill Strickler

The Strickler brothers were prosperous cattle farmers in the Euclid area, north of Crookston. One of the brothers lived on one side of the road where his children went to Warren for school, the other Strickler cousins went to school in Crookston. Bill Strickler saw the importance of continuing the Winter Shows, so he donated a large amount of money, and consequently, the main Winter Shows arena was named after him.

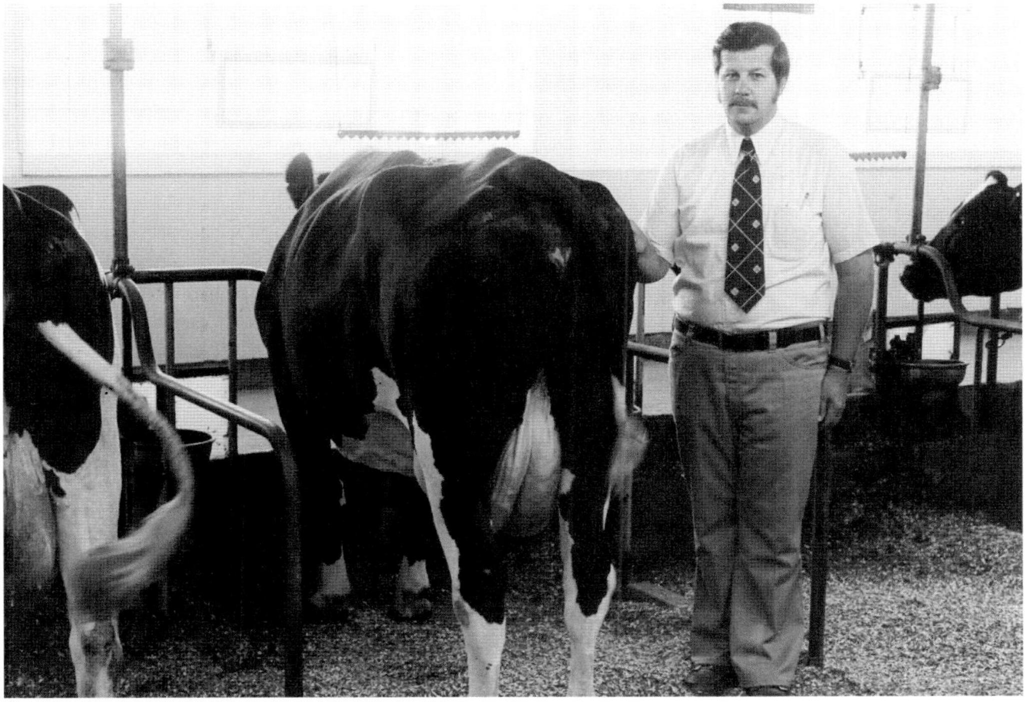

Dr. George Marx, the Dairy Researcher

Dr. George Marx spent a lot of time in the lab doing research on the latest technology for the dairy industry. A cheese factory was located in the town of Gentilly, east of Crookston. It became known for advanced practice in producing milk and its products. In fact, by some reports, the Catholic priest would give an hour sermon, and half was devoted to the latest research done to produce better milk and cheese! (NWROC.)

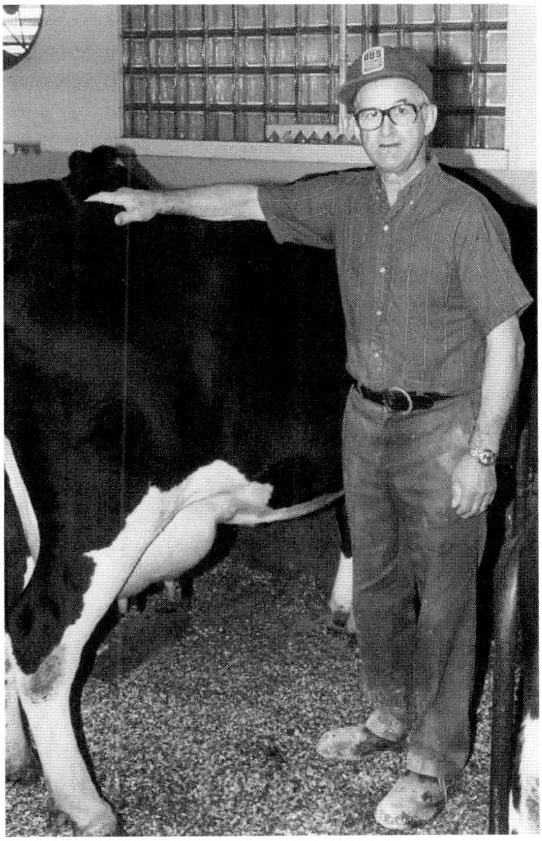

Marvin Chandler, the Dairy Attendant

This picture was taken of Marvin Chandler in September 1983. Marv would get up at 5:00 a.m. and head to the dairy barn at the Experiment Station to milk the cows. After 38 years of doing this, he was ready to retire. When Superintendent Youngquist saw Marv would receive a higher pension if he stayed on one more year, he asked Marv not to retire and work in the lab with Dr. Marx. Marv will be forever thankful to his boss, Dr. Youngquist, who was looking out for him. (NWROC.)

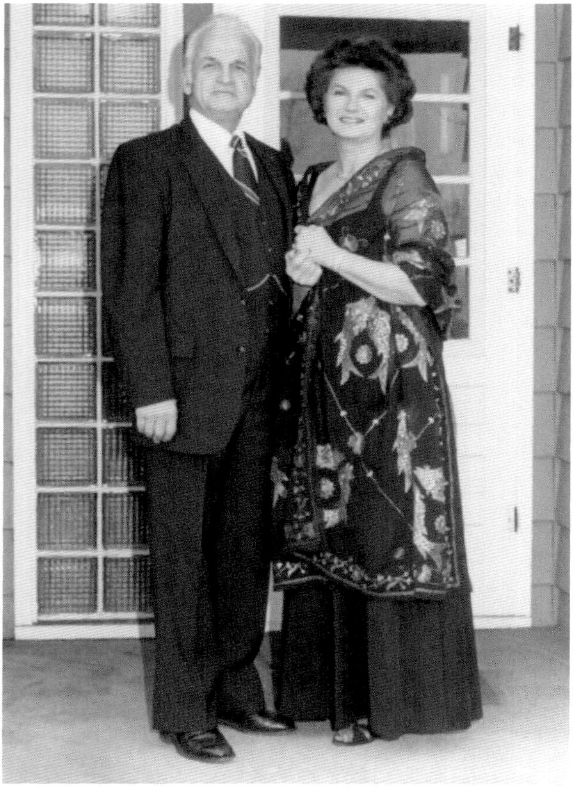

Regent Stanley Sahlstrom and Ludmilla "Mil" Sahlstrom
Dr. Stan Sahlstrom and his wife, Mil, moved to Crookston when he was named provost of the University of Minnesota Technical Institute (UMTI) in September 1965. Stan was known as a dynamic motivator; his wife was known as a gracious hostess. Mil claimed her husband's veins "flowed maroon and gold"; he was so dedicated to the University of Minnesota. On October 12, 1984, Sahlstrom resigned from UMC to become a University of Minnesota regent the following year. (Photograph taken by John Zak.)

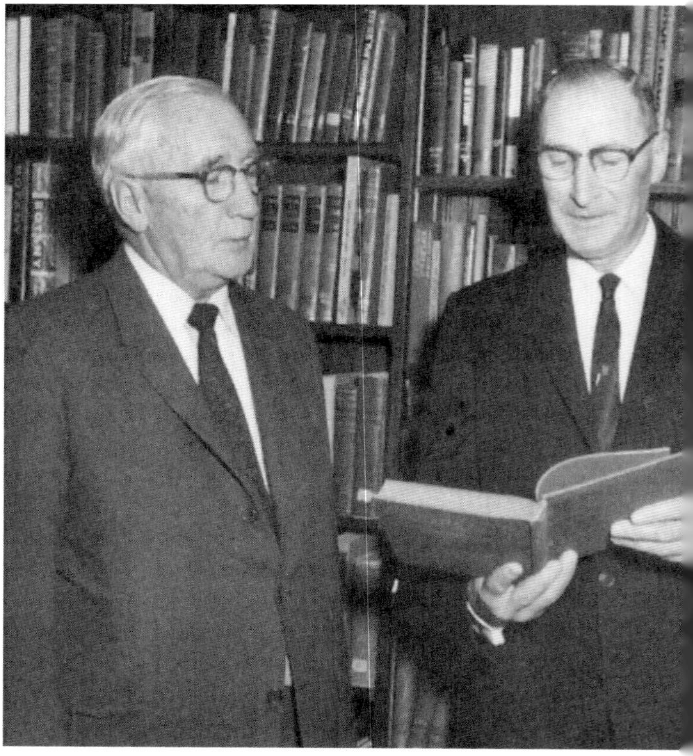

Judge James Montague and Regent Herman Skyberg
Judge James E. Montague (left) was a judge of district court from 1934 to 1949, replacing Judge William Watts. Montague was a well-known authority on Polk County history. He and University of Minnesota regent Herman Skyberg are shown checking out a book at the newly remodeled library in Kiehle Hall. Skyberg had a farming background in the Fisher area and did much for the NWSA campus as an alumnus. There is a dormitory named after Skyberg on the UMC campus.

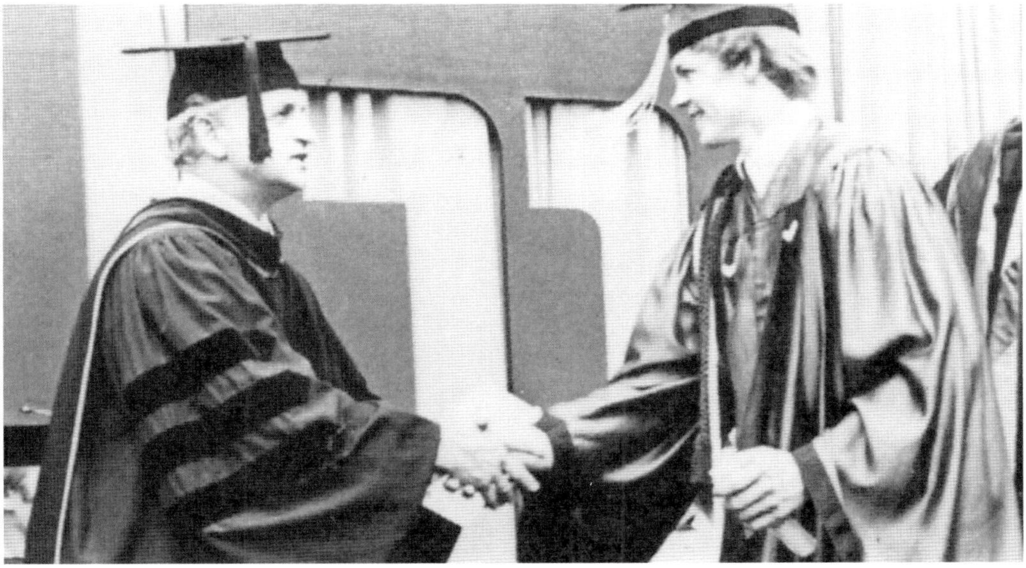

Provost Sahlstrom

Provost Stan Sahlstrom had a ready handshake for everyone he met. Sahlstrom traveled up and down the Red River Valley recruiting the first Tech students and, with his people skills, was able to start up a university from scratch. During the summer of 1965, Sahlstrom was "selling the institution." No high school was missed, and by the fall of 1966, two hundred students showed up to register. During job interviews, Sahlstrom made it known that he expected the teaching faculty to live in Crookston and not commute from afar.

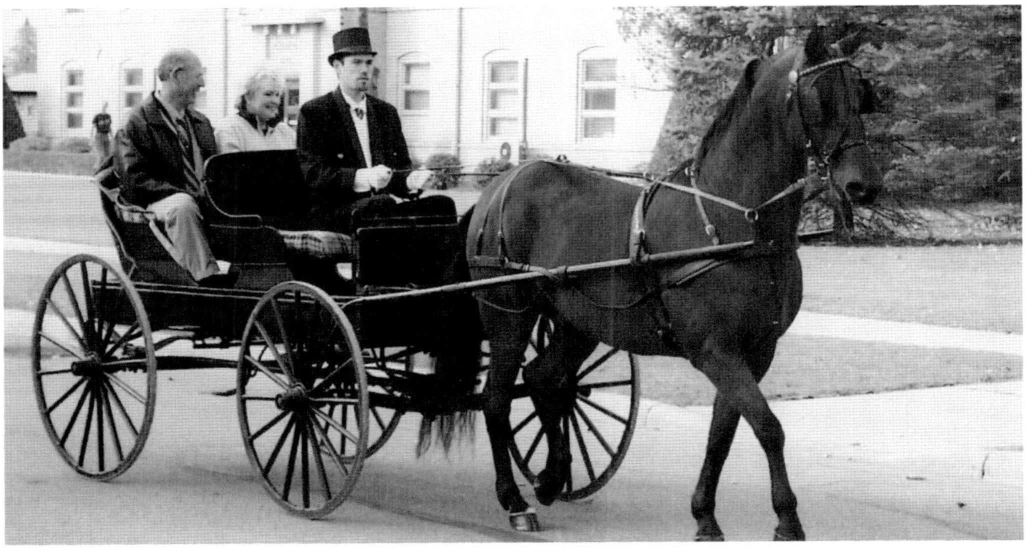

Chancellor Don and Mary Beth Sargeant

Eventually, the title of UMC's leader changed. Provost Sahlstrom bequeathed the thriving campus to Chancellor Don Sargeant in the spring of 1985. Dr. Don and Mary Beth Sargeant had originally come to Crookston to be a part of the UMTI in June 1973. In 1991, the UMC campus began a five-year program to build student and faculty confidence in using laptop computers for instruction. The campus has been nationally acclaimed as one of the first laptop universities ever since. (Courtesy of Bernie Elseth.)

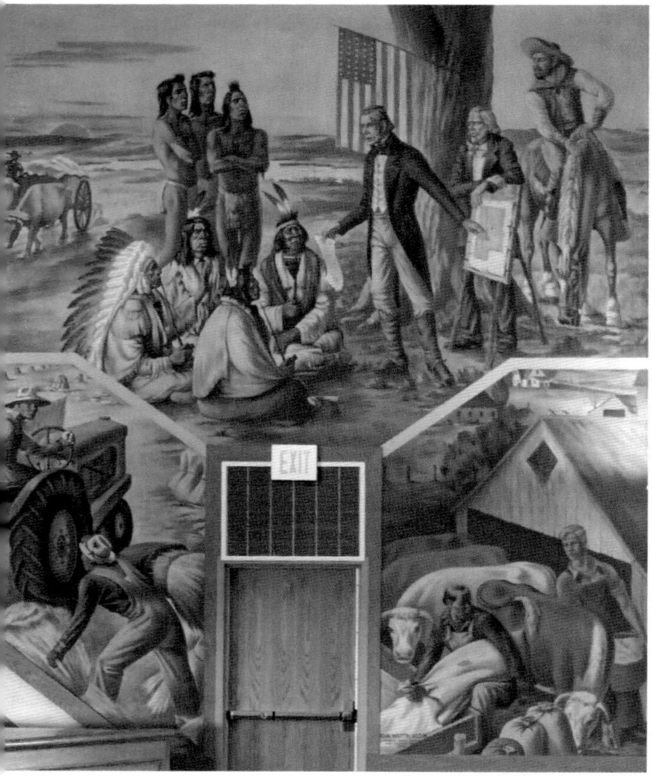

John Martin Soucha, Artist
John Martin Soucha's east mural in the Kiehle Auditorium continues the narrative begun on page 2. Native Americans are sitting with peace pipes while the white man is referring to a map of the Red River Valley. The use of oxcarts, followed by tractors, shows the progress made. All appears peaceful. According to the federal agency from Washington, DC, that got involved with this WPA project, it was completed in 1942, ten years after its inception. It was a gift from the NWSA class of 1932. (Photograph taken by Steve Hannah.)

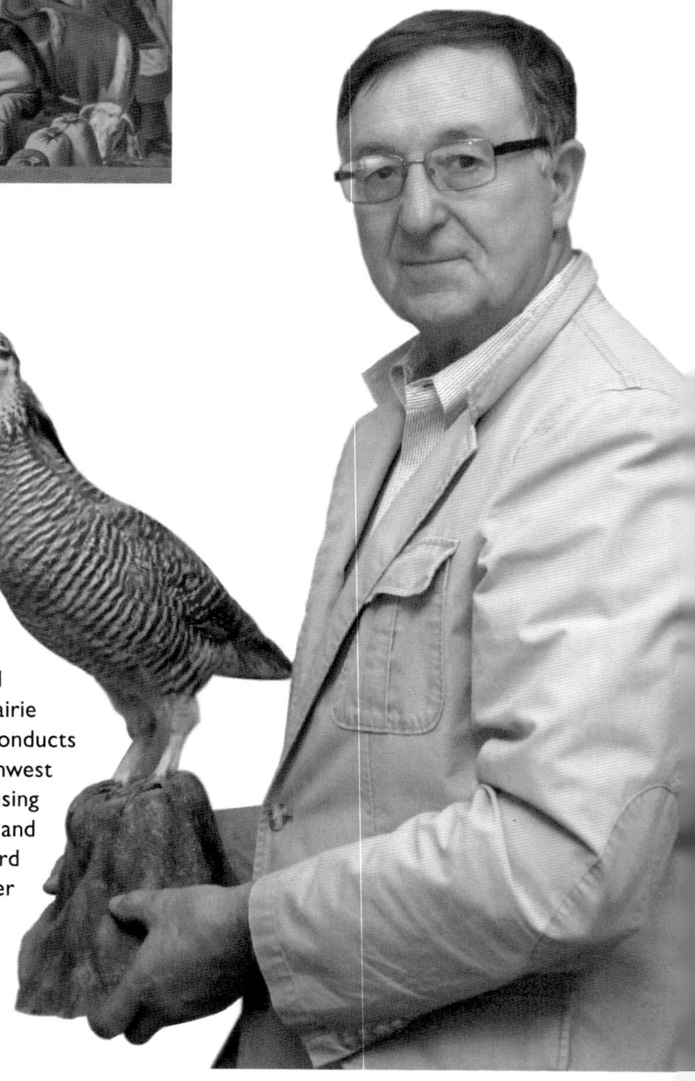

Dr. W. Daniel Svedarsky
Dr. Dan Svedarsky has been at UMC since 1969, for 45 years. Svedarsky has studied the nesting and brood-rearing ecology of greater prairie chickens in Minnesota. He also conducts wildlife research with the Northwest Research and Outreach Center, focusing on tallgrass prairie restoration and management using fire and prairie bird management, especially for greater prairie chickens. (Photograph taken by Steve Hannah.)

CHAPTER SIX

Public Servants and God's Servants

Advisedly, religion and politics are two topics that should not be discussed at family gatherings. Too many arguments have involved a politician's voting record or a clergyman's sermon. On the other hand, in Minnesota, it is always safe to discuss the weather. The weather in Crookston may be just as intractable as politics and religion, but because it is out of man's control, it is a benign topic for discussion.

However, the topics of politics and religion fit nicely together into this chapter because both have historically been a basis for public service. Laws are formed through politics and are ordered to be upheld, and the Ten Commandments and gospel are respected and upheld in the religious community. When policies are put into place that hinder the people, the politician is voted out. If a politician listens to his or her constituents, then he or she is in for the long haul of representing the people. That is democracy, and this is how long-serving political legends are made.

The United States is blessed with the rule of law as set forth in the Constitution by the founding fathers. Firefighters, police and patrolmen, and others who served in the military to protect democracy are to be respected. This short chapter gives honor to those who keep the fear factor out—making sure a ruling tyrant does not take over. A few decades into Crookston's history, the early 20th century brought an influx of the freedom-seeking Scandinavians. Once acclimated to American life, many Norwegians held positions of power in Crookston.

In the case of religion, there are many different faiths represented in Crookston. In this chapter, no mention is made of the churches outside of the old Catholic cathedral or the newer Trinity Lutheran Church. See Images of America: *Crookston* for information on other local churches that made an impact on early Crookston. This book focuses on the individuals who were legendary in their own right, for good or naught.

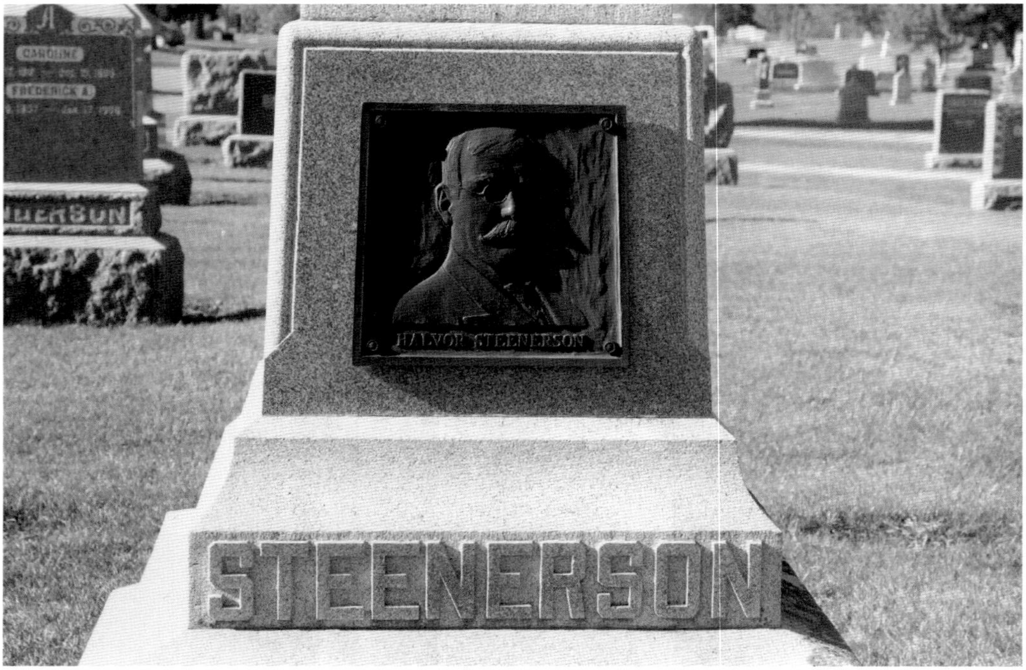

Hon. Halvor Steenerson

In Crookston's peaceful Oakdale cemetery, it is easy to find several prominent memorials dedicated to the Steenerson clan. At the entrance, there is a memorial honoring the Honorable Halvor Steenerson. On March 23, 1905, Congressman Steenerson secured a big Spanish war gun for Crookston. It sat on the northwest corner of the old courthouse lawn. The gun was melted down as scrap metal during World War II. In 1906, as a person with Norwegian roots, he tried to get a Leif Erickson statue for Crookston but failed.

Halvor was born on June 30, 1852, in Dane County, Wisconsin. After studying law, he moved to Crookston in 1880. He was the county attorney for a short time from 1881 to 1882, was a Minnesota senator from 1883 to 1887, then spent a longer time as a US Representative from Minnesota's 9th District from 1903 to 1923. Halvor was married in 1878 to Mary Christopherson, and they had four children. Clara and Benjamin lived in their home on Houston Avenue; the other two children died earlier. (A sad and unsolved puzzle surrounds Benjamin's death.) Halvor died on November 22, 1926, in Crookston at age 74 years.

According to a few *Crookston Daily Times* headlines, the following shows that he worked hard for his constituents no matter if they were Native American or Norwegian. In January 19, 1907, Congressman Steenerson introduced a bill on Indian affairs and by July of that year, Halvor was adopted by the Chippewa tribe. On September 26, 1907, the Red Lake Indians aired their grievances to Halvor. Subsequent to that in December 28, 1907, he introduced a drainage bill to Congress. In April 29, 1909, he was the honored speaker at the American Scandinavian society. On July 13, 1912, he addressed the teachers at NWSA. Superintendent Selvig was no doubt a friend of Halvor's with similar Norwegian roots.

Perhaps Halvor was best known for the "Steenerson Grain Rate Case," where he represented Elias Steenerson, who was an extensive grain farmer in the Climax, Minnesota, area. The case involved the question of the power of the state through a commission to regulate and fix charges for railroad transportation. The case was most stubbornly contested before the Minnesota Railroad and Warehouse Commission and twice carried to the Minnesota Supreme Court. The 15-percent reduction ordered by the commission was finally sustained and acquiesced to by the railroad company. (Photograph taken by Steve Hannah.)

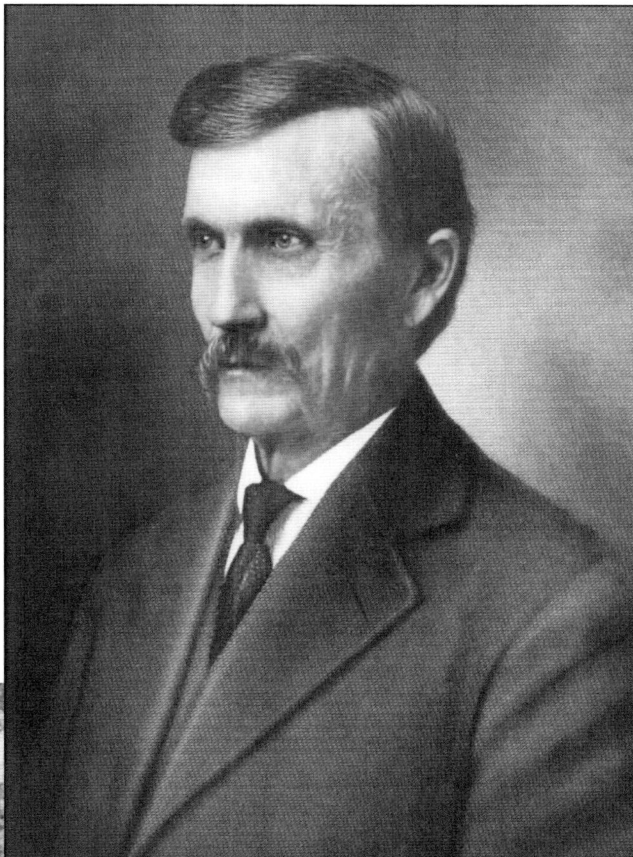

Judge William Watts

Judge William Watts was born on June 9, 1850, in Ontario. Watts came to Crookston in January 1878. He was married to Edith E. Webb, whose father, Rice Webb, was one of Polk County's pioneers. The Wattses had four children. Watts was county attorney from 1882 to 1888, then he was the judge of district court from 1899 to 1934. He documented many memories about Crookston's early years in the *Polk County Centennial* book that came out in 1979. The family photograph below was taken in 1937 in front of Judge Watts's residence at 519 North Ash Street. From left to right are son William, Edith, Watts, and his sister. (Below, courtesy of Jessie Brolsma.)

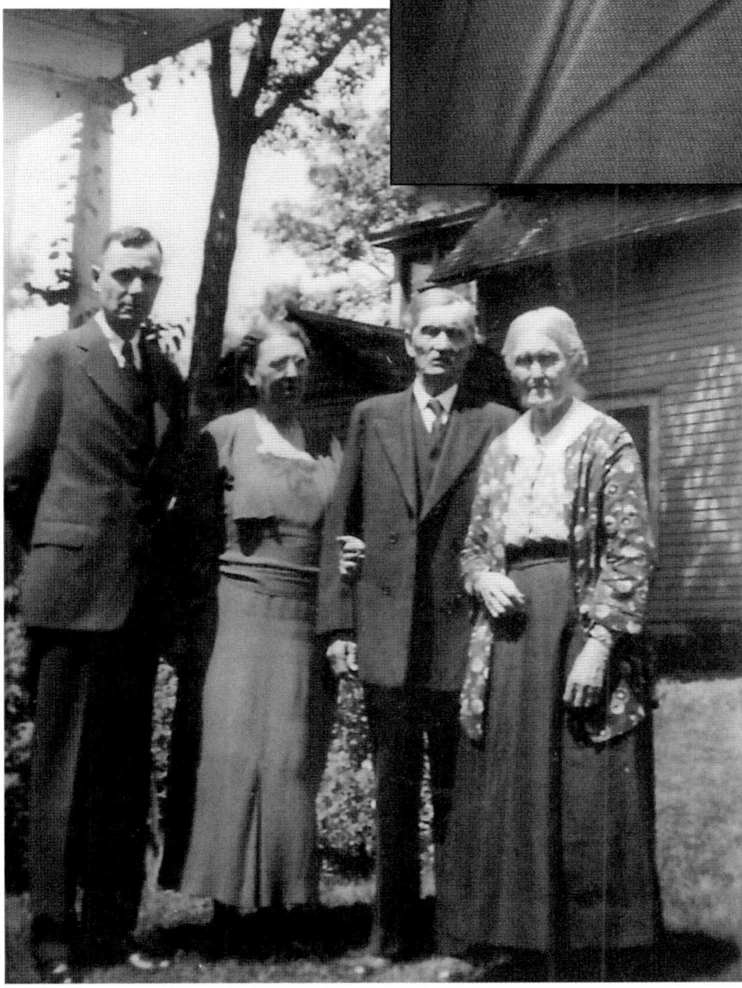

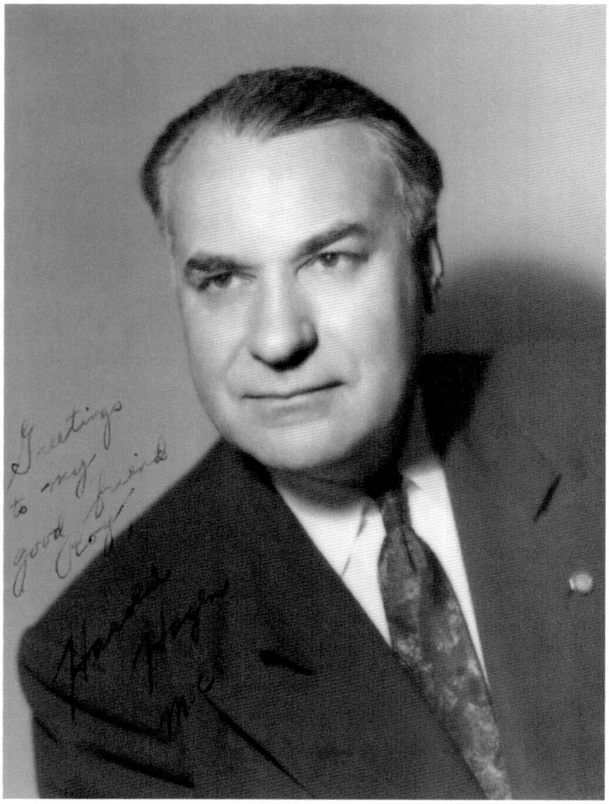

Minnesota Representative Harold C. Hagen
Harold C. Hagen was a Minnesota representative for 12 years (1943–1954) in Washington, DC, after R.T. Buckler (1935–1941). In a surprise, upset victory, Coya Knudson beat Hagen in his seventh election. His legislative interests were flood control, Ojibwe Indian welfare, agriculture, rural electrification, conservation, postal and social services, World War II, and veterans' affairs. Earlier, Representative Hagen had been a journalist (editor of the *Polk County Leader*), a businessman (1923–1933), and a professional automobile racer in the 1930s. (Courtesy of Minnesota Historical Society, St. Paul.)

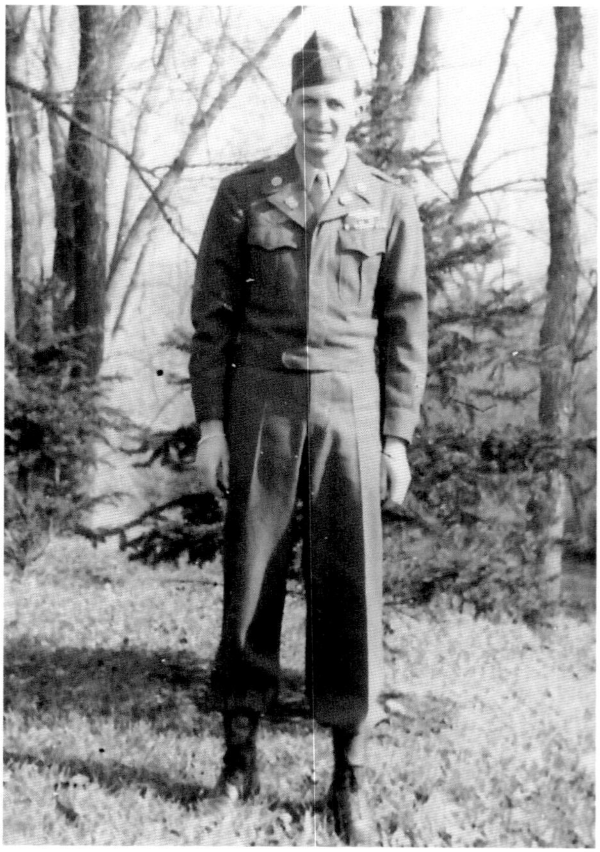

Bernie Lieder in Uniform
Bernard "Bernie" Lieder was born in 1923 to a German-speaking farm family near Hanover, Minnesota. He served in the US Army in France, Belgium, Holland, and Germany during and after World War II (1943–1946). The 102nd Division, in which Bernie served, started in France and ended up near Berlin and on the River Elbe. He says the Combat Infantry Badge added $10 to his $50-per-month pay! Bernie Lieder came to Crookston as a county engineer turned politician. (Courtesy of Bernie Lieder.)

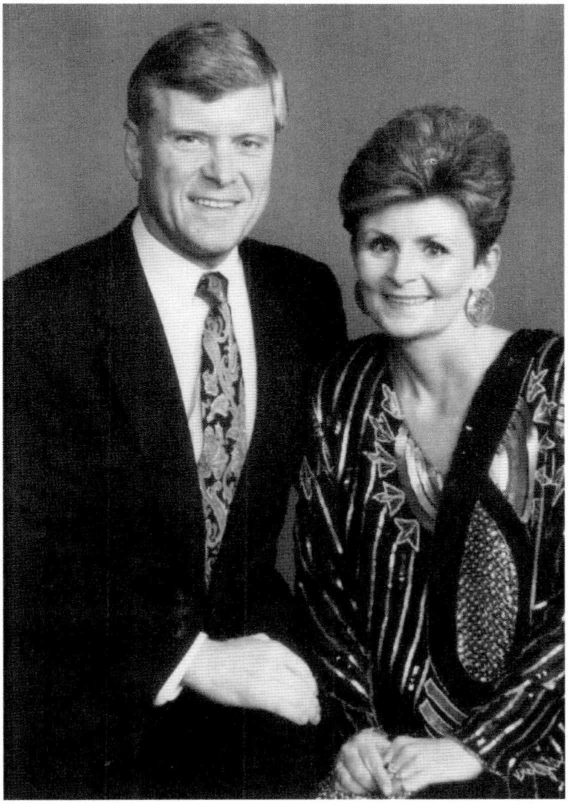

Senate Majority Leader Roger Moe
Roger was a hometown Crookston boy who later taught in Ada, Minnesota, before he became senator for the 2nd District and senate majority leader. In the 1980s, Senator Moe played a major role in UMC's campus. On December 1, 1988, Roger was reelected as state senate majority leader. He is pictured here with his wife, Paulette. (Courtesy of Janet Moe Solheim.)

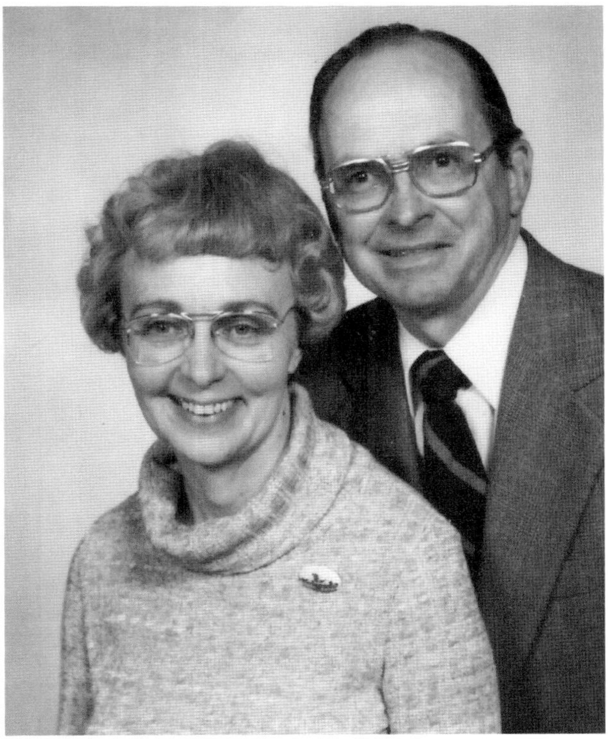

State Representative Bernie Lieder
State representative Bernie Lieder for District 2A is pictured with his wife, Shirley Lieder. As a former county engineer in the 1970s, Bernie's expertise showed through in the following committees: transportation policy, transportation finance, and commerce. He tried to get the Highway 75 bypass approved, and by the fall of 1985, he and Sen. Roger Moe announced that the Minnesota Department of Transportation had approved it. Lieder served from 1985 to 2011. (Courtesy of Bernie Lieder.)

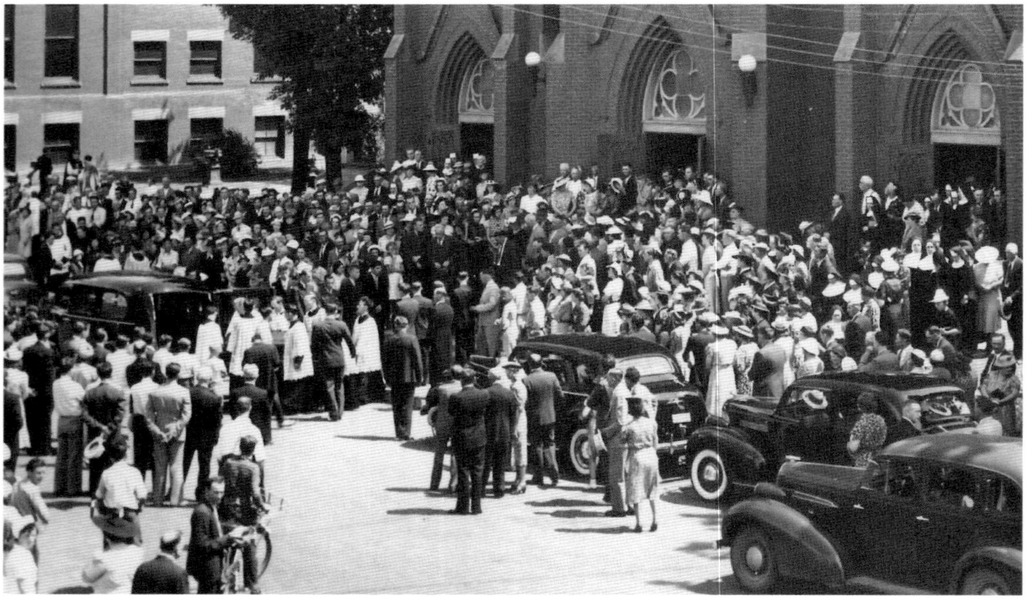

Catholic Bishop Timothy Corbett
Bishop Corbett's funeral in 1939 is pictured in front of the Cathedral of Immaculate Conception, which was built in 1912, soon after his arrival to Crookston from Duluth. On May 31, 1910, a hopeful Bishop Corbett said, "Keep your eye on budding Crookston." Corbett had a diocese with less than 20,000 Catholic scattered over his territory of 17,000 square miles. He knew that in order to build it up under his leadership, it would require prayer and work instead of weeping and lamenting. (Courtesy of Sr. Laurian Lasha, OSB.)

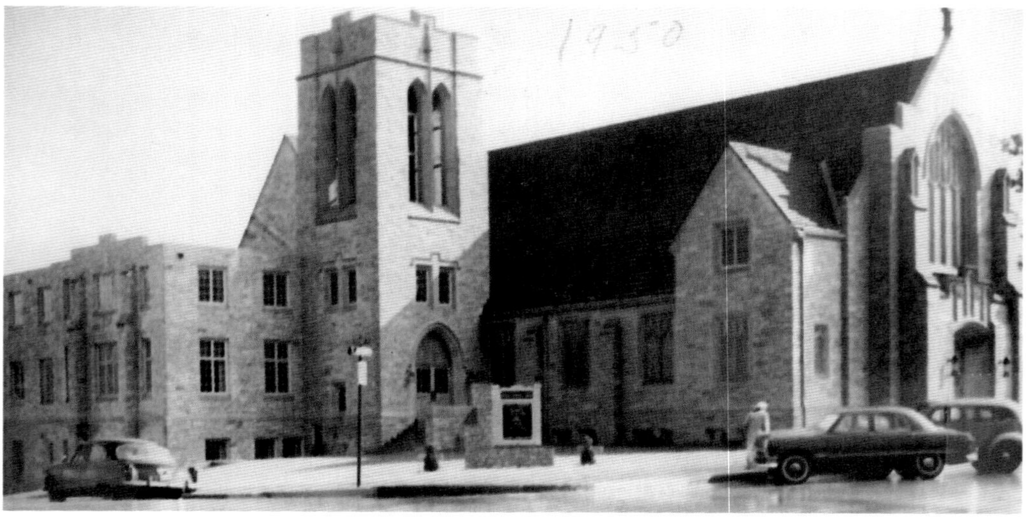

Trinity Lutheran Church
Trinity Lutheran Church was built after the spring flood of 1950. (See the aerial view on page 14.) There was money among the congregants for a church with beautiful stained-glass windows, a pipe organ with choir loft off to the side, and a balcony in the back. The two side-by-side Lutheran churches on South Broadway baffles many people in Crookston. At one time, there were two Pastor Hansons representing the Our Savior's Missouri Synod and Trinity Lutheran Church.

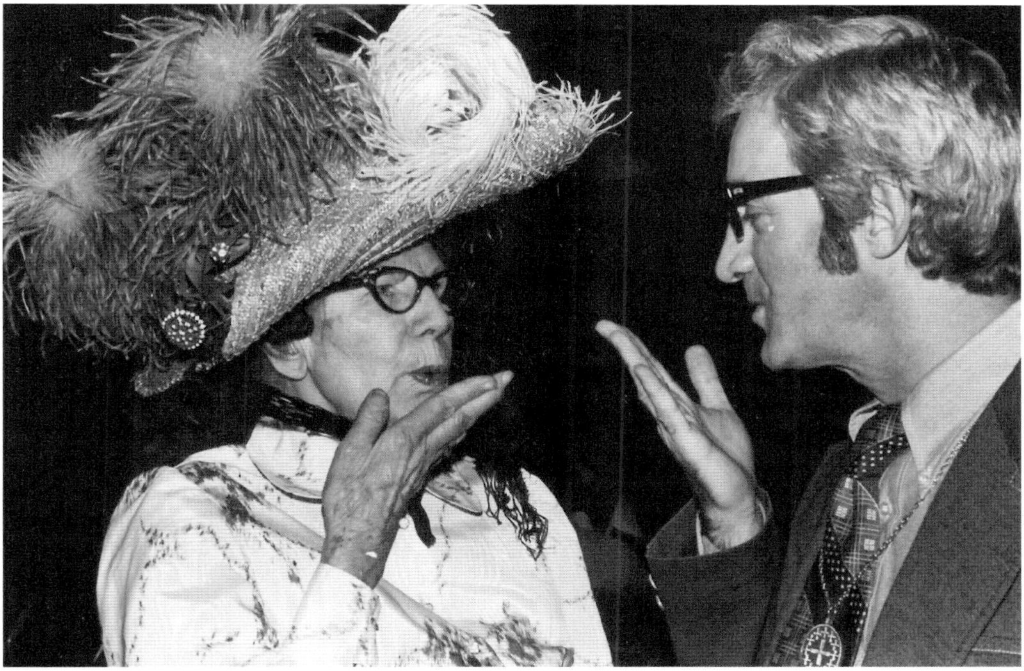

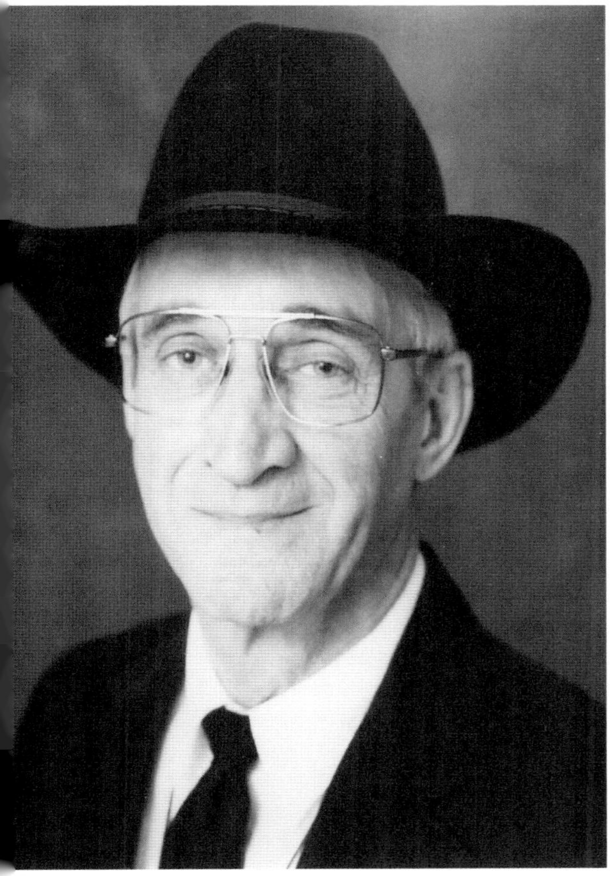

Emma Johnson and Pastor Jim Hanson

Above, Trinity Lutheran Church pastor Jim Hanson is talking with Emma Johnson, the wife of jeweler E.W. Johnson. She was known for her hats and other eccentricities. Pastor James Hanson served at Crookston's Trinity Lutheran Church for 17 years. He acknowledged there were many lonely, frightened, hurting people who needed someone to listen to them, pray with them, and walk with them. He was born in Bemidji on October 1, 1929, the third of four sons born to Rev. A.E. and Marie Hanson. He graduated from St. Olaf College in 1950 and continued his seminary training at Luther Seminary in St. Paul. Upon graduating, he married his roommate's sister, Ramona Kompelien on June 16, 1954, two days after his ordination. They served in parishes in Montana, Crookston, and in Texas. (Left, courtesy of Timothy Hanson.)

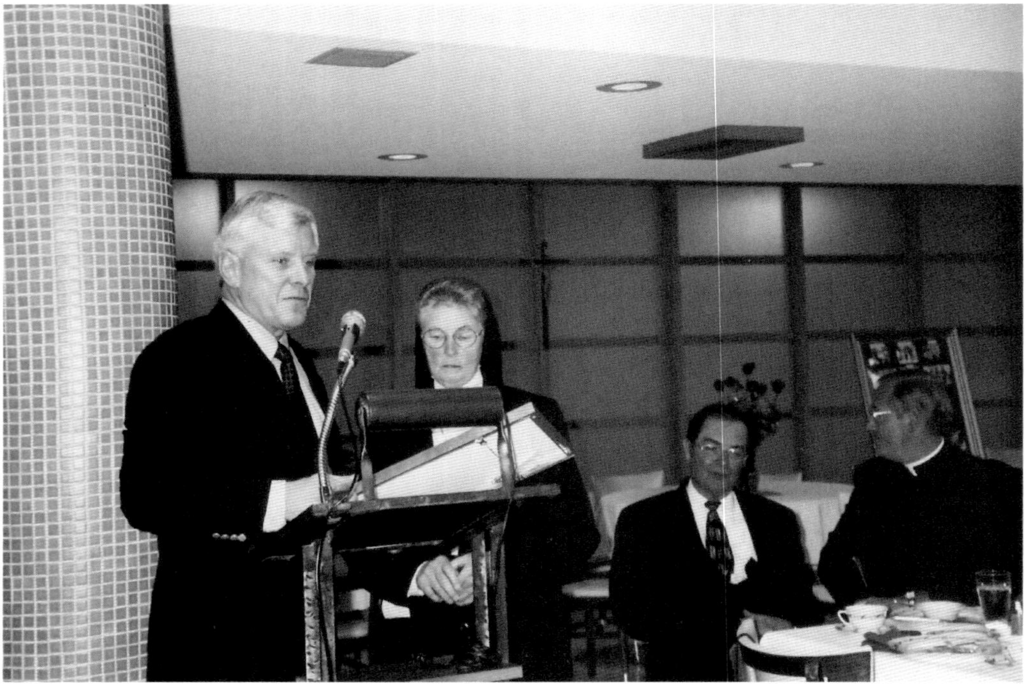

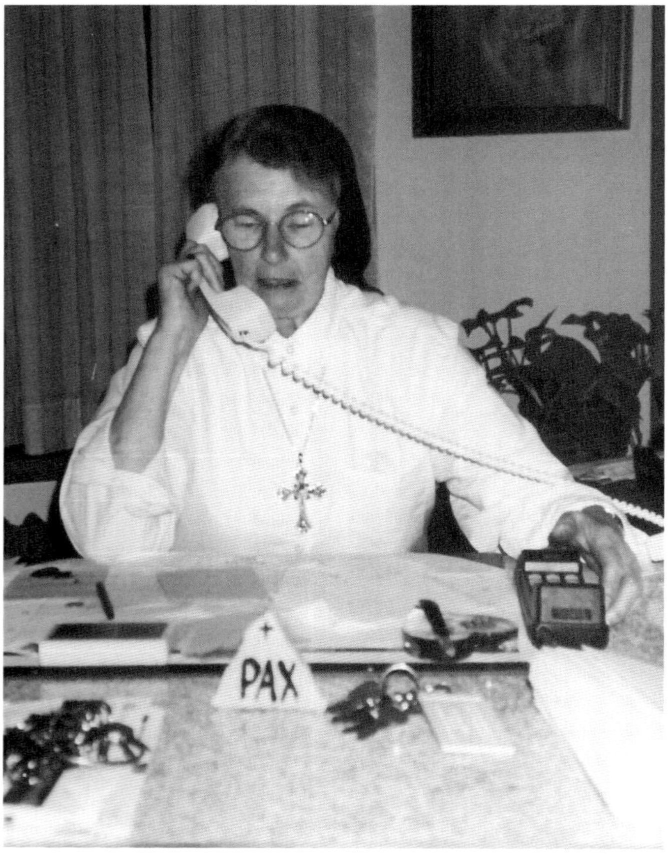

Sen. Roger Moe and Sr. Justina Violette
As Senate majority leader for many years, Roger Moe had the honor of celebrating many people's achievements. One of those people was Sister Justina (Violette) who was known as the "Mother Theresa of the North." She was the third of 16 children born in a French Catholic family in Red Lake Falls. She was a sister for more than 60 years and a member of Mount St. Benedict since 1938. Because of her 30 years of helping those in need, she was named the Top American Missionary for 1999 by a Catholic group. She started out by distributing food outside the bishop's house. In 1986, Sister Justina founded the Care & Share homeless shelter in the former Catholic grade school. (Both courtesy of Sr. Laurian Lasha, OSB.)

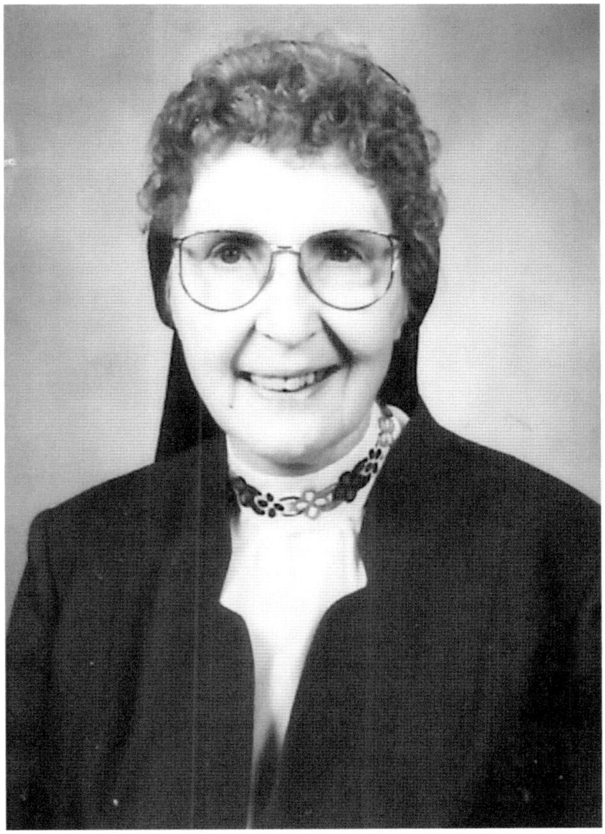

Sister Carmella, Piano Teacher Extraordinaire
Sr. Carmella (Florence) Buckley was the second of nine children born in her family in Pine City, Minnesota. Her name was changed in 1931 when she became a novice, and she made her perpetual commitment in 1935. While commenting on her passion for music, she wrote, "I love teaching music, and because this is what I have done for years, it has added to my happiness. Music has many 'healing' qualities for my students and also for me. I miss directing liturgical music, which was my greatest love, but I've done a lot of that, and one can't go on forever. But the music can live on in our hearts." She died at age 99 but was still playing a lively tune at age 95! (Both courtesy of Sr. Laurian Lasha, OSB.)

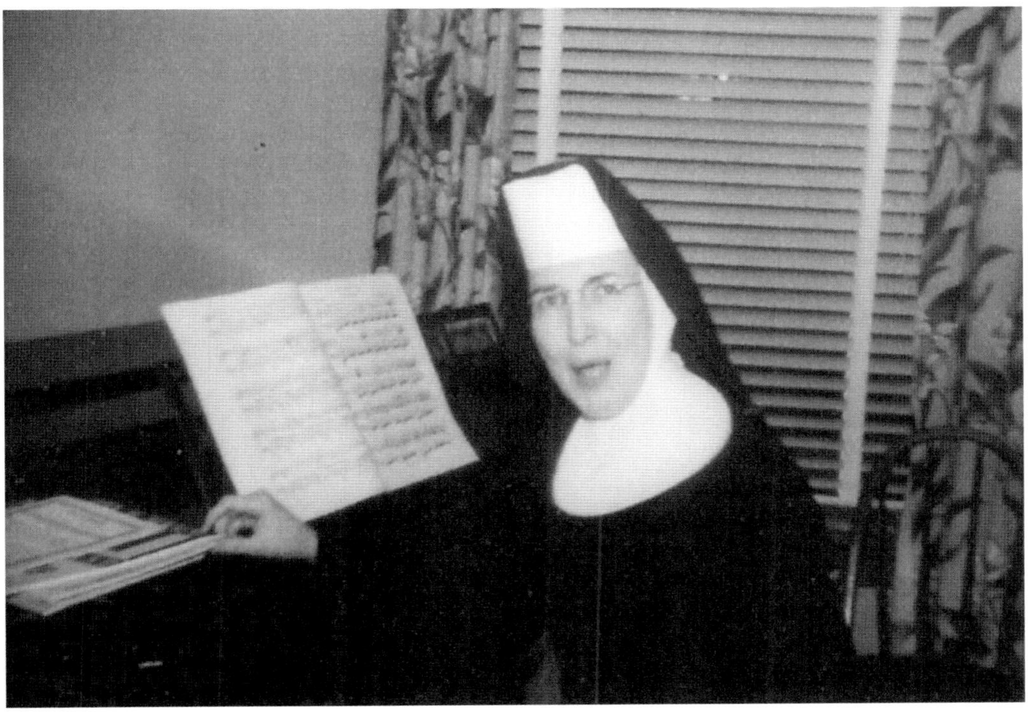

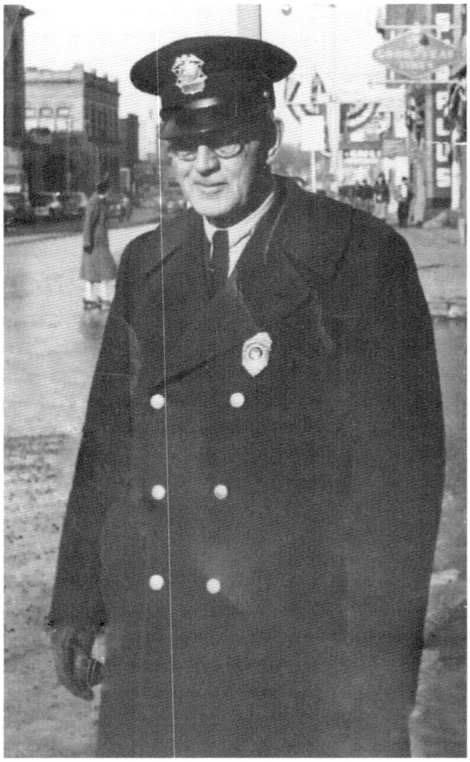

Police Chiefs Milton and Harry Dillabough
Milton V. Dillabough was born in Crookston on February 1, 1883. At age 15, he started working on the railroad for four years. Before he worked on the police force, he spent 20 years, from 1902 to 1922, building telephone lines in the United States and Canada. When he became a patrolman, work was tough, with long hours (12-hour shifts, seven days a week) and without the convenience of a patrol car. By 1928, a policeman's pay amounted to $128 a month. In the 1930s, three shifts were incorporated into a 24-hour day. Milton served as police captain from 1928 to about 1948. During that time, a Harley-Davidson motorcycle with a side car was the first mechanized vehicle used by the police department. The first patrol car was introduced around 1938. In 1940, the Crookston Police Department consisted of eight men. Harry Dillabough, Milton's son, served as police chief from 1958 to 1969. (Both courtesy of Patti Dillabough.)

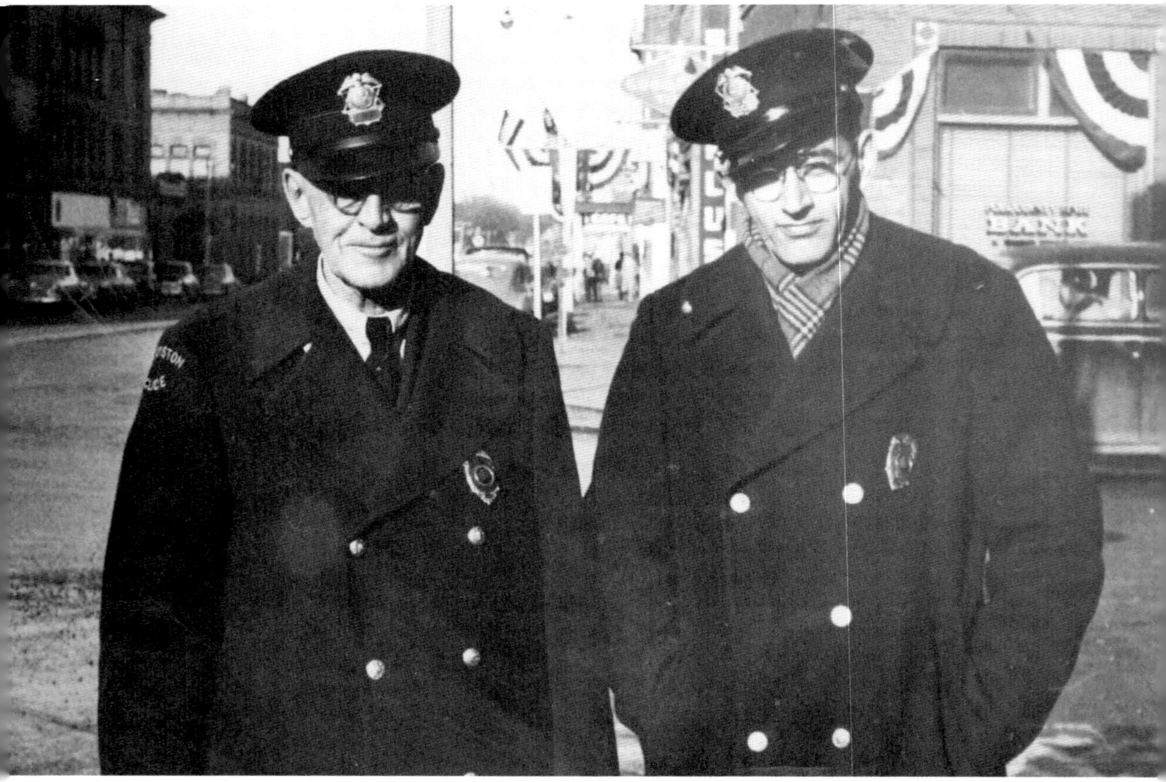

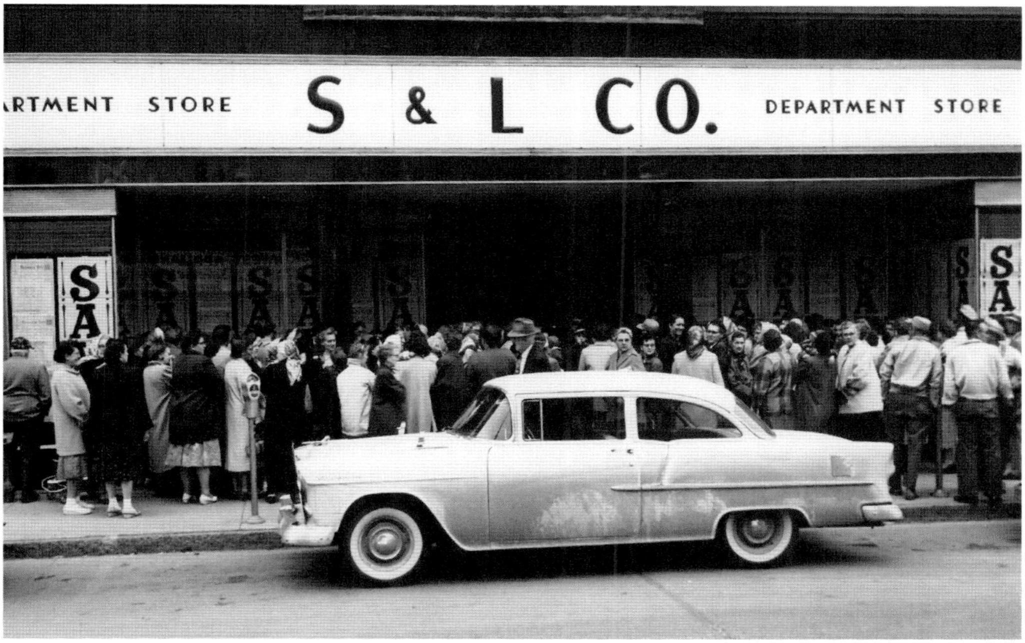

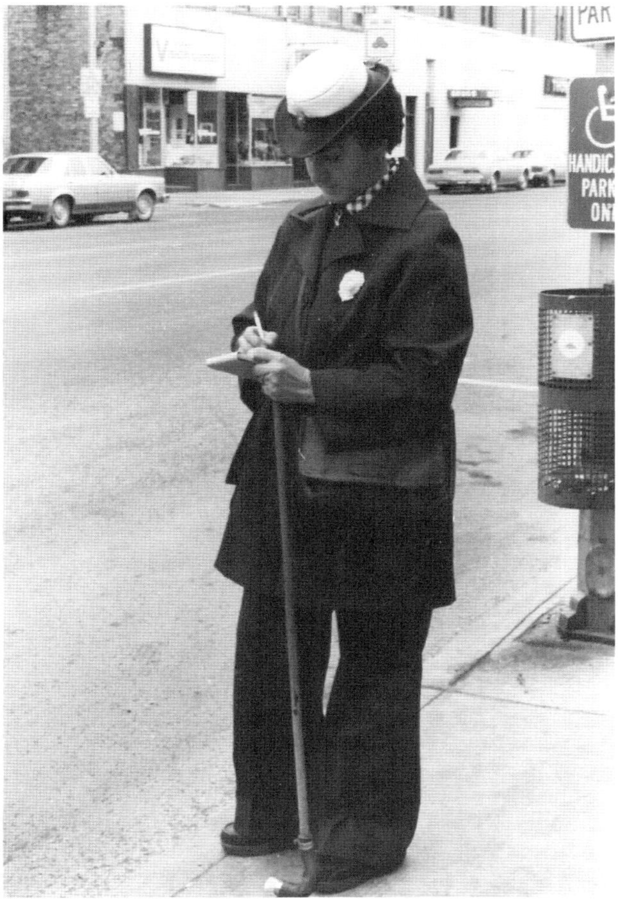

Verleth Oftelie, Meter Maid

Pictured above, in front of the S&L Company Department Store were parking meters and a big crowd for a sale. (See page 42 for the meters in front of Sundet's Toy and Hobby Shop.) Verleth Oftelie, the legendary meter maid, walked the beat for 21.5 years. She officially ended her career on December 31, 1988. She would put chalk on tires and return an hour later to see if the car was still there. When Verleth first started writing parking tickets they were 50¢. By the time she ended, overtime parkers were fined $3. The ticket would read: "Sorry, you have violated our parking ordinance." (Left, courtesy of Cliff Oftelie Jr.)

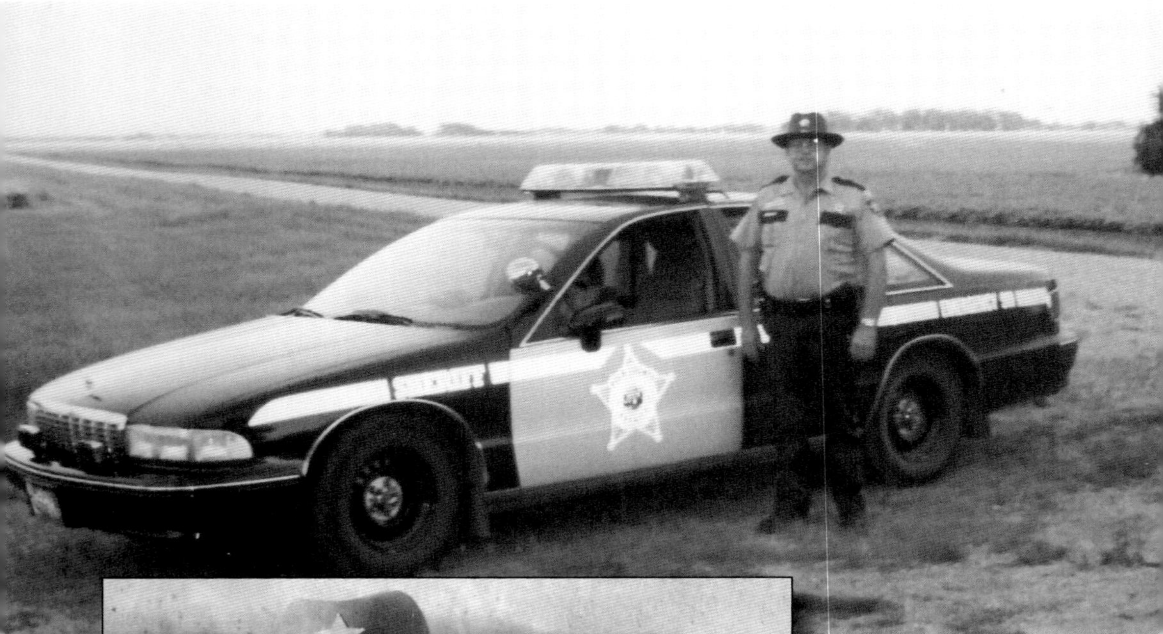

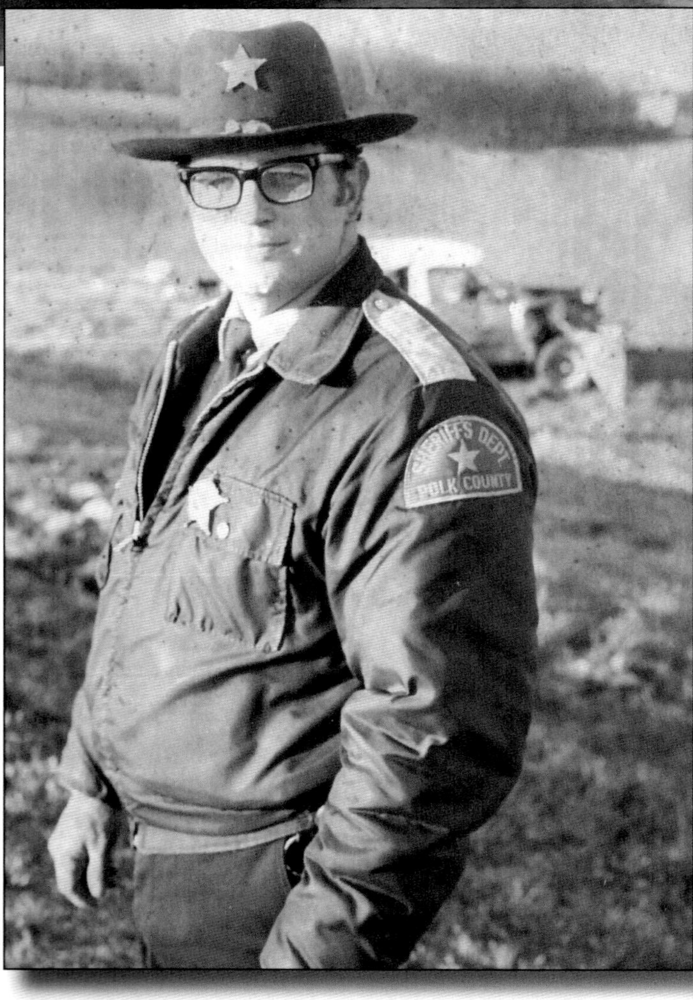

Highway Patrolman Walt Keller

Walt Keller (1951–2012) is pictured in front of his highway patrol car, in his patrolman's uniform. Sgt. Walt Keller had been a deputy with Polk County for nearly 28 years after coming to Crookston in 1976. He served in virtually every position the sheriff's office department had, from patrol duty and investigations to domestic family issues, car fatalities, shootings, and all things in between. He said the key to law enforcement was community involvement. He was active in Rotary and the American Legion clubs. (Both courtesy of Margie Keller.)

CHAPTER SEVEN

Competing against the Clock

In Crookston, many potential champions have raced against the clock. This is true for car owners who did not want to get a parking ticket when the meter maid made her rounds (see page 87). Many deserving athletes are not in this small book. Certainly, there are those who were legendary in their own minds. For example, the guys who played endless hours of foosball at the bowling alley or those who played the popular card game Smear on the bus while traveling to an away football or basketball game. Through the years, Crookston has had a fair share of state champions in major sports, but this book is far too short to list them all.

It is exciting to witness racing against a stopwatch or timer, no matter what the sport or season. Who can forget the many rousing hockey games in the old sports arena off East Robert Street, when the Cathedral Mount hockey players would rally against the Central High School players? The fierce competition in that sport produced better hockey players as a result. Crookston is proud of John Noah's hockey performance in the 1952 Olympics.

In winter, Crookston has had lots of snow, especially in 1966. The urge to still be able to get around must have fueled the rage to own a snowmobile. It certainly captured the enthusiasm of competitors like Dale Cormican and Roger Janssen. These two racers featured in this chapter were heroes in one elementary schoolboy's estimation. During one of the International 500 snowmobile race, this youngster pretended sickness to miss school. He wanted to watch out his bedroom window to the east to see the racers zoom parallel to Highway 75, one mile away. His mom was wise to him, thus he was relegated to a west bedroom to convalesce the whole day. He missed out on the entire race. Racers rode from Winnipeg to Crookston for the first leg of their journey, keeping their snowmobiles at the Winter Shows Building before taking off for St. Paul as their final destination. Imagine the boy's sheer disappointment the next day when he was "feeling much better" to find out that his whole class had gone to the finish line near the Winter Shows to see the racers up close. He admitted that he never feigned illness again.

During the summer months, baseball and fast- and slow-pitch softball were taken very seriously in Crookston. Many Crookstonites also fondly remember the outdoor swimming pool where the public library is now. Splashing on the low end or jumping off the high board were spectacular things to do in front of those admirers of such feats. Now, Crookston has a year-round, Olympic-size indoor pool that it can be proud of, where swimmers can compete against the clock.

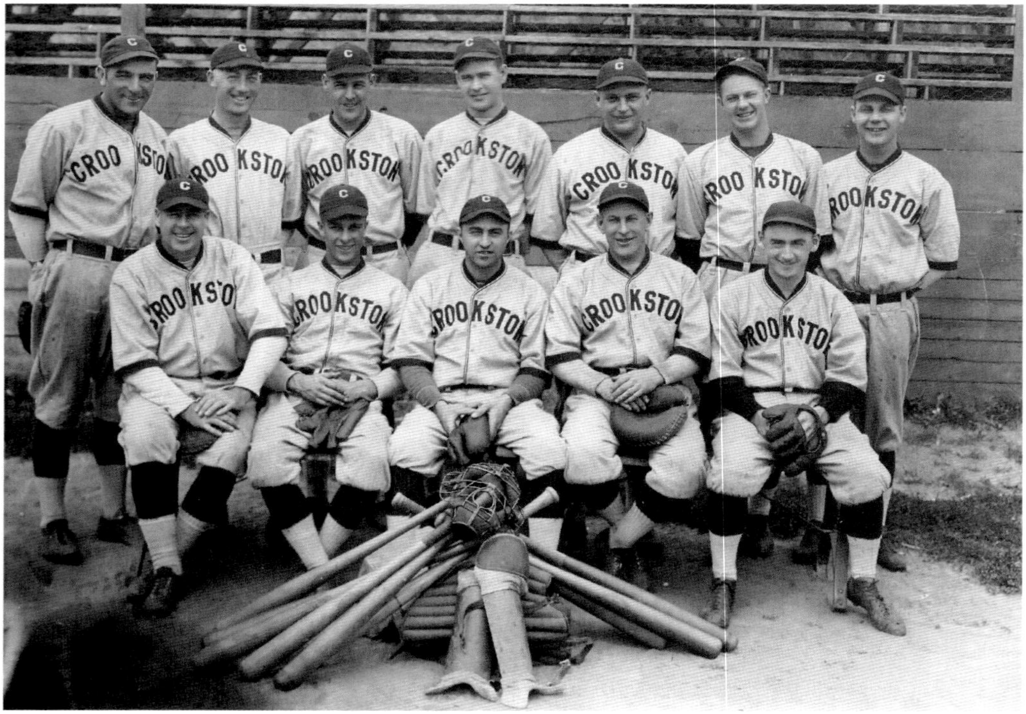

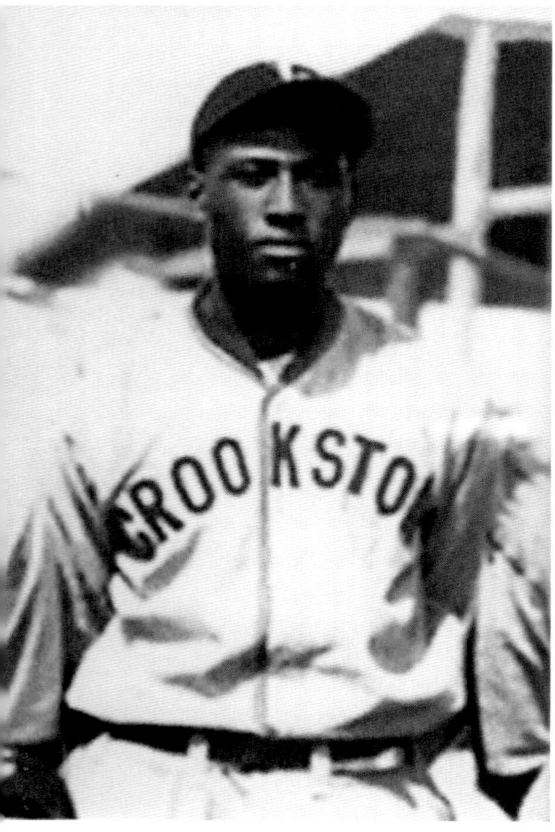

Crookston Champs in the Northern League
In the late 1920s and 1930s, Minor League Baseball's Northern League had the following teams: Crookston Pirates, Winnipeg Maroons, Grand Forks Chiefs, Fargo-Moorhead Twins, Duluth Dukes, Superior Blues, Eau Claire Bears, and the Wausau Lumberjacks. The 1928–1929 Crookston champs are, from left to right, (sitting) Arthur Leonard "2-Bagger Andy" Anderson; pitcher Beryl Millet; Paul Dudley (Red Owl Store manager); Pete Tulley; and Mr. Feller; (standing) Clarence Peltier, Vernon Peltier, Karsten Roisum, Maynard Stardig, Sid Parnus, Milton "Skip" Hendrickson, and Ed Vinje.

Chester "Chet" Brewer
Chester Arthur "Chet" Brewer (January 14, 1907–March 26, 1990) played baseball for 24 years all over the world and 44 of the 48 continental United States. He played in Bismarck, North Dakota, in 1935–1936 but mostly for the Kansas City Monarchs. He helped coach a young Jackie Robinson. He died in Whittier, California, at the age of 83. Of all the places Brewer pitched, he claimed he loved Crookston best; he played there just one summer, in 1931.

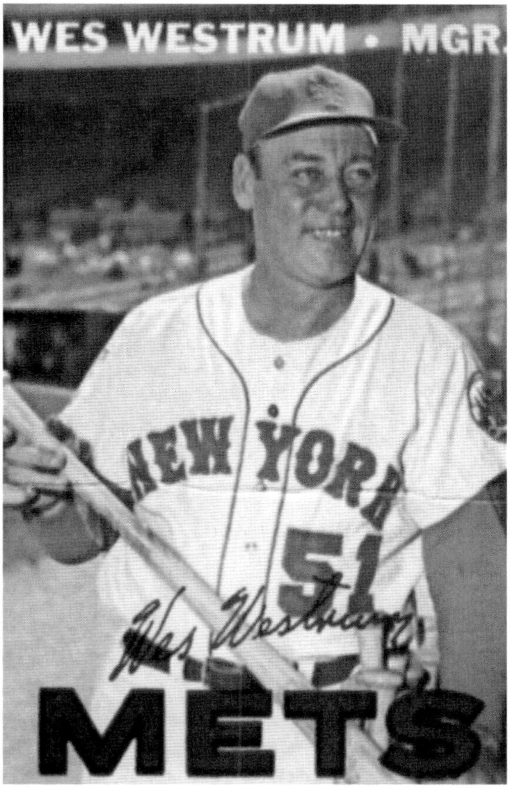

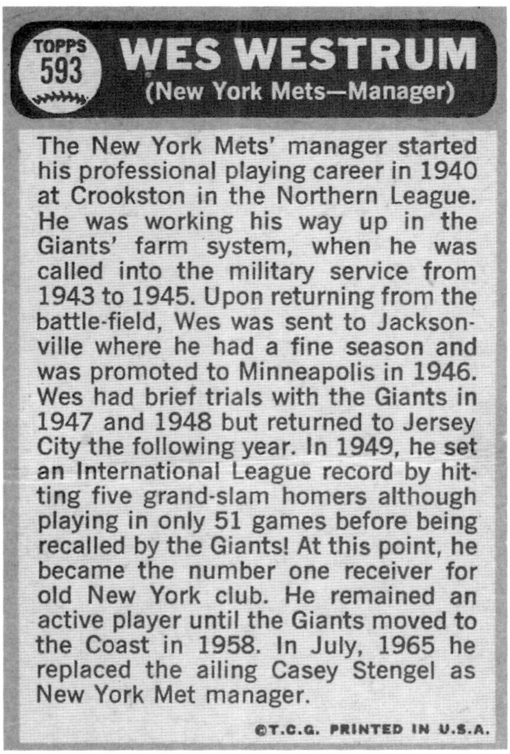

TOPPS 593

WES WESTRUM

(New York Mets—Manager)

The New York Mets' manager started his professional playing career in 1940 at Crookston in the Northern League. He was working his way up in the Giants' farm system, when he was called into the military service from 1943 to 1945. Upon returning from the battle-field, Wes was sent to Jacksonville where he had a fine season and was promoted to Minneapolis in 1946. Wes had brief trials with the Giants in 1947 and 1948 but returned to Jersey City the following year. In 1949, he set an International League record by hitting five grand-slam homers although playing in only 51 games before being recalled by the Giants! At this point, he became the number one receiver for old New York club. He remained an active player until the Giants moved to the Coast in 1958. In July, 1965 he replaced the ailing Casey Stengel as New York Met manager.

©T.C.G. PRINTED IN U.S.A.

Wes Westrum
Wes Westrum's baseball card front and back proves he was a famous player. Westrum started his professional playing career in 1940 at Crookston in the minor-league's Northern League. While he was working his way up in the Giants' farm system, he was called into the military and served from 1943 to 1945. Upon returning from the battlefield, Wes was sent to Jacksonville where he had a fine season and was promoted to Minneapolis in 1946. Wes had brief trials with the Giants in 1947 and 1948 but returned to Jersey City the following year. In 1949, he set an International League record by hitting five grand-slam homers. He played there in only 51 games before being recalled by the Giants. (Both courtesy of Cliff Oftelie.)

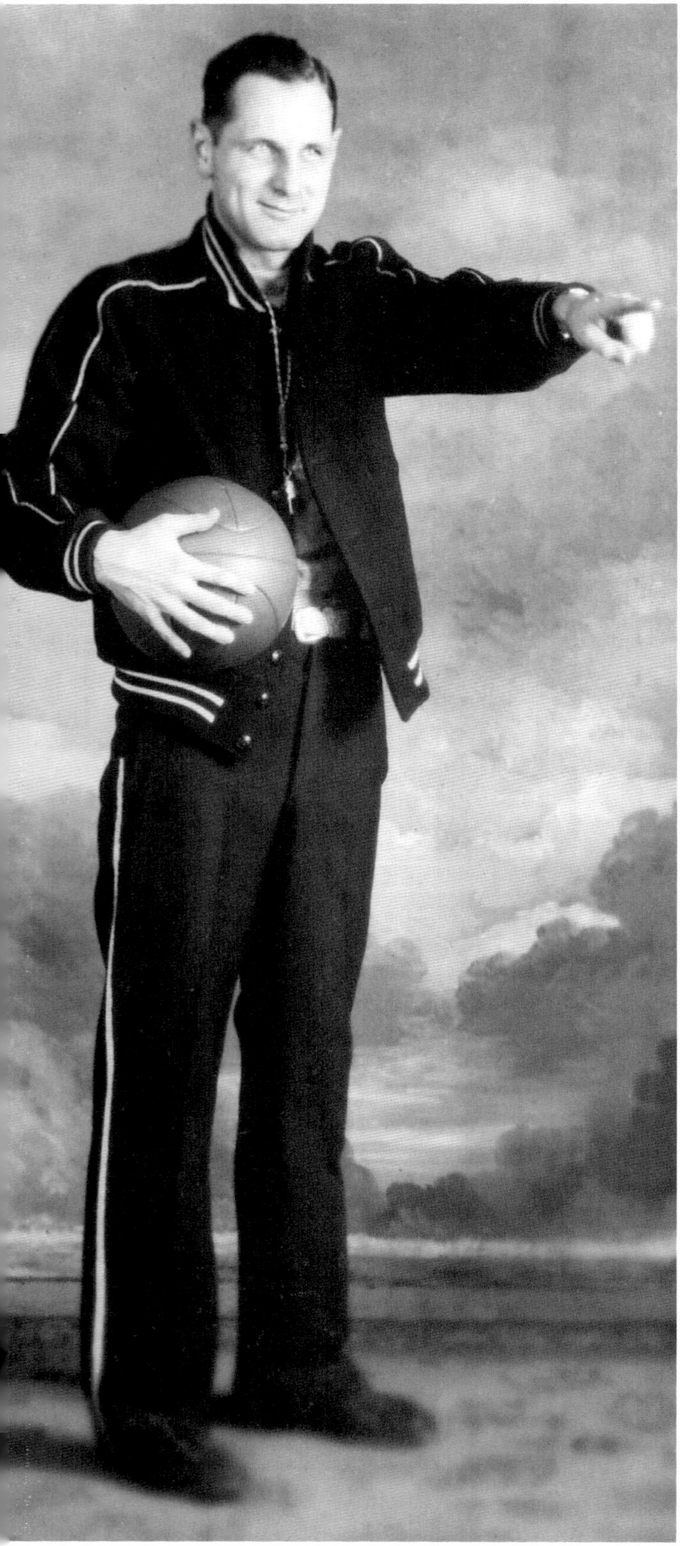

Herschel Lysaker

Herschel Charles Henry Lysaker had three sons: Pepper, John, and David. The father and sons were all involved in football—one was a player for the Aggies, another was a coach. During one game, all four Lysaker men were pitted with or coaching against each other.

Herschel was born on October 29, 1910, in Twin Valley, Minnesota, where he grew up and graduated from high school in 1928. In 1932, he graduated from Concordia College, Moorhead, with degrees in teaching and coaching. On October 10, 1932, he married Esther Hoialmen in Twin Valley. He taught and coached at several places in North Dakota. In 1942, he attended the US Navy Preflight Coaching School in Iowa, and the family later moved to Crookston, where he was a teacher, coach, and athletic director for Central High School. In 1944, Herschel became a teacher and coach for Northwest School of Agriculture, Crookston. From 1966 until retiring in 1977, he worked for UMC as an athletic director, coach, and vice provost. After retirement, UMC's Lysaker Gymnasium was named for him.

Herschel never served in the military, but he made sure that he met the bus for every returning soldier and followed the kid home, trying to recruit him for the football team. He also had a love for music and played his clarinet since he was a child. He sang in the church choir for 50 years and taught Sunday school for 25 years. He was a baseball commissioner for city teams in Minnesota for many years. When he retired from UMC, he knew he would miss the students. "The most rewarding part is the friendships I've built up with hundreds of kids over the years. That's the real joy of teaching, what people outside the teaching profession don't understand. You see the kids you may have helped out, and you see how they've turned out in later life," he said.

Herschel died on February 9, 2006, at age 95, in the Villa St. Vincent Nursing Home. (NWROC.)

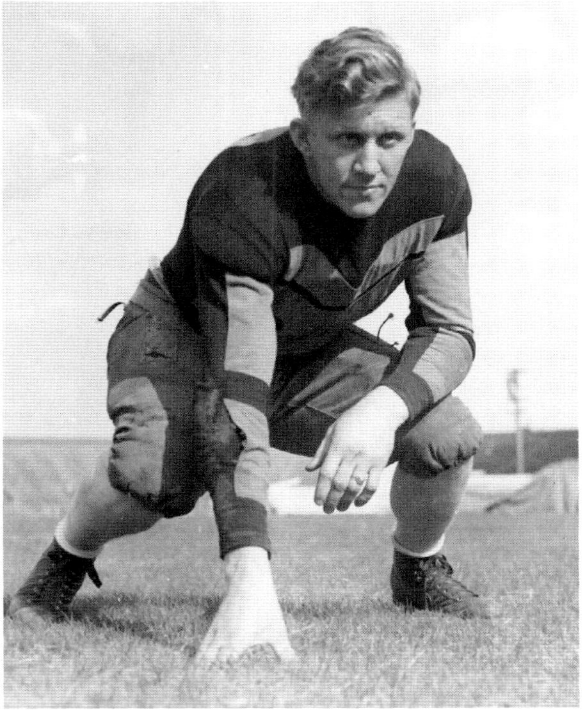

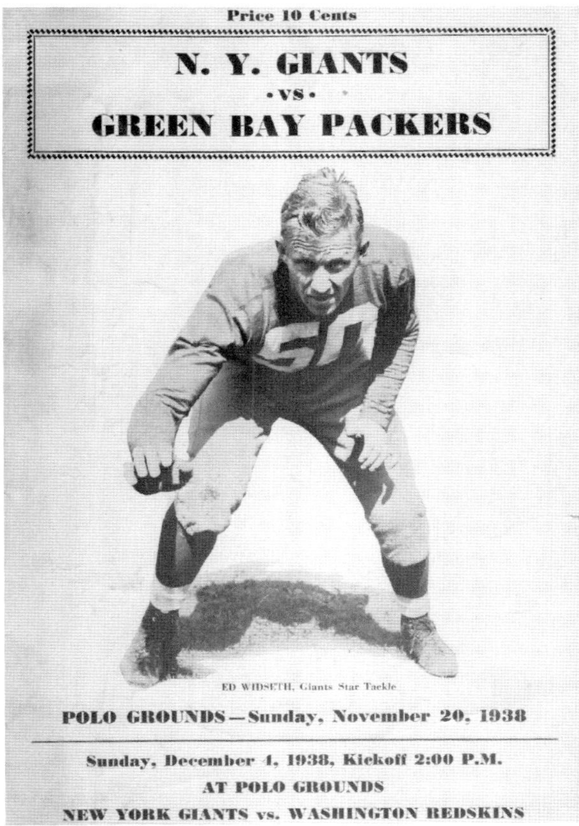

Edwin Widseth The football field on the south side of UMC is named Ed Widseth Field. Ed was born in Gonvik, and his hometown was McIntosh where he was recruited by Hershel Lysaker for the NWSA. The top photograph shows Widseth when he played tackle for Bernie Bierman's Golden Gophers from 1934 to 1936. Their record for three seasons was 23-1. His official biography at the College Hall of Fame, into which he was inducted in 1954, reads, "A slashing, driving invader, Widseth used his 6-2, 220-pound body to pummel opposing players, relentlessly advancing until the ball carrier was within his grasp and quickly felled." In 1936, Widseth was named to the Associate Press All-American football team. He played for the New York Giants from 1937 to 1940 and was an all-NFL player for three consecutive years. When he was finished playing professional football, he ran a grocery store in the Twin Cities. Widseth died in 1998 in St. Paul, Minnesota. (Both courtesy of Greg Widseth.)

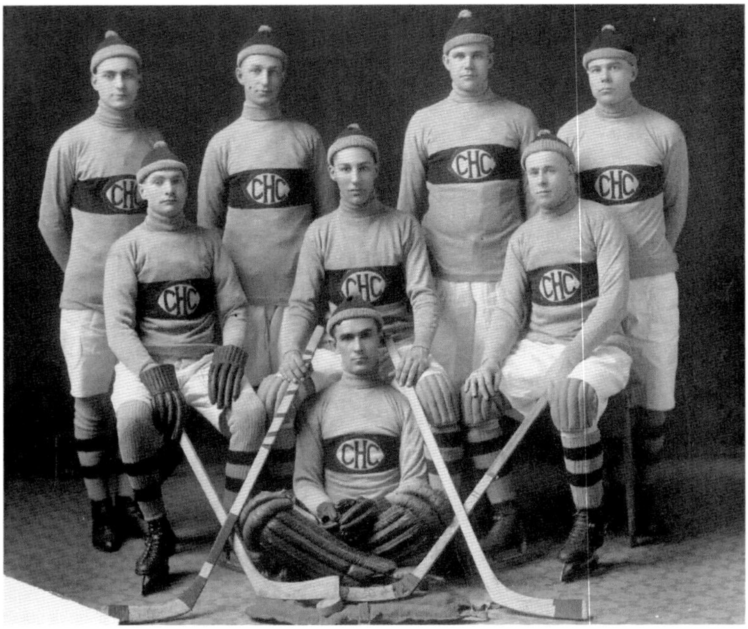

1916 Crookston Hockey and John Noah

The Crookston Hockey Club started about 1916. Pictured are, from left to right, (sitting) Bill Herbert, Earl Gramer and A. Leonard Anderson; (standing) Armand Viau, Joe Herbranson, Bill Hansen, and Butch Hansen. The goalie on the floor is George Charboneau. Below, note the helmetless hockey players of the 1950s. John Noah represents Crookston skating behind the goal cage. Back in those days, a goal judge would stand over the net to verify whether the puck went into the net. Also note there is no Plexiglass protection from errant pucks for the fans either.

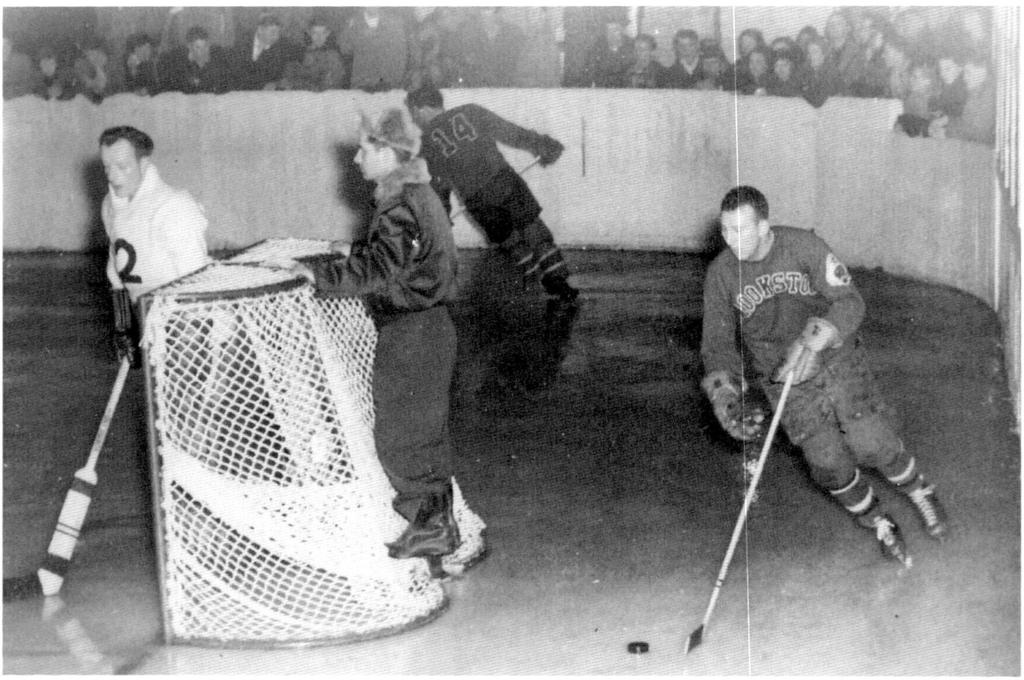

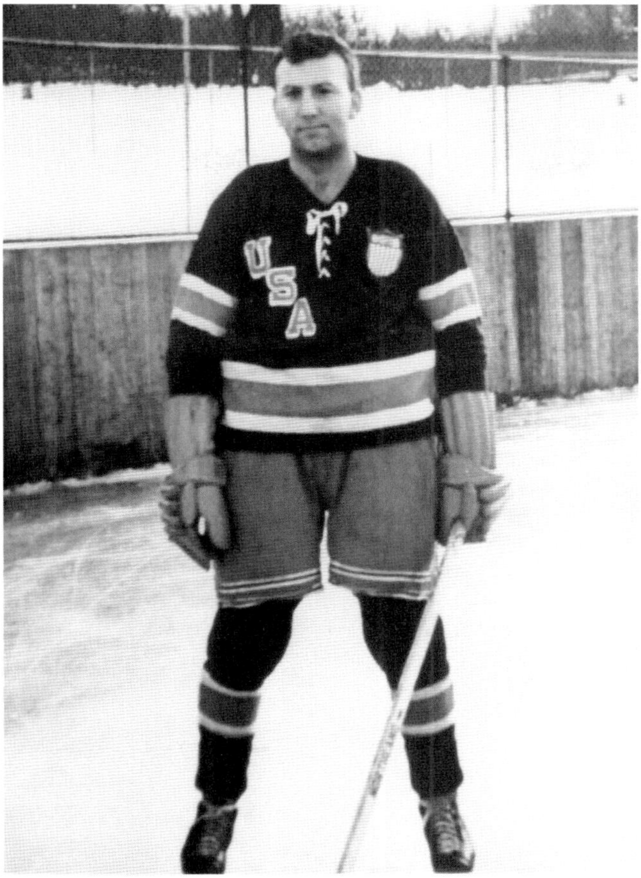

John Noah, 1952 Olympics Hockey Player

John Michael Noah was on the US Olympic hockey team in 1952, helping the United States win a silver medal. The team played in the 1952 Winter Olympics in Oslo, Norway, after it had traveled with the US national hockey team to countries like England, France, and Switzerland. What kept the team from the gold medal was a loss to Sweden.

Noah had played hockey since seventh grade for Mount Cathedral School. After graduation, he entered the University of North Dakota and played on the 1948 Sioux team that marked UND's entrance into major hockey competition. While playing a game in Ann Arbor, Michigan, Noah scored the winning goal, a 6-5 triumph. Noah saw UND emerge from the bottom of the heap to the top from that point on. Noah spent hours practicing in UND's unheated, old facility, labeled "the barn," that was nothing compared to the $100-million complex underwritten by Ralph Englestad. Noah also spent a lot of time at UND's football stadium. Noah graduated with the class of 1951 and was inducted into the Sioux Athletic Hall of Fame. Later, he played for the Crookston Pirates, an amateur hockey team that won the 1951 National Amateur Championship with a win over the New York Mets.

Noah was born on November 21, 1927; he had seven sisters and three brothers. Of his two brothers, two are Catholic priests and another is an attorney in Crookston. His ethnic background is Lebanese. His mother had come on her own from Lebanon to the United States to give her children opportunities; this vision was shared by his dad as well. John Noah had said, "We live in a great country; you can't beat the United States."

After his stint playing on the Olympic team, Noah was drafted into the Army and was assigned to Fort Leonard Wood, Missouri. He was discharged in April 1954 and returned to Crookston. Noah currently lives in Fargo, where he has been very active in mental health organizations.

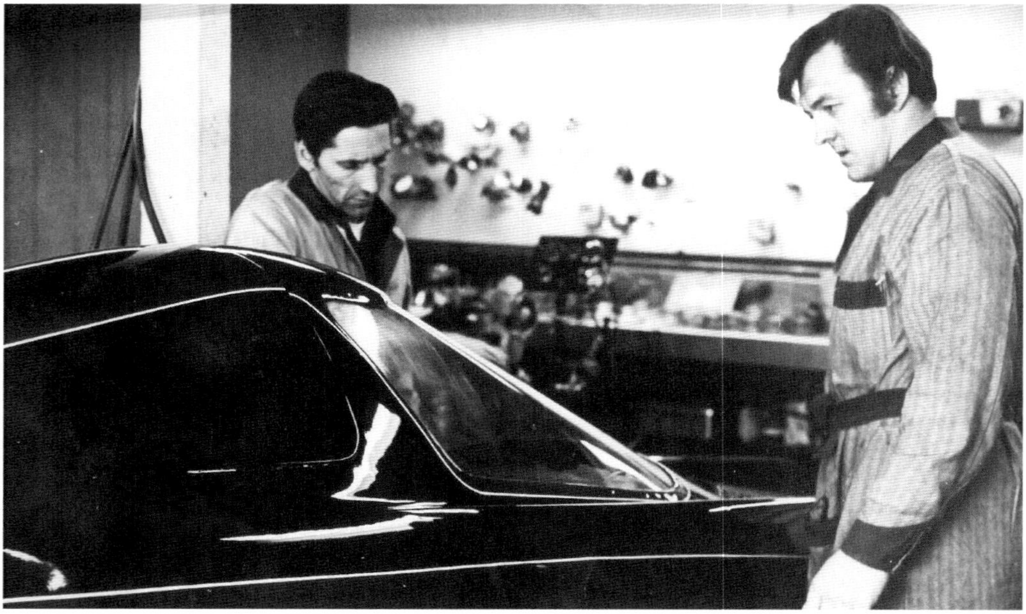

Dale Cormican

Pictured with legendary mechanic Denny Ray, Dale Cormican (right), born in 1944, was inducted into the Snowmobile Hall of Fame in 1997. Cormican was written on the hall of fame plaque as "one of a handful of snowmobile racing originals who forged the profile of the sport in the very early days." He made headlines when he won first place in the St. Paul–Winnipeg International 500 race two consecutive years, 1968 and 1969, on Arctic Cat Panthers. He was successful at racing "not only because he had a dominant machine but because he had superior riding ability and a great engineering mind." Today, he is the owner of Cormican Construction, which does road work throughout the region. He spends winters inventing in a well-equipped shop at his home on Maple Lake. He holds a number of patents including one for a plastic racing ski. (Both courtesy of Brandon and Shawn Cormican.)

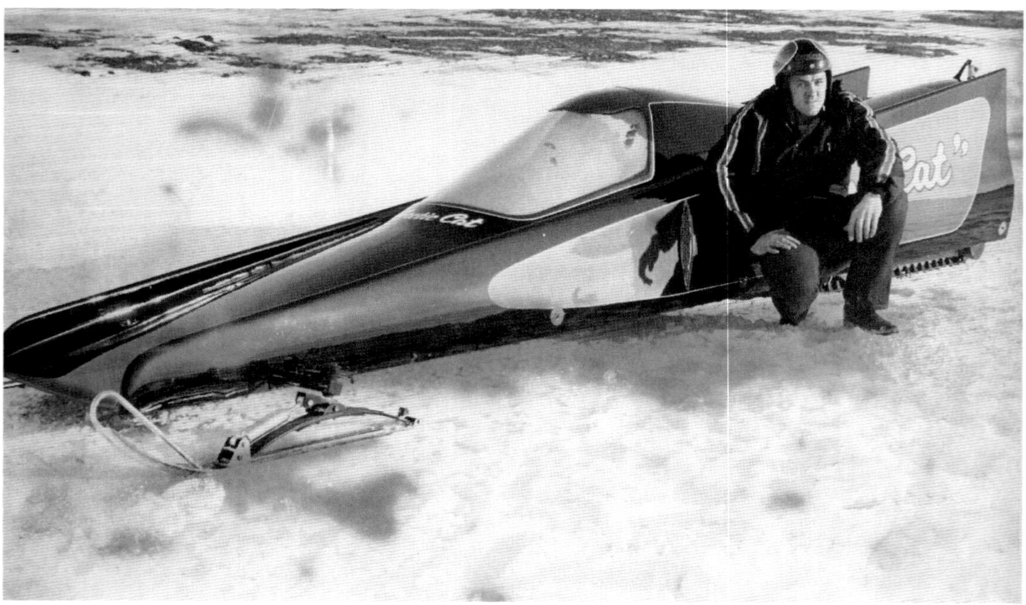

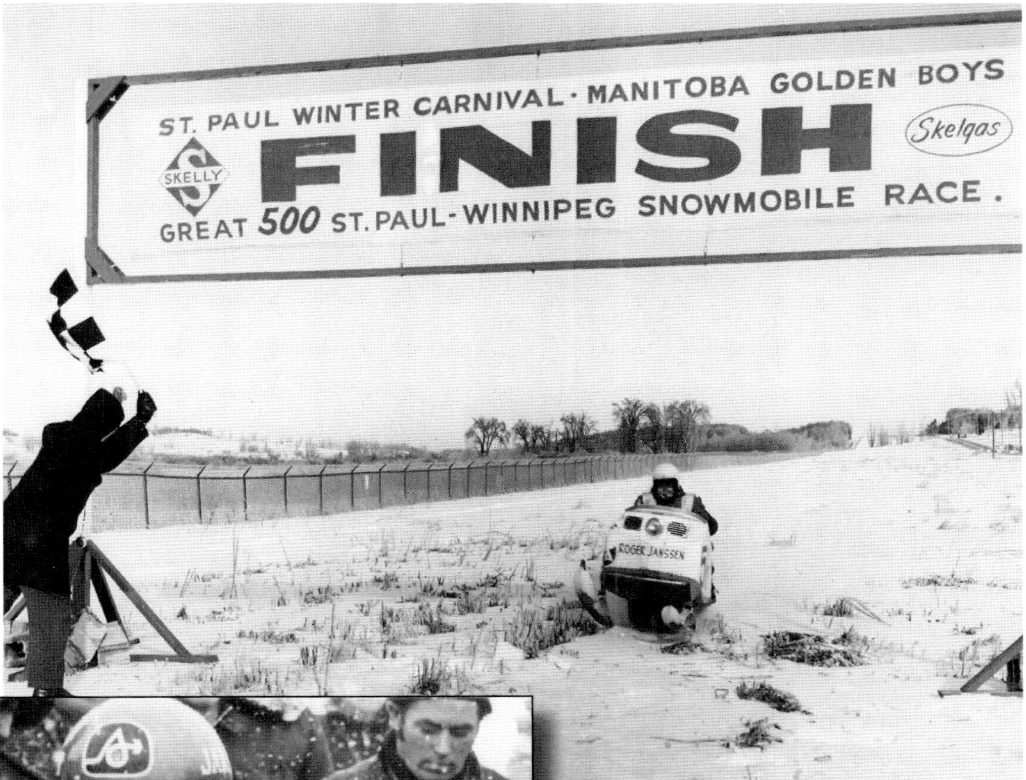

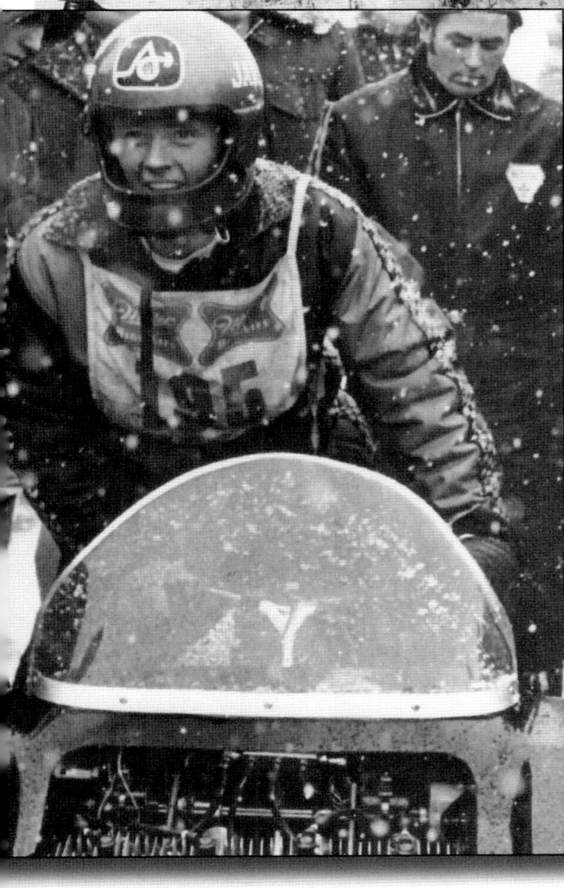

Roger Janssen

In the above photograph, Roger Janssen is at the finish line of the St. Paul-Winnipeg 500 snowmobile race in the 1960s when snow was plentiful. Roger graduated from Central High School in 1958. He also graduated from soapbox racing to snowmobile races. In his 10 years of competing in the 500-mile race to St. Paul, he always finished in the top 10. His son John told a story about his dad's driving ability. Roger had racing instincts even while driving beet trucks during the harvest season. Before the 75 bypass, beet trucks went right through downtown Crookston. When Roger would see ahead that a red light was about to happen and other beet trucks were forced to stop, he would idle slowly and pass the stopped truck when the light turned green and get ahead in line at the beet factory to dump his beets. Once a racer, always ready to get ahead of the next guy! (Both, courtesy of Roger Janssen.)

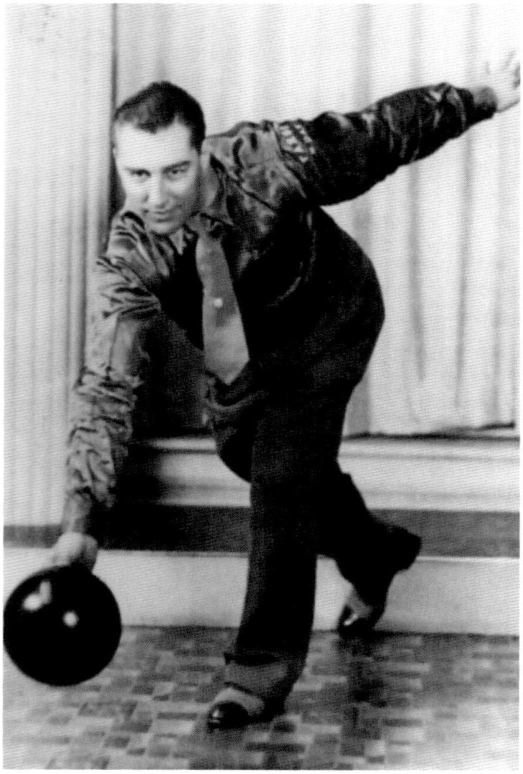

Earl Peter Gramer

Earl Peter Gramer was the quintessential all-around athlete. He was a hockey player (see page 94) and a professional bowler in Chicago, as seen in the studio shot to the left. There used to be a bowling alley on south Main Street where the bowling pins had to be manually set up after each strike. Gramer's son Earl Bryant Gramer later built and owned the automated Corral Lanes Bowling Alley until he sold it in 1978. Gramer was also a billiards player. He traveled the region as a trick-shot extraordinaire, under the moniker "The Masked Marvel" since he hid his identity by wearing a mask. He twice took on world-champion billiard player Cowboy Weston in exhibition matches. He beat Weston in one match, and his grandson Dan Gramer wears that world championship ring to this day. (Both courtesy of Ron Gramer.)

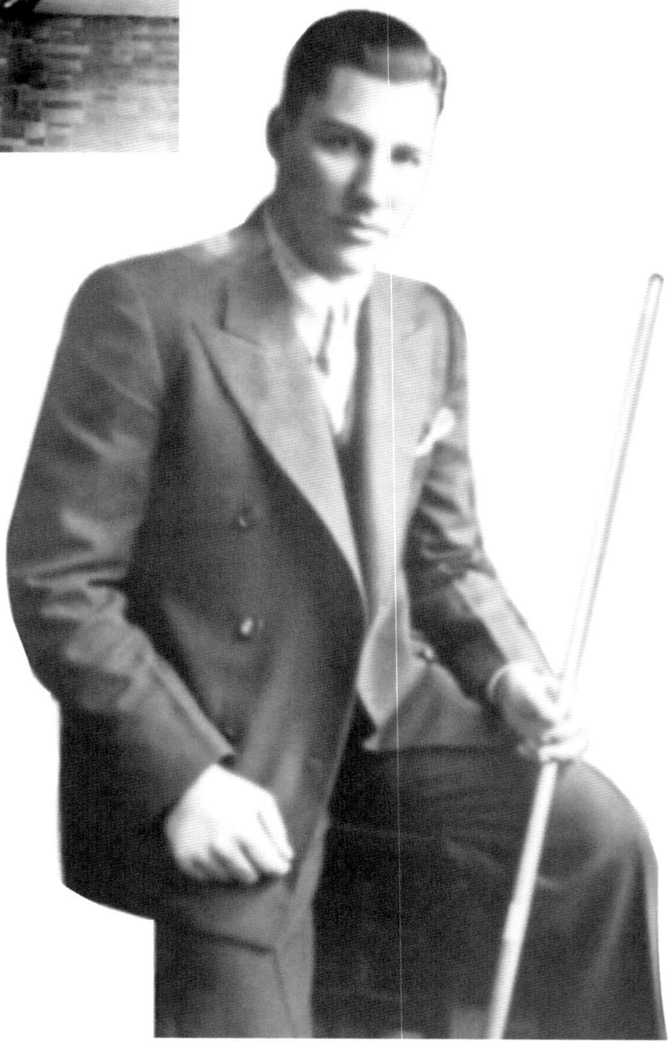

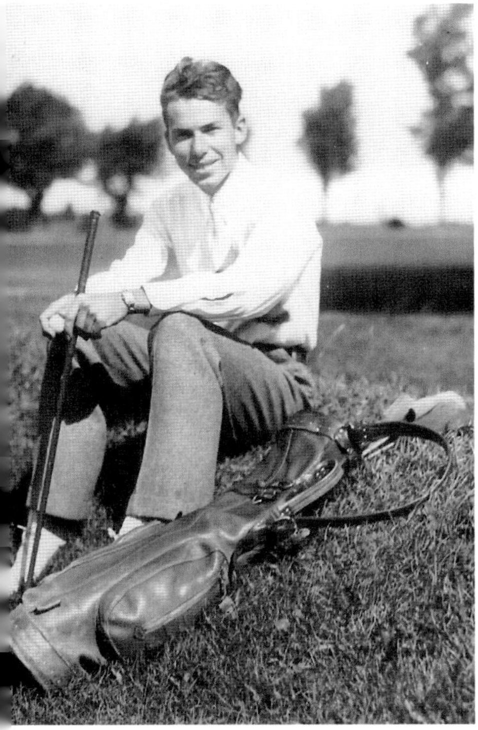

Ernotte Hiller

Crookston's Minakwa Country Club named the Ernotte Hiller Memorial Golf Tournament in memory of a man who won it 15 times. When Hiller attended the University of Minnesota in Minneapolis, his golf team won the Big Ten title in 1938. Ernotte played regional tournaments, including the Birchmont, which he won in 1935. In the Pine-to-Palm tournament, he was a medalist in 1936 and runner-up in 1946. He took over his father Charles Hiller's business. (See page 34.) (Courtesy of Matt Hiller.)

Crookston Central High State A Track Winners

In the spring of 1974, the Crookston Central track team competed against the clock and won the Minnesota State A track title. Note the plethora of trophies this team amassed thanks to its coaches' skills and the intensity of these runners. Pictured are, from left to right, (first row) Don Moore, Nate Hanson, Jeff Radi, Leonard Devos, and Jon Burkhardt; (second row) coach Les Drechsel, Mike Ranum, Bert Ranum, Robin Larson, Tom Longtin, Jeff Potter, coach Al Droen, and coach Murray Warren. (Courtesy of Leah Warren Volker.)

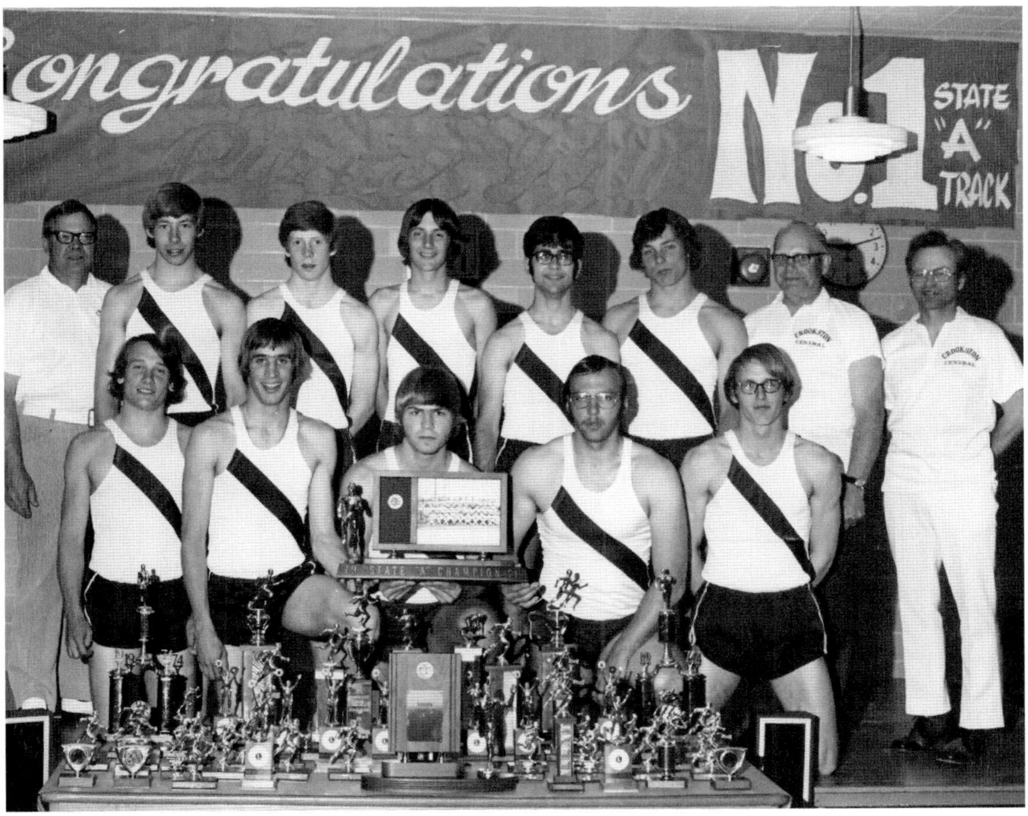

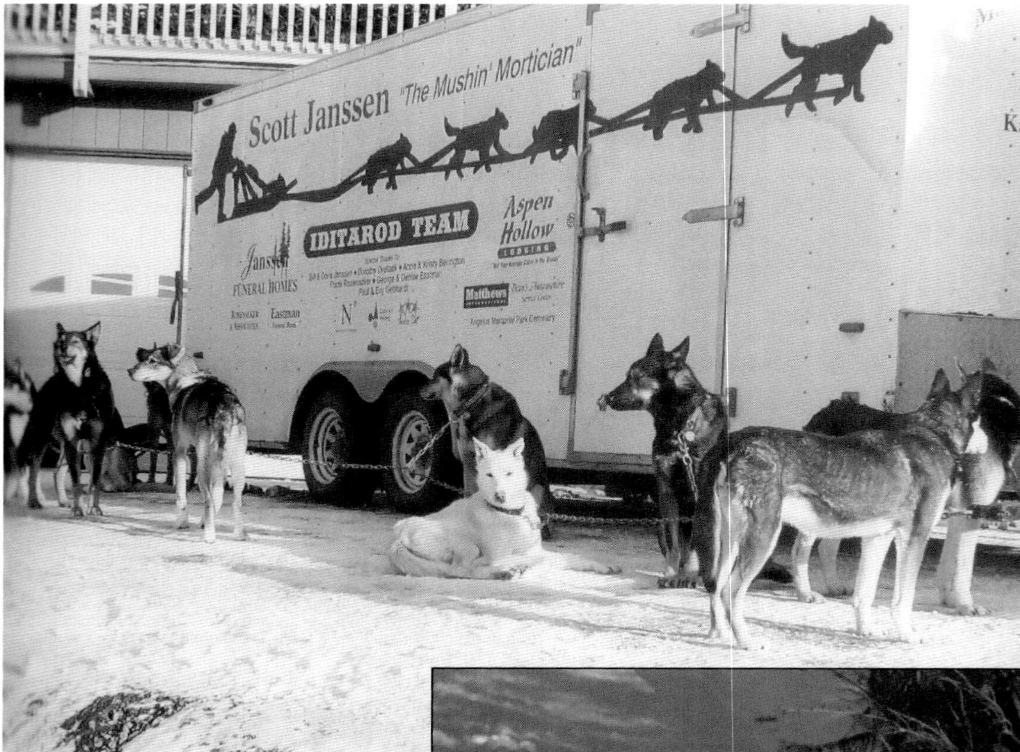

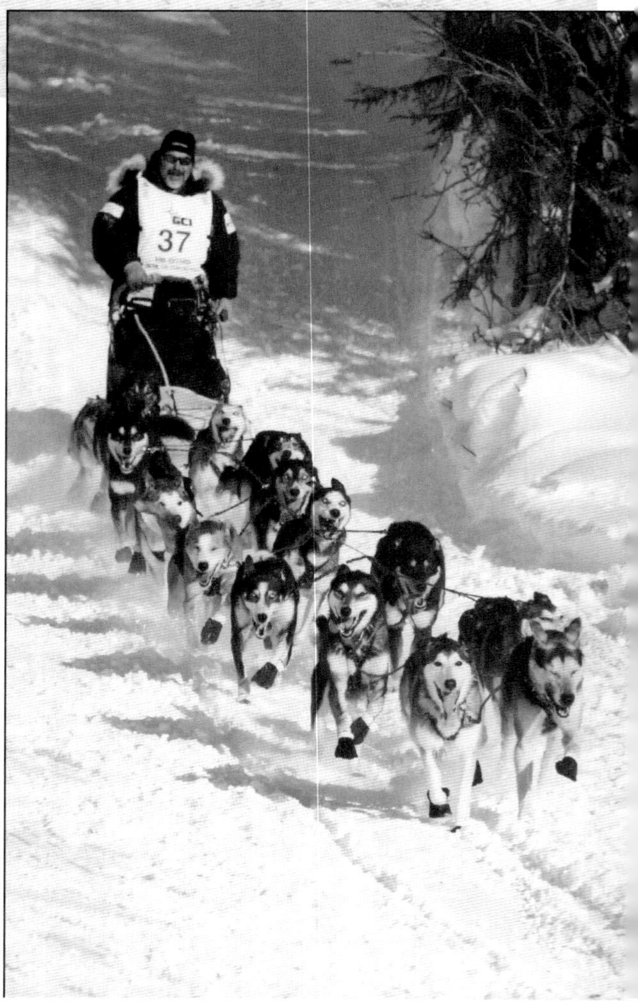

Scott Janssen
Most people do not know that on January 27, 1917, James J. Hill's son Louis W. Hill brought a film crew through Crookston to film the dogsled race that went along the Great Northern Railroad, running north and south along Highway 75. Fifty years later, snowmobiles took the same 500-mile route from Winnipeg to St. Paul. Scott Janssen, a former Crookstonite, now lives in Alaska but still considers himself a Minnesota boy. Perhaps the fact that his relative Roger Janssen raced snowmobiles helped Scott make the jump to compete in the Iditarod. Scott, known as the "Mushin' Mortician," claims that being a finisher of this 1,000-mile race is an achievement. For him, the most important thing along the Alaska trail is to take care of his dogs. As long as they are happy, healthy, and fed, he will never be left stranded in the middle of some very open and untouched, but beautiful, place. (Both courtesy of Bill and Lois Janssen.)

CHAPTER EIGHT

Performing in the Spotlight

Musical talent emerged immediately in the fast-growing town of Crookston. Many of the settlers brought with them instruments from the old country, such as violins and accordions. Some toted their brass instruments to toot. And some simply sang and harmonized with others in church or in the many other musical groups that had sprung up. These were led by many different band directors, including G. Oliver Riggs, Arthur Wasshausen, and T.W. Thorson, who is remembered by many older people as "Mr. Music." In the old days, John Philip Sousa's visits to small cities like Crookston ignited an interest in young people to want to march and play in a band in a parade.

Crookston had its own piano dealership. Piano and voice lessons were encouraged among the young. People felt they had to prove they were refined and polished and not a "country hick" who could not read music. There were women's glee clubs and men's choruses. Crookston had as many fine barbershop quartets to care for men's spirits as it had barbershops to care for men's heads.

Vaudeville was all the rage at one point and Crookston hosted actors and actresses in its venues, such as at the Grand Theater and the theater in the Opera Block. During the Roaring Twenties, flappers dominated the stage. For some priests and other clergy, going to the movie theater was considered a sin. Having a pump organ heaving out hymns was considered far better than listening to the player pianos grinding out music in the early black-and-white silent movies.

The Crookston Civic Music League brought world-class talent to Crookston Central High auditorium. Its excellence continues to this day. The musically inclined also performed Easter oratorios with soloists singing their parts in "Elijah," "Seven Last Words," and other sacred pieces. Crookston put on plays and musicals, like *Brigadoon*, *The Music Man*, *Oklahoma*, and many others. Past veterans of the Crookston Community Theater include directors Dean and Cindee Brown; it continues today with many talented actors.

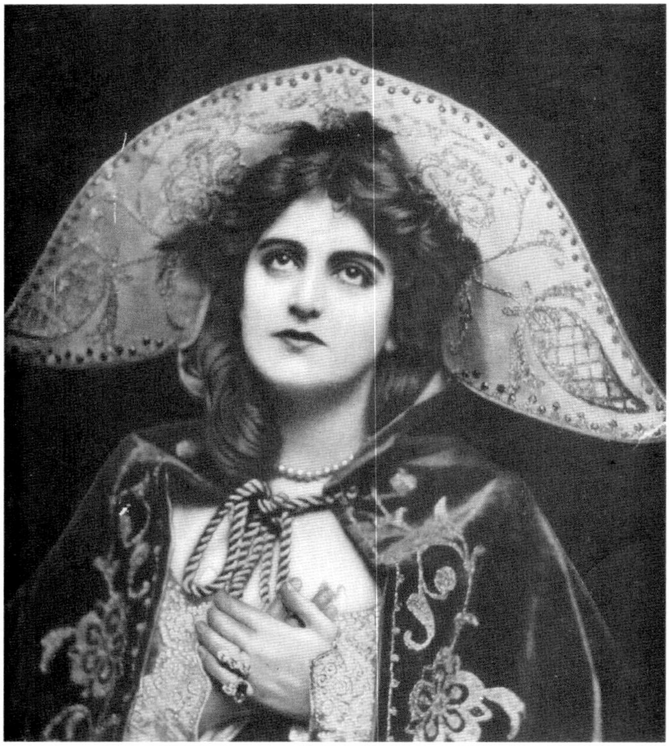

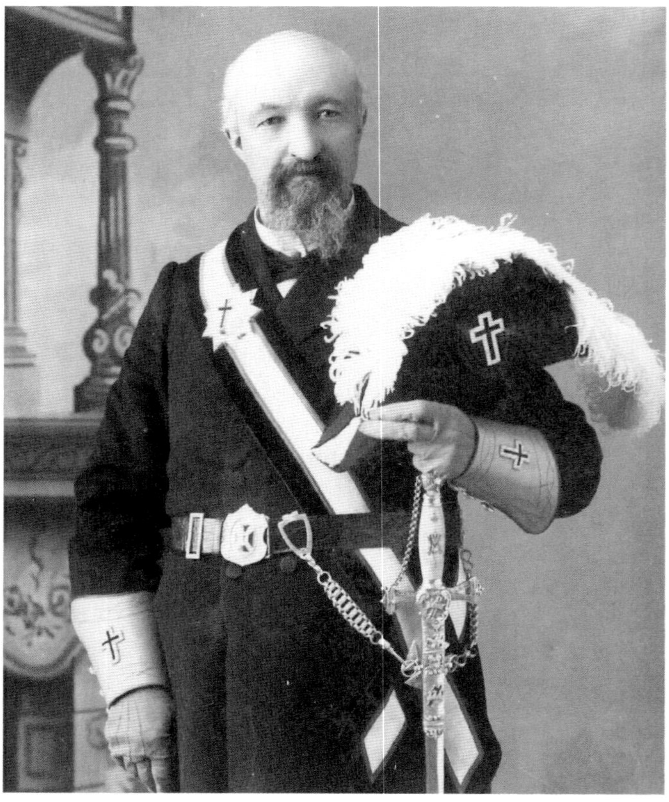

Charles and May Mix
Mary Lincoln Shapleigh (also spelled "Shapley") is pictured dressed in her vaudeville costume. Her stage name was May Mix. Her father, Thomas C. Shapleigh, built their home in the Woods Addition back when some laughed that he had to take out so many trees. On September 28, 1882, Mary Shapleigh and Charles Mix spoke their vows in Crookston. On September 28, 1907, they were honored as the "old settler couple" and celebrated their silver anniversary. On August 24, 1942, May Mix died. Maj. Charles Henry Mix was a romantic, national figure in the early years and one of the most distinguished in Crookston's history. Originally from Connecticut, he came West in 1852. He enlisted for service during the Sioux War in 1862 and was with the Independent Cavalry Battalion on its memorable march to Pembina. After colorful experiences in Indian affairs, he was employed by the Great Northern Railroad, and for some years, he was a station agent at Crookston.

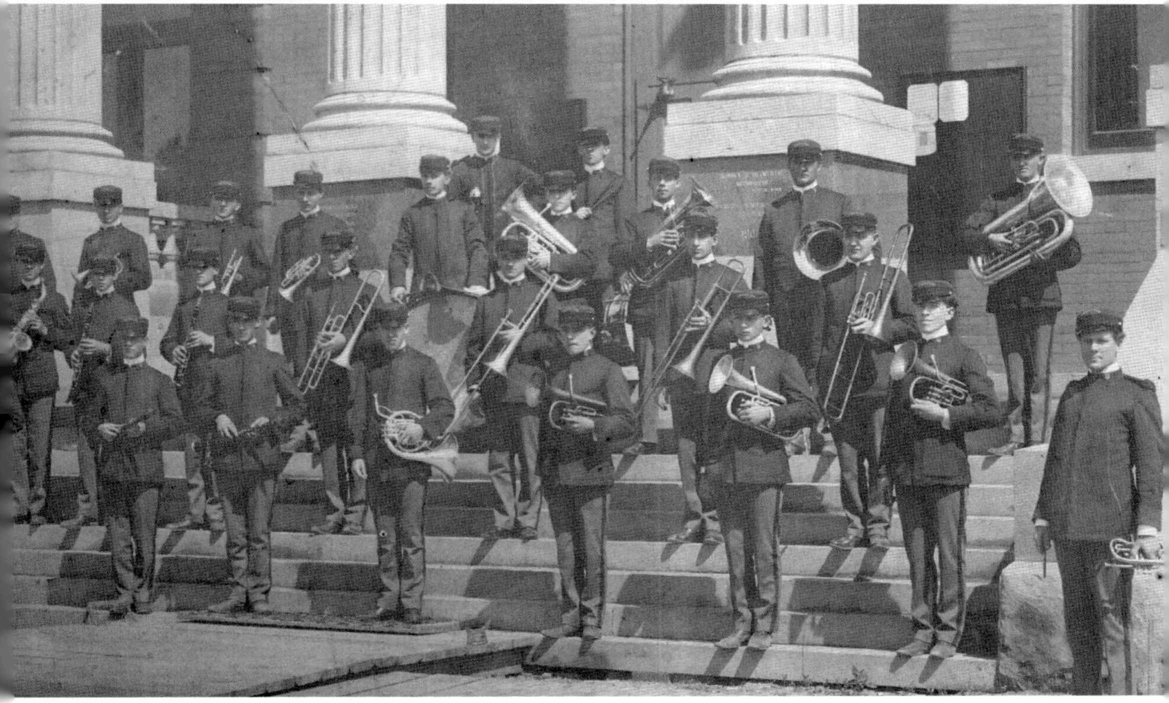

G. Oliver Riggs, the Original "Music Man"

G. Oliver Riggs (first row, far right) was the musical forefather of many of Crookston's great music traditions. A graduate of Oberlin's Conservatory of Music, 28-year-old Riggs arrived in Crookston in 1898. Riggs was a talented band director and a cornet and violin soloist. His wife, Islea, had studied piano in Chicago and accompanied the Crookston band. Bandmaster Riggs, his wife, daughter Rosalie, and infant son are all buried at the Crookston cemetery.

According to Riggs's great-granddaughter Joy Riggs of Northfield, Minnesota, G. Oliver Riggs was an enthusiastic organizer, like the Harold Hill character in the play *The Music Man*, but he was also a gifted instructor. Joy stated that he "was no Harold Hill, he honestly wanted to bring quality music to every place he went."

Band director Riggs's musicians played for musical comedies and vaudeville shows at the Opera House between 1898 and 1906. Under his direction, the city band played outdoor summer concerts on a portable bandstand and played indoors in the winter at the opera house. In April 1905, he received a gold-trimmed baton from his band members who valued his directing skills. Businesspeople paid subscription fees and received tickets for the concerts. Joy continued, "He kept his musicians busy all year long, with weekly summer concerts that sometimes attracted more than 1,000 people."

At the turn of the century, few public schools had music programs, so Riggs organized the city's first boys' band of 30 members. He left in 1909 to direct bands in Grand Forks, Washington State, and Montana, and when he returned to Crookston in 1914, he worked to build up the boys' band into a 75-piece group. Riggs also directed the Northwest School of Agriculture band in 1916 and 1917.

G. Oliver Riggs left Crookston in 1919 to direct bands in Bemidji and St. Cloud. He served as president of the Minnesota Bandmasters Association in 1929, and he lobbied the Minnesota legislature to pass the band tax law in 1927, which allowed towns to levy a tax to fund community bands. He passed away at age 76 in 1946 in Bemidji.

Others standing on the steps of the county courthouse in this photograph are John Rusk, Henry Theilon, O.W. Peterson, Elmer Ellington, Irwin Burkhart, Harry Burkhart, Ted Eiken, Norm Mossefin, W. Ellingson, Ed Mossefin, Dickman, Burt Gourley, Fred Walker, George Johnson, Albin Johnson, John Boh, H. Fischer, Art Kirsch, B. O'Neil, T. Johnson, Jim Heng Gail Dunleavey and Louis Barrett.

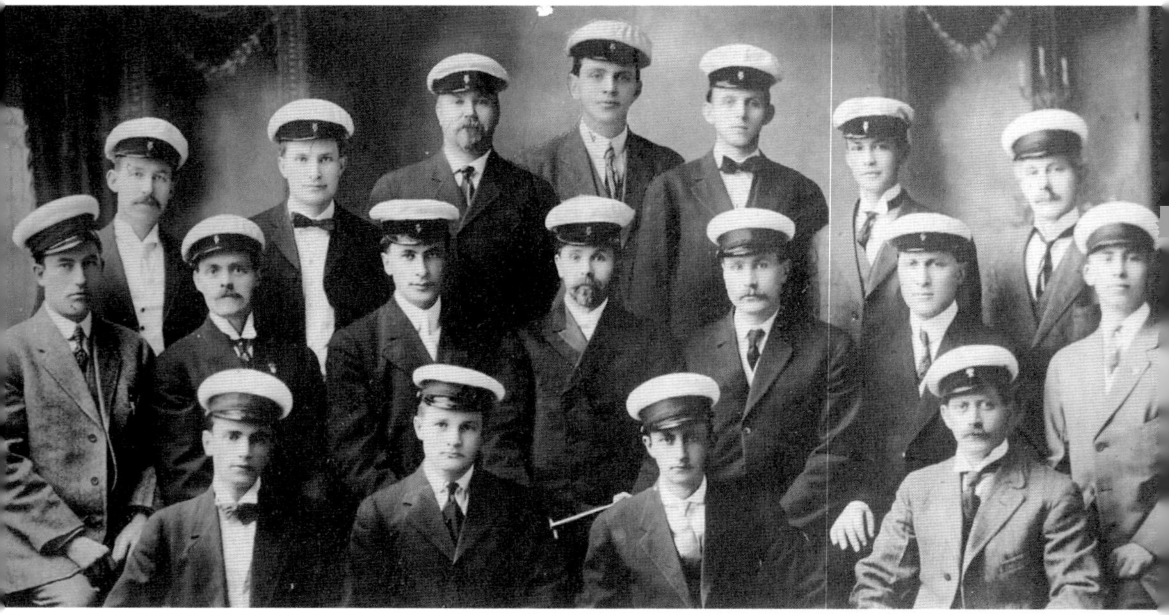

Famous Northwest Singers
T.W. Thorson brought male singers from different parts of the Red River Valley, and their group continued to expand to almost 100 men. As Hywel C. Rowland put it back in the early 1940s, "this group has learned how to sing with sympathetic unity, smooth flowing legato line, beauty of tone, accuracy of intonation, clarity of diction and imaginative interpretation." Rowland added, "T.W. Thorson should know that he is held in high honor by his chorus and community."

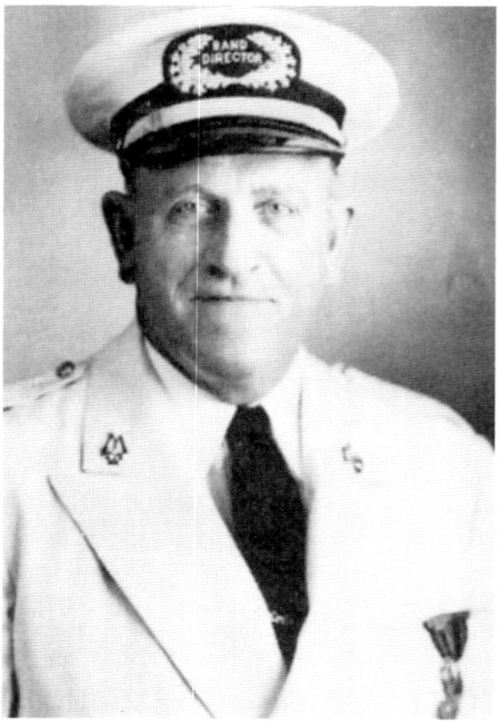

Theodore W. Thorson
T.W. Thorson was known as "Mr. Music" throughout Polk County. Even though Thorson was asked to be the first US Navy Band director, he instead accepted the position as supervisor of music in the Crookston public schools. Once in Crookston, he formed the a cappella choir and directed orchestra and band for 28 years. He was involved with the Rotary Club and Civic Music League. He was president of the Polk County Historical Society until his death. He and his wife, Lilian, were honored as "Pioneer Couple" in 1973. T.W.T. died on September 29, 1973.

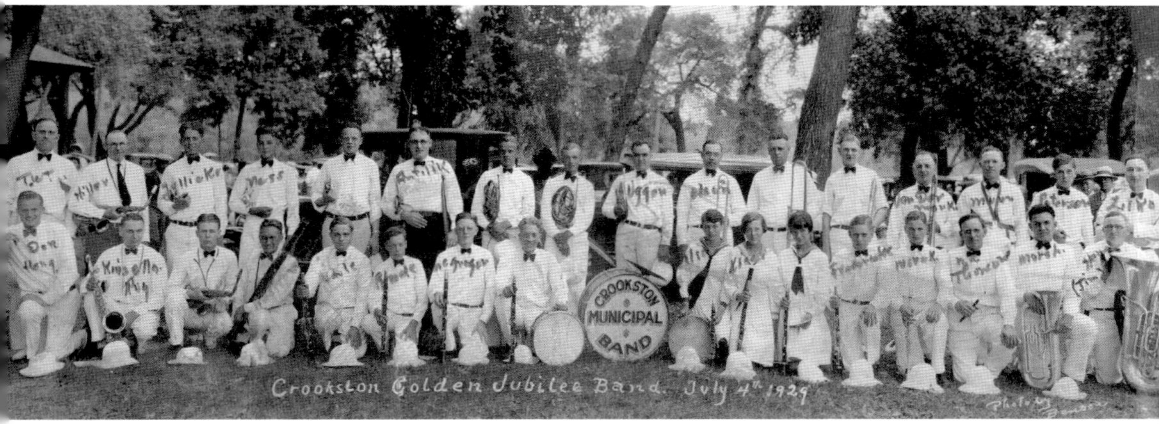

Crookston Golden Jubilee Band

Fourth of July in 1929 meant a Central Park concert that brought in many appreciative listeners. Pictured are, from left to right, (first row) Don Heng (trombone), Roy Knisella (sax), unidentified (sax) unidentified (bassoon), ? Ule (clarinet), ? Rude (clarinet), ? McGregor (clarinet), ? MaCrosst (clarinet), unidentified (drums), Vic Kiser (clarinet), unidentified, ? Frederick (clarinet), ? Novak (flute), N.A. Thorson (piccollo), ? Marsh (tuba), and Jim Heng (big trombone); (second row) director T.W. Thorson, Charles Hiller (saxophone), ? Gullickson (trumpet), ? Ness (trumpet), unidentified, ? Antolik (trumpet), unidentified (French horn), unidentified (French horn), ? Uggen (trumpet), ? Olson (trombone), unidentified (trombone), unidentified (trombone), ? Van der Mork, ? Munn (percussion), ? Peterson, and ? Zilko.

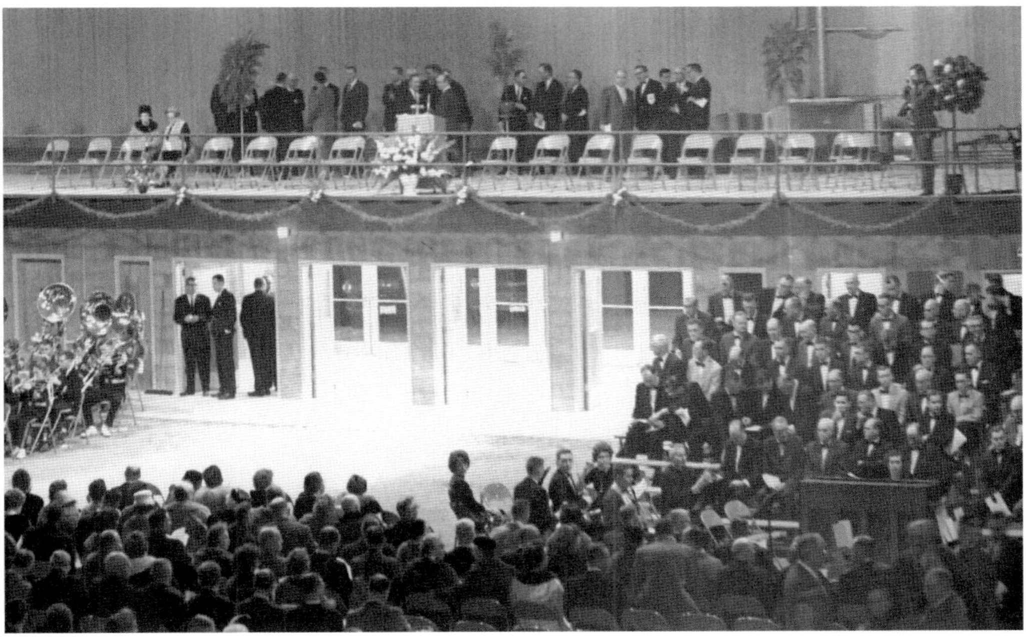

Northwest Singers Reunion

In 1962, the dedication of the newly built Red River Valley Winter Shows Building brought together many dignitaries from a 14-county region. The Northwest Singers reunion also took place at this happy affair. Half of the original singers were in the chorus, with their suit and ties and perhaps somewhat rusty voices. T.W. Thorson was directing while the band played nearby.

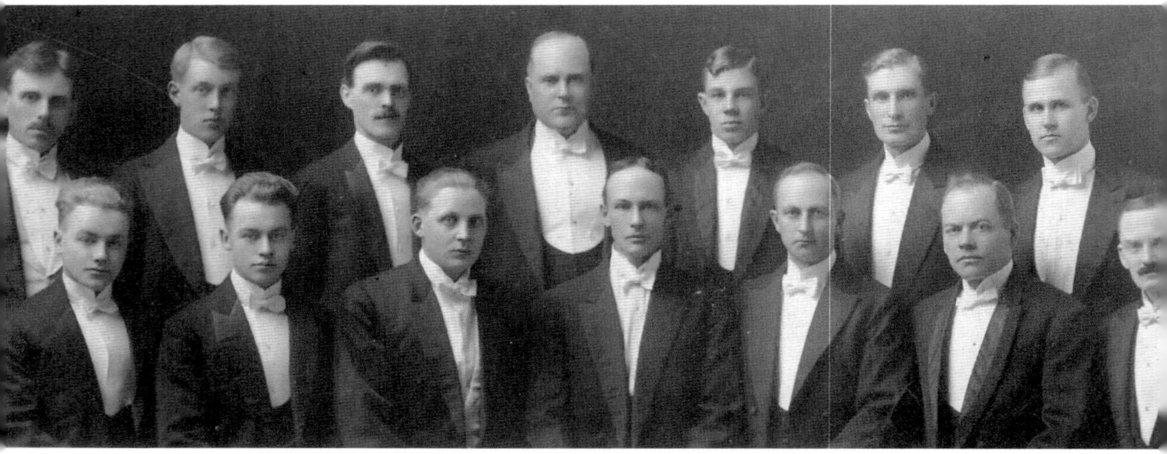

Viking Male Chorus and Sons of Norway Dancers

Pictured above are, from left to right, (first row) William Bangen, Christian Bangen, Ingvald Morken, director O.W. Peterson, Andy Carlson, John Saugstad, and John Hjelmeland; (second row) N.A. Thorson, Adolph Kvamme, M.G. Selvick, Dr. Jacob S. Kjelland, Henry Espe, Adolph Morck, and Paul Onstad.

The photograph below shows many of the Sons of Norway Dancers from the Crookston area. Others who are unidentified are from Fisher and East Grand Forks. They are, from left to right, (first row) four unidentified, Margaret Toutges (center), Agnes Larson, and Mona Brevik (second from the right); (second row) Raymond Egeland, Nig Gunstinson, unidentified, Andy Clemenson, Marion Gunstinson, Ole Thise, Myrtle Bain, unidentified, Olaf Omlid, and Omar Bain. (Above, courtesy of Julia Aune, of Washington, DC.)

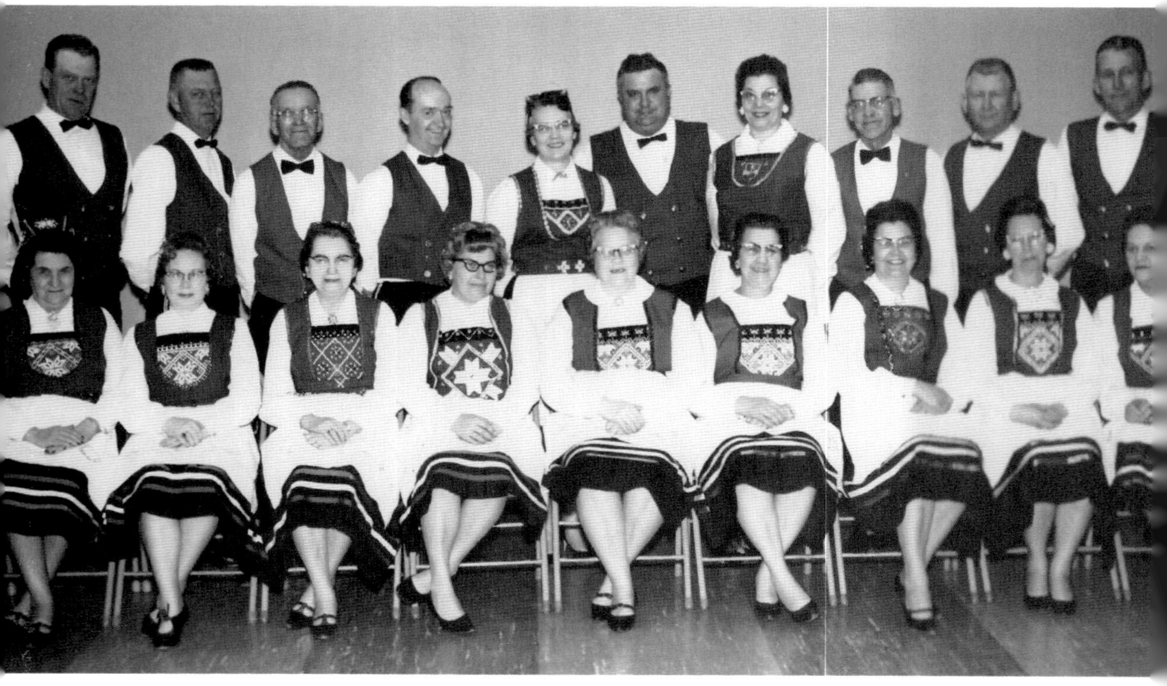

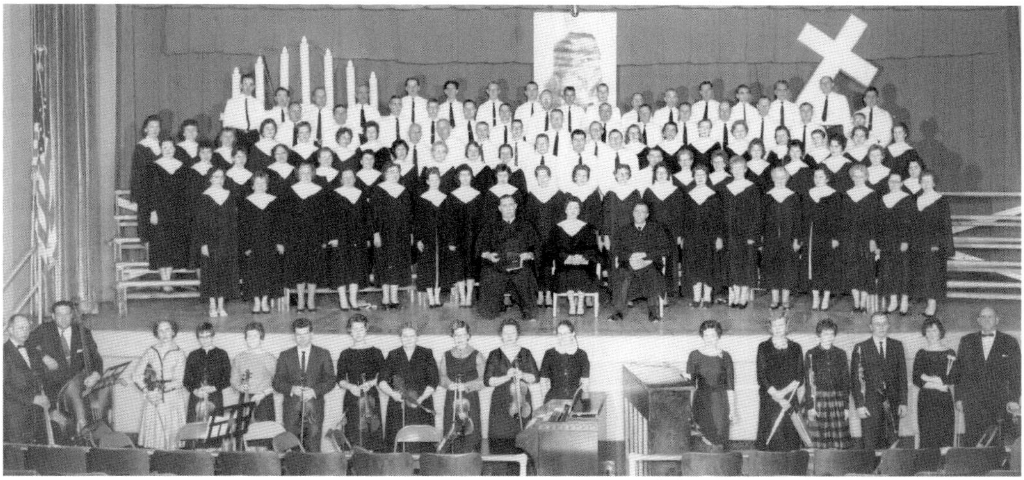

Easter Oratorio Concerts
T.W. Thorson directed Trinity Lutheran Church's senior choir from 1929 to 1970, more than 40 years. In this 1961 photograph, the Easter oratorio is the "Seven Last Words." Director Thorson presented annual Good Friday oratorio concerts with combined church choirs and orchestras held at the Central High School auditorium. T.W. is standing on the far right, behind the organ is Alpha Morck, and the first violinist next to her is Merle Miller. Garfield Reichert, sitting on the right on the stage, is the bass soloist.

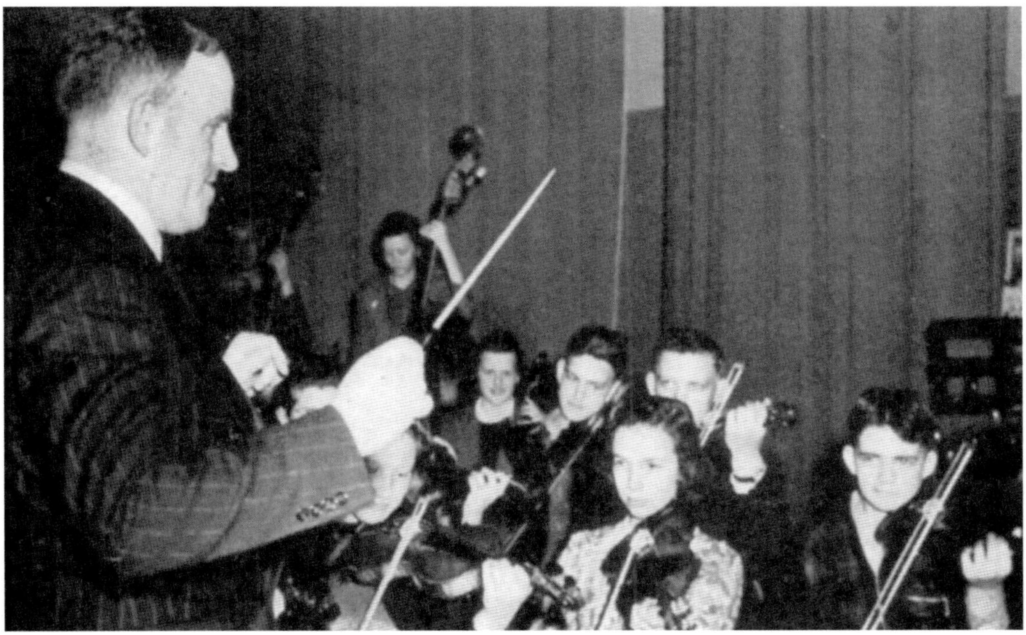

T.W. Thorson, Mr. Music
T.W. Thorson moved to Crookston from Fertile in 1929. By 1932, he was supervising the school music department with an a cappella choir, orchestra, and band. When he retired from the Crookston public school system in 1960, three music teachers replaced what he had started. Behind TWT's right sleeve is Merle Stone Miller playing first chair violin. Doug Carey is playing on the far right. Merle directed the high school orchestra in the 1960s and 1970s.

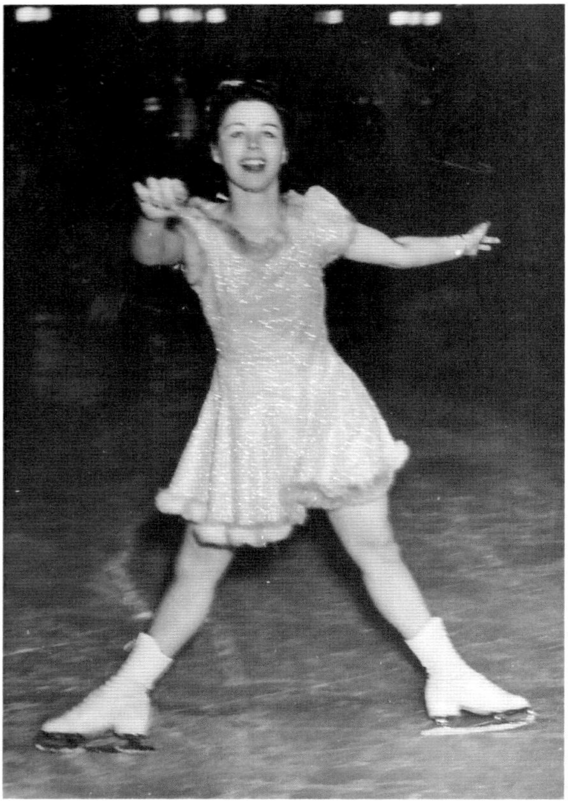

Eleanore Maves and Family

Eleanore Maves was born in Pueblo, Colorado, on September 29, 1917. She married Russell Maves on November 12, 1938, and they moved to Crookston where she dedicated her energies to her family and the community. For 21 years, she directed and produced the "Ice Follies," an ice-skating revue, sponsored by the Crookston Jaycees. She spent more than 30 years as an active member of the hospital auxiliary and formed the Candy Stripers. Eleanore was a part of the theater group called the Cathedral Players. She also started the entertainment group called Eleanore's Octet, which performed for 20 years until 1988. Eleanore died at her Maple Lake home on December 4, 1995. Pictured below are Eleanore's husband, Russell Maves, and their children Gary and Nancy skating; younger daughter Cindy is not pictured. (Both courtesy of Nancy Maves Thomasson.)

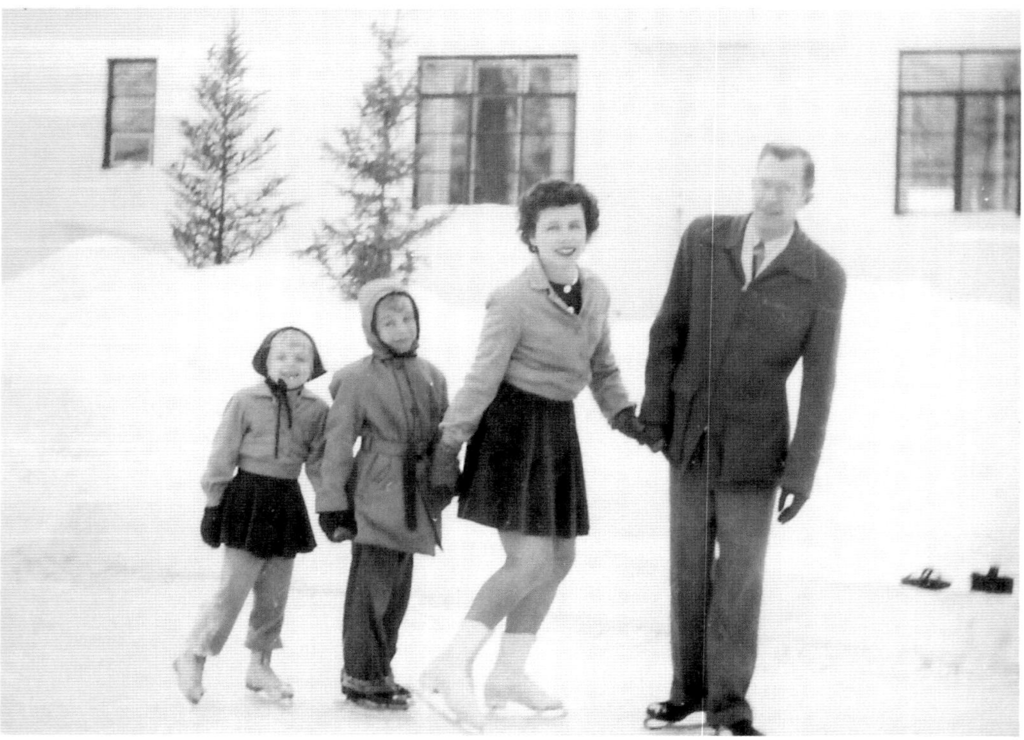

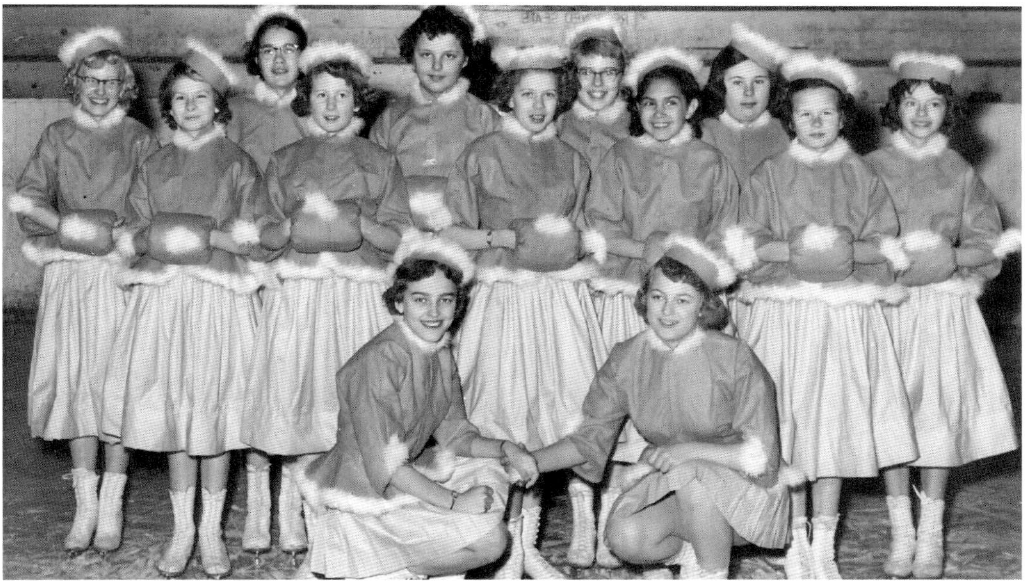

Eleanore's Ice Follies and Eleanore's Octet

The Ice Follies were directed for many years by Eleanore Maves. In order to get more practice time in the ice arena, she knew she had to involve the boy hockey players in the annual event. This was much to the dismay of the hockey coaches, but delight to the young girls in rabbit fur hats and muffs. A few of the girls identified are Jill Janecky, fourth from the right, and Sandy Waller, kneeling on the right. Also in the photograph are Kathy Hodgeson, Jean Reff, Kathy Larson, and Pat O'Boyle.

Pictured below is Eleanore's Octet, without Eleanore, who was always the director. From left to right are Pat Nimens, Burt Menard, Joanne Westberg, Al Brekken, Kay Miller, Dennis Marcusson, and Pat Bergen. They were a group for about 20 years, singing for many charitable events.

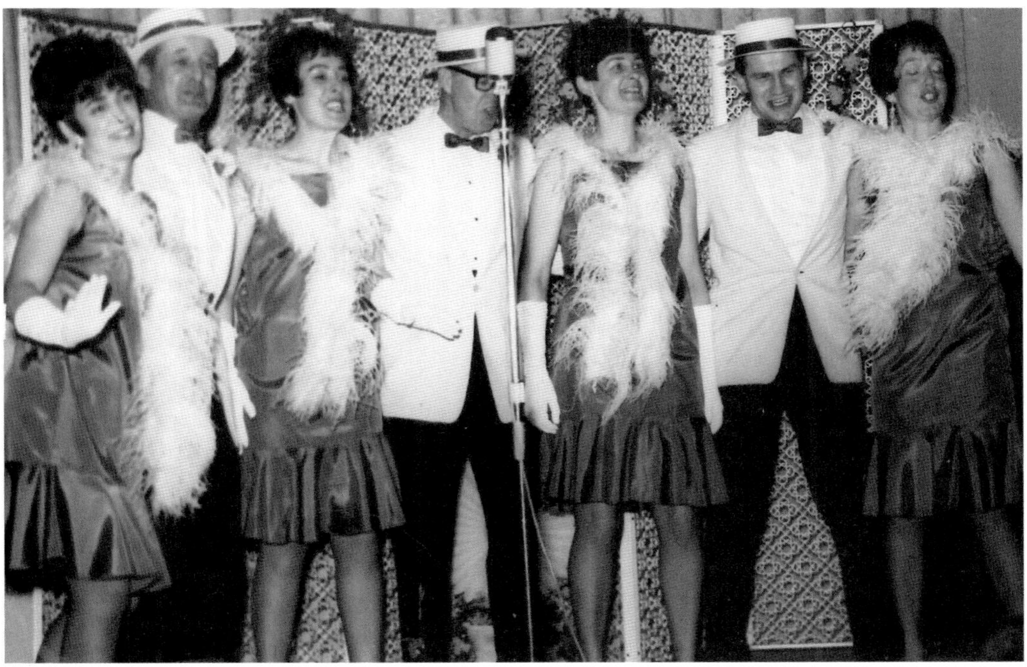

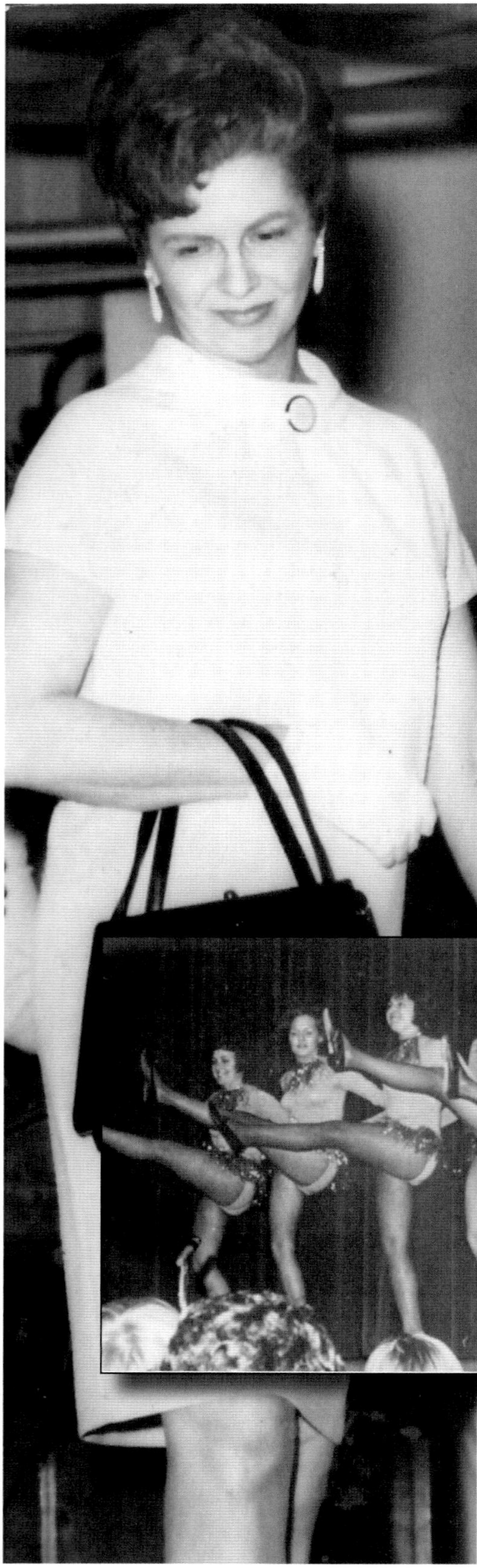

UM Technical Institute Faculty Frolics
The Faculty Frolics was always a big hit among the close-knit group of faculty members and their wives in the early days of the tech institute. Represented in the chorus line below are, from left to right, Ellen Leake, Mary Beth Sargeant, Clara Hodgson, Jeannine Windels, Jan Opgrand, Chris Habstrit, Diane Bachmeier, and Karen Johnson. Another act in 1973 was by Betty Brecto; she appeared in a skit called "Sewing Tips from Mrs. Hips." She demonstrated how, by proper use of dressmaking hints, one could reduce from "pleasingly plump" to a beautiful "36-24-28." Another favorite number was put on by the glamorous Mil Sahlstrom (pictured at left), who was born in Yugoslavia. Dressed as a vamp, she would sing while holding a long-stemmed cigarette holder sitting by the piano. Mil's stage name was Lilli Marlene, and her persona was inspired by actress Marlene Dietrich.

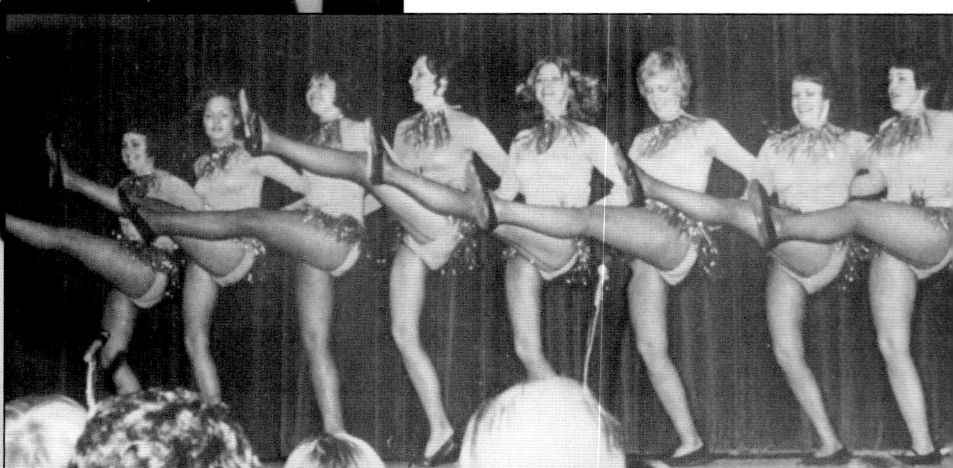

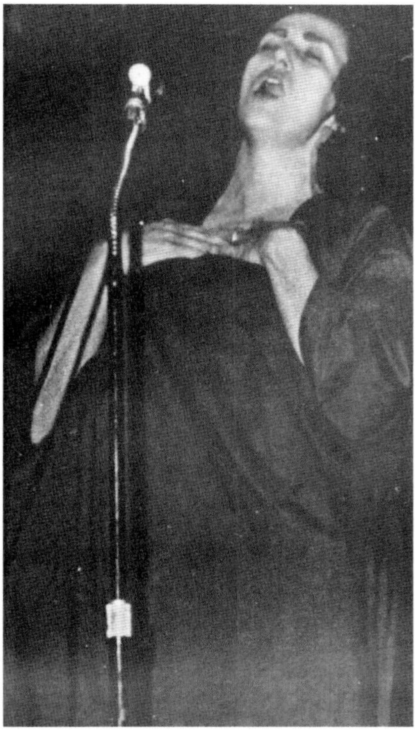

Mary Ann Knotek

Mary Ann Knotek was impersonating Kate Smith. Typically the steady-handed accompanist, Mary Ann and Jeannine Windels coordinated much of the Faculty Frolics in the early 1970s to raise student scholarship money. Mary Ann has played organ almost every Sunday at St. Paul's Lutheran Church ever since she and Dale Knotek arrived to Crookston—for 46 years, Mary Ann has led the hymn singing for at least 2,300 worship services at a good and steady clip, not counting Advent, weddings, and funeral services.

Marcoux Corner

Marcoux Corner is the landmark intersection of US Highway 2 and Highway 32. This area was originally settled by Edward Marcoux in 1927 and was used as a roadhouse and tavern. In 1994, Marcoux Corner became the stage name for an a cappella group composed of Crookstonites Kevin Taylor, Eric Barnum, Brent Thorson, and Eric Patenaude. In 1997, baritone Eric Barnum left the quartet to compose, so Josh Beasler replaced him. The quartet appeared in Fargo to perform for Pres. George W. Bush, and they opened a show for the Beach Boys. The group disbanded in 2007. (Courtesy of Deanna Pautenaude.)

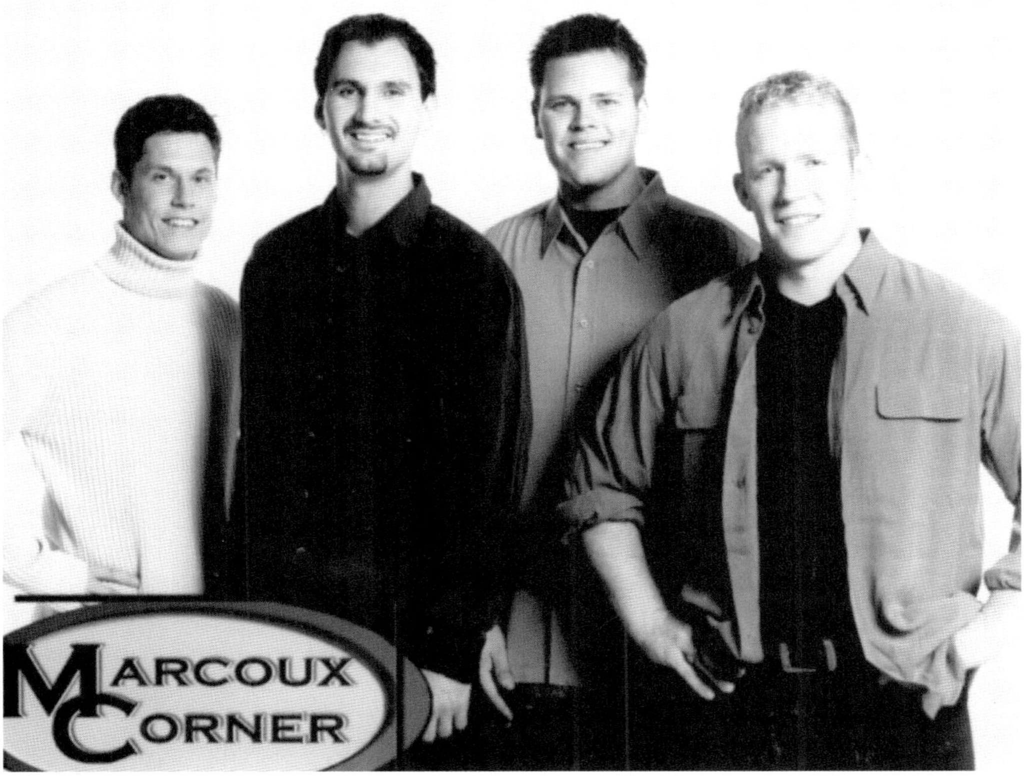

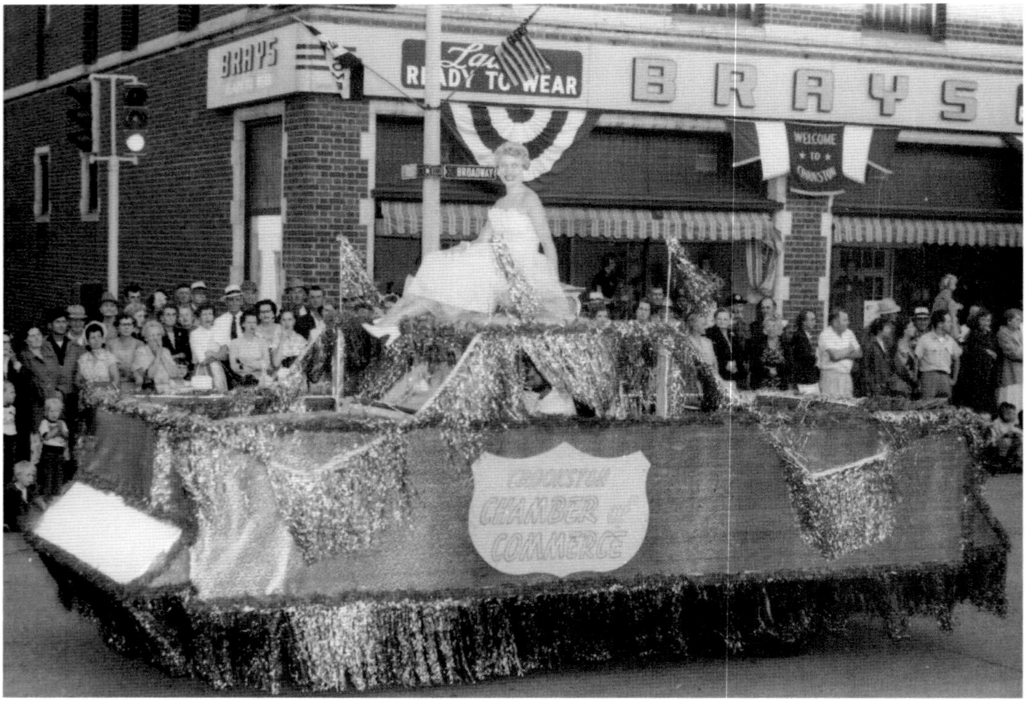

Miss Crookston Denise Johnson and Country Girl Renee Rongen

Denise Johnson, Miss Crookston, represents the Crookston Chamber of Commerce in a 1954 parade. Her float is going past Brays Ladies Ready to Wear store, which later became the upscale women's Town and Country store in the 1960s and 1970s. The top floor of the Eagles Building is where the KROX radio station started out.

The photograph below shows Renee Wall Rongen atop a John Deere tractor and mower. Renee graduated from Central High School in 1979 and is widely known as a touring professional speaker and humorist throughout the United States. She has written several books: *Grandy's Quilt*, *A Gift for All Seasons*, and most recently the popular, *Fundamentally Female*. (Courtesy of Renee Rongen.)

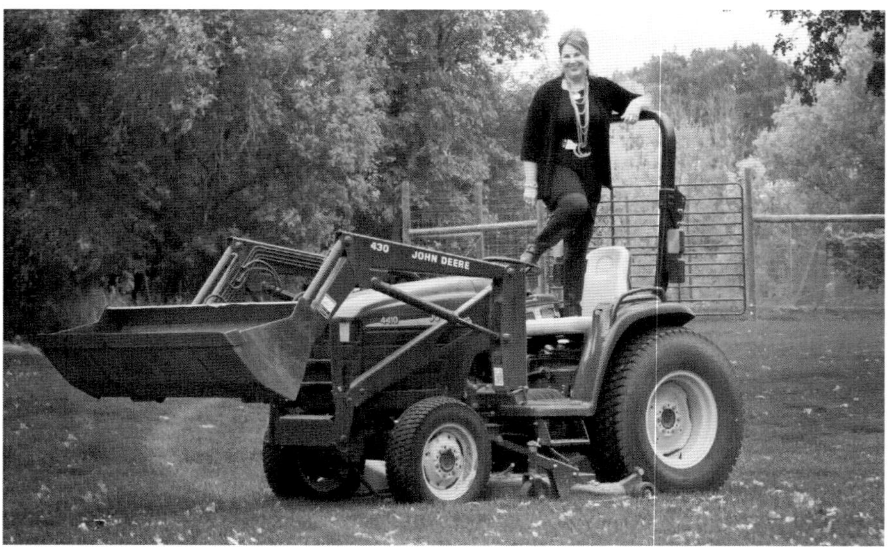

CHAPTER NINE

Remarkable Women

Today, some might be dismayed that too much credit is given to the men, as if they were the sole movers and shakers in the early Crookston community. Indeed, men held political office, were the war heroes, athletes, and early businessmen. But, what about the women? There is a Ukrainian saying that the man might be the head of the house, but the woman is the neck that turns his head. In many cases, that was true a century ago. Many of the successful men of the Crookston community had a wife who did the behind-the-scenes work of meal preparation, cleaning, and raising their children—and really, much more.

The earliest Crookston dwellers and farmers were cutting logs for firewood or the family's log house, building barns, tending to the livestock, tilling the soil, going to town for supplies, and being the fix-it man for everything around the farmyard. Meanwhile, the farmers' wives were doing the meal preparations, raising the children, raising poultry, milking cows, canning, sewing, and doing all else that needed to be done around the house and farmyard. From this pioneering era, Crookston has the tradition of women as hard workers. Yet, or maybe partly because of their home chores, Crookston women noted in this chapter were dogged in their ambitions to make things better for Crookston's education, civic leagues, and so on. For the farmer's wife, the winter months provided more time for this.

World War II brought more women into farm work and almost all war effort jobs to replace sons who had been deployed. But the invention of labor-saving appliances did much to ease women's burden in the prosperous postwar period. Crookston women living in the city had electricity early on, so they were the readers, the ones up on the news. They also had newspapers and wrote letters back to the Old Country. Some were active in their churches or were members of ladies aid groups or other societies. Some of these women volunteered in organizations to aid those less fortunate. The American Red Cross needed many able-bodied women to help during World War I. Soon, women were thinking outside of the professions of secretary, teacher, and nurse. This is true especially of those who made a mark for themselves, outside of being married. Among these, secretaries, teachers, librarians, and curators of local history are focused on in this chapter.

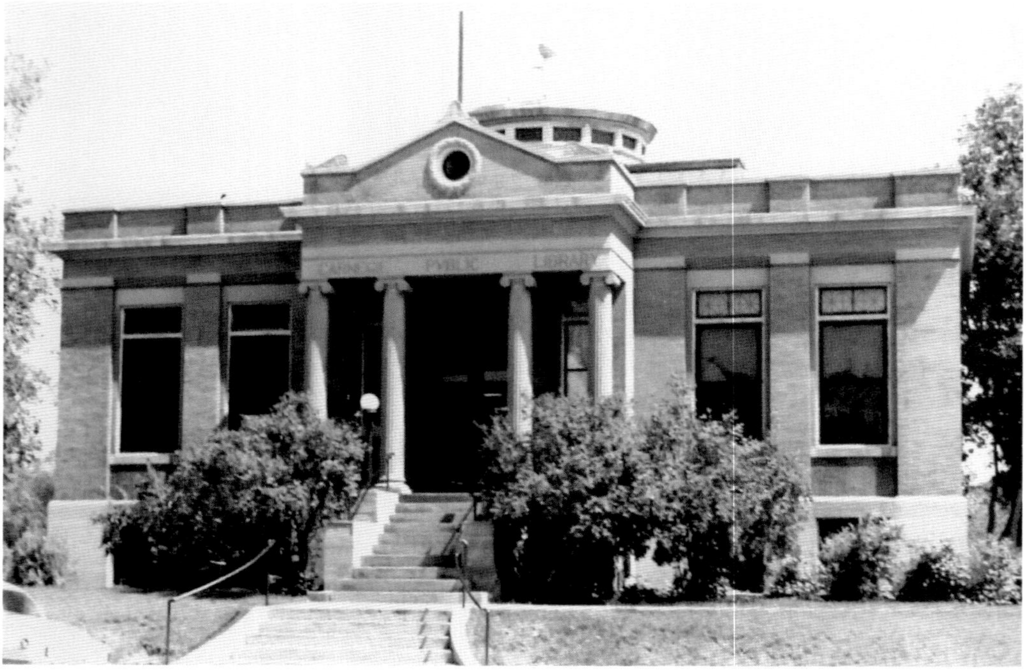

Elizabeth Lommen, the Quintessential Librarian

After the Crookston mayor had sought $35,000 from the Andrew Carnegie Foundation for a community library in March 29, 1902, Elizabeth Lommen was able to successfully secure a lesser amount of $17,500. Although Lommen obtained the Carnegie library funds in late 1903, it was five years before the grand opening. It was an auspicious, two-hour affair in November 1908 with G. Oliver Riggs's band in attendance. Congressman Halvor Steenerson gave a speech about Andrew Carnegie's generosity after a prominent Crookston resident, David H. Turner, gave four large jardinieres as gifts to the library.

The practical work of maintaining the library consumed Lommen's life. Having helped create it, she was capable of keeping things orderly in the beautiful new library. The entire first floor was arranged so that she was able to see every portion of the first floor while she was seated at the check desk. All the floors were covered with a heavy cork carpet that was entirely noiseless. The main consideration was to have a quiet place for readers and those who wanted to study.

Someone described Lommen in the following as the quintessential librarian:

> Miss Lommen . . . kept a struggling library at first alive and helped it then grow stronger. Miss Lommen was a tall, slender lady, quite austere in appearance. She wore glasses, often dressed in a white shirtwaist with high collar and a long black skirt. Outwardly she was very stern—one look over the top of her glasses or occasionally one shout of "quiet!" kept perfect order in the library. There were no problems of discipline in those days when Miss Lommen was about. Inwardly, she was a very kind hearted person.

After a 22-year career as city librarian, Lommen resigned on July 24, 1924. On September 28, 1937, the *Crookston Daily Times* reported that the pioneer resident had relocated to Fordville, North Dakota, to be close to her sister Addie. Lommen ended her 1924 article with, "I have been loyal to the library board and the public, I have found the people kind and courteous. The children have been quiet and well behaved through it all; the time has passed quickly and pleasantly. A great deal more could be said but to avoid making it too long, I close, thanking you for the kindness shown me through my library work."

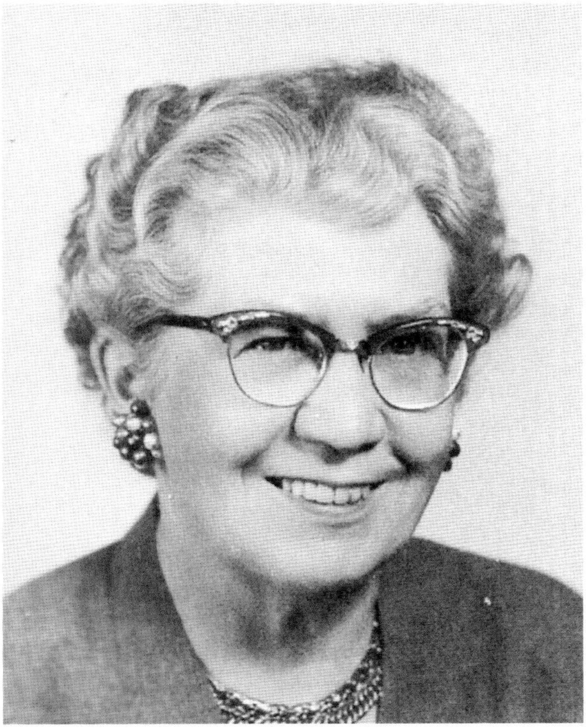

Instructor Retta Bede
Retta Bede, for whom UMC's Bede Dining Hall is named, was much loved on the Northwest School of Agriculture campus. Bede retired in July 1957 after 32 years of teaching home economics. She taught the farm girls who were boarding away from home how to work long, hard farm-wife hours and how to bake, preserve, and can. Though never married, she was like a second mother to many of the boys and girls who lived on the NWSA campus.

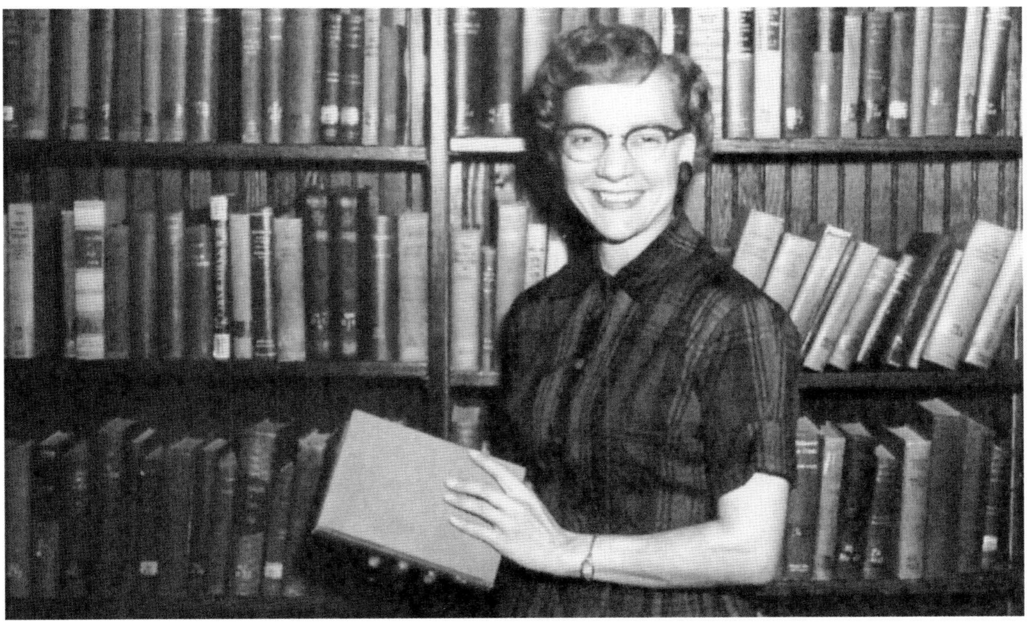

Librarian Berniel Nelson
Even though Berniel Nelson, UMC's librarian who retired after 47 years of service, would never admit it, she was the one who held together the reunions of the Northwest School of Agriculture. She knew everyone from that era and continued on through Provost Stan Sahlstrom's leadership. She saw all the transitions that occurred with each change of leader, from superintendent to provost to chancellor. Berniel, even when retired, continued to work closely with the NWSA reunions.

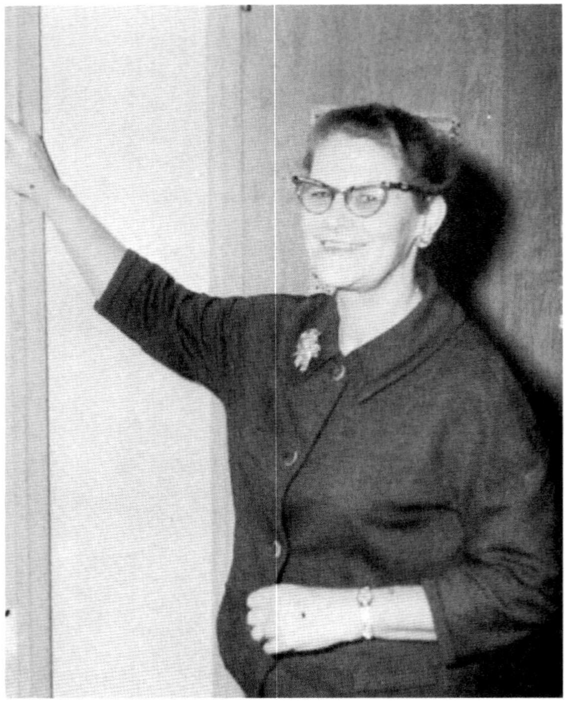

Alpha Morck

Alpha Morck was employed by the Crookston Public School System for many years as a Latin and Spanish teacher. She was also the organist at Trinity Lutheran Church for many years under T.W. Thorson's direction. As a single woman, she looked regal and elegant in her professional dresses. One 50-year high school reunion had special significance: she finally married the man she had known and dated back in high school. Alpha became the second Mrs. Ole Syverson in her early 80s.

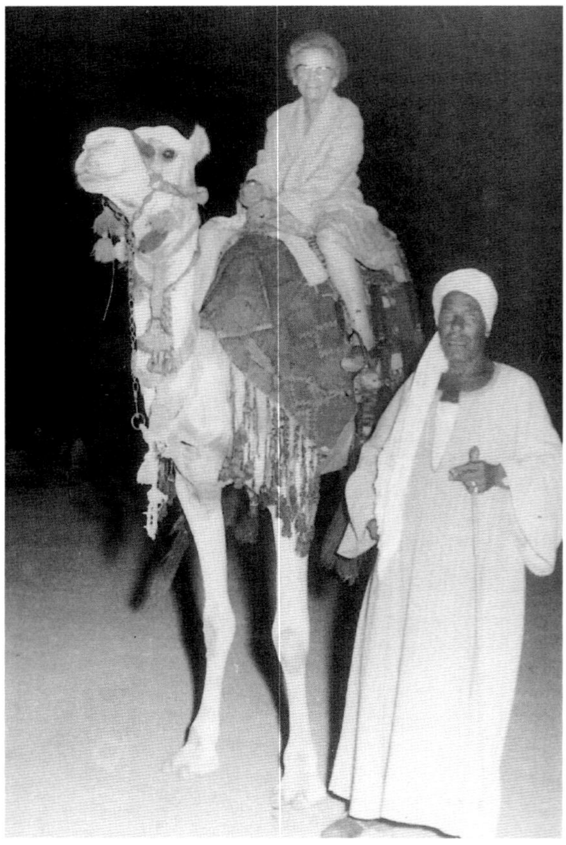

Henrietta Holte

Henrietta Holte, Dr. Halvor Holte's widow, traveled widely and considered herself a curator. She always wanted to ride a camel in Egypt. At the age of 88, she checked it off her bucket list. Henrietta was most known for all the Native American Indian artifacts she had collected. She wrote a book that listed thousands of these items and their origins. Henrietta was very active in Indian welfare work and was officially adopted by the Chippewa tribe and given an Indian name, Waganningo Quay, meaning "Woman of Morning Star."

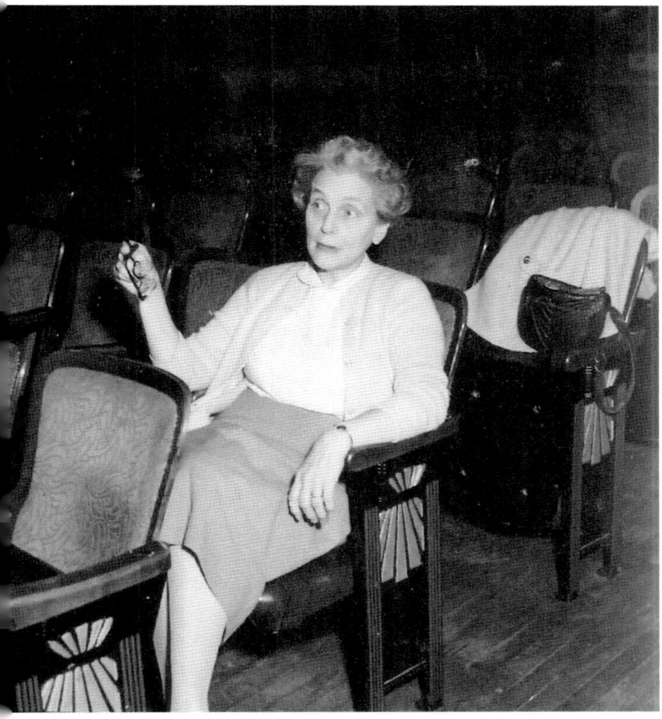

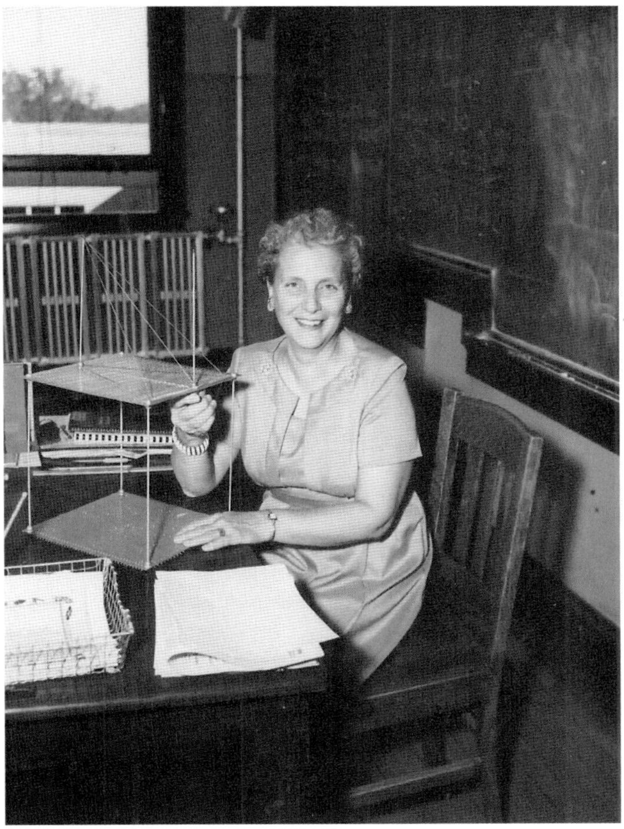

Evelyn Probstfield
Evelyn Probstfield (Gesell) had a prominent grandfather in the Moorhead, Minnesota, area, R.M. Probstfield. He kept a diary about a round-trip from Moorhead to Pembina on the Red River; it lasted eight days and three hours. After 22 years of service on the Crookston High School teaching staff, Evelyn Probstfield retired in June 1965. She had taught speech, drama, and mathematics and had been in charge of drama and speech activities the entire time. In drama competition, her plays won the regional events and they advanced the state level five times during her tenure.

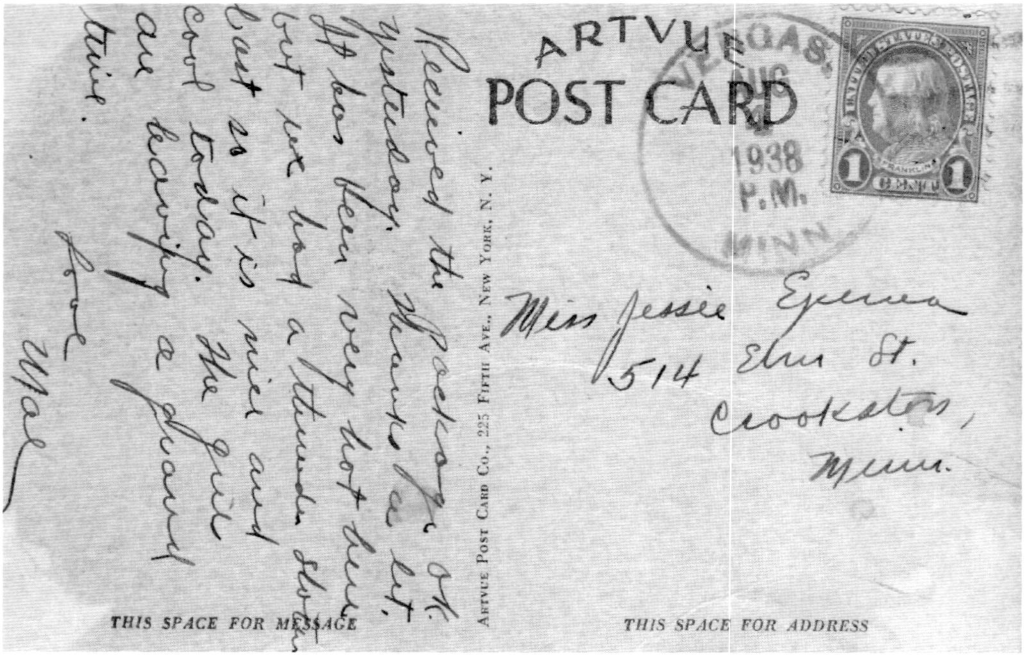

Postcard from Mae Rideout
On August 4, 1938, Mae Rideout wrote a postcard to Jessie Epema who worked for Mae as household help at her 514 Elm Street home. Jessie took care of Mae Rideout's house while Mae was the business manager at the Northwest Clinic. Jessie said Mae was very kind to her. When she got married to George Brolsma Jr. on September 7, 1940, Mae helped with planning and used flowers from her garden for Jessie's wedding ceremony. Born in 1920, Jessie Epema Brolsma (right) is seen with her sister-in-law Agnes Brolsma. Jessie was born and lived on a farm three miles west of Crookston. During her senior year at Central High School, Jessie lived and did household chores for Judge William Watts and his wife, Edith, at 519 North Ash. She remembered Edith saying that her ancestors arrived on the *Mayflower.* Jessie also worked at the R.T. Buckler farm one summer as domestic help. She also lived with the Dr. Russell Sather family. (Right, courtesy of Jessie Brolsma.)

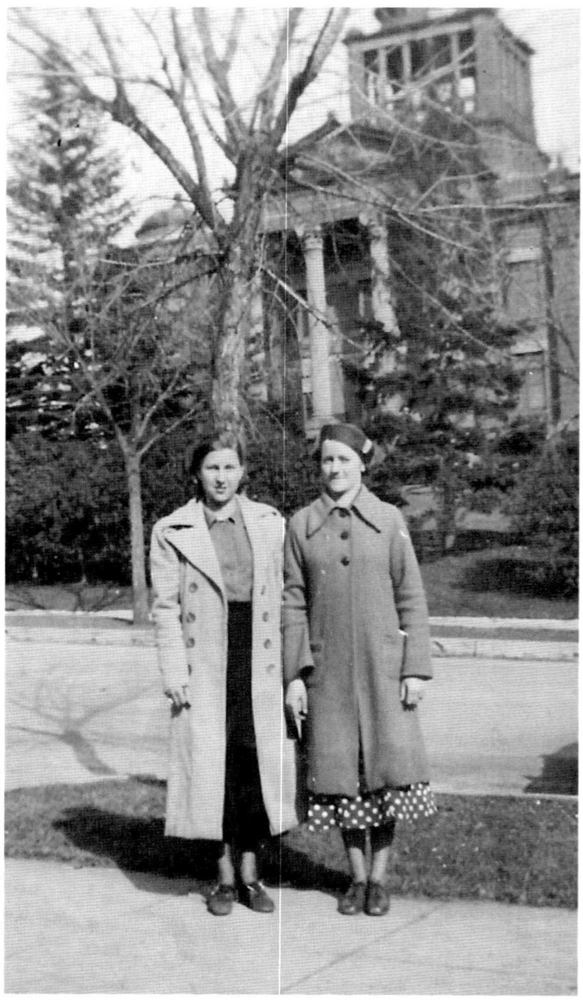

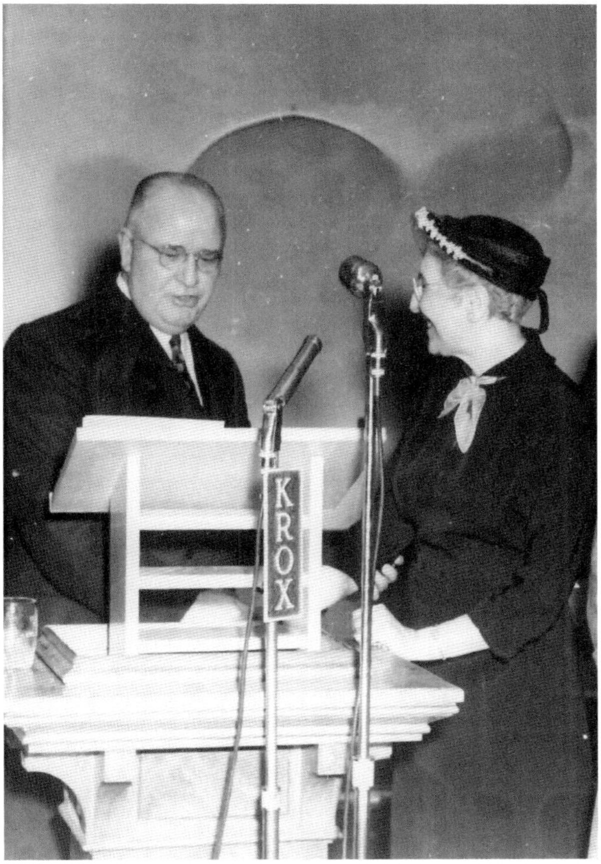

Mae Rideout, Exceptional Overachiever

On April 12, 1954, Minnesota State Supreme Court Justice Roger L. Dell of St. Paul presented the *Book of Golden Deeds* award to Mae Rideout at an annual affair. When receiving the reward Mae said, "All of the things I have done in the past have been a success only because the people who were behind me had faith in me." She also said that she had fun in all of the things she participated in, and she did not see why she should receive an award for having fun. Below, Mae Rideout is receiving the honor of "Woman of the Year" on March 8, 1954; she received it again in 1971. Standing are, from left to right, Mae's sister, Edna Young; Evelyn Andrews, 1954 Business and Professional Women's Club president; Clara Berg; and Ida Tvedten, the first club president. Ida had served as a Red Cross nurse in World War I.

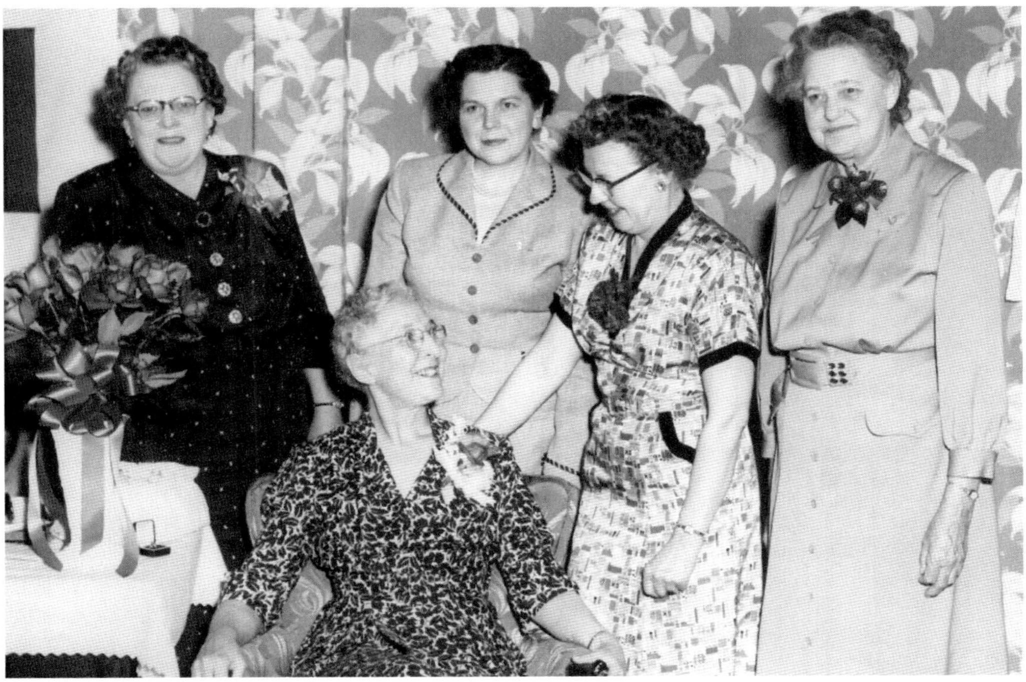

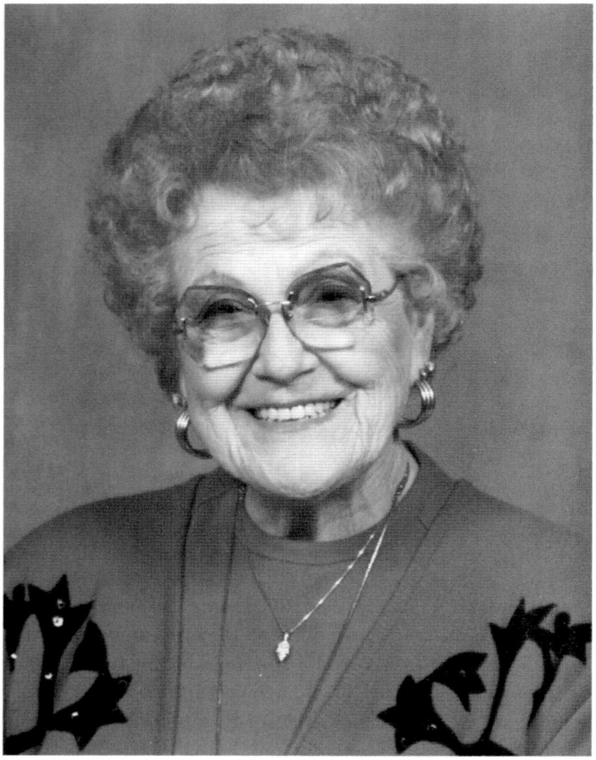

Vicki Dragseth Irwin

Vicki Dragseth Irwin was born on July 27, 1915, and was married to Andy T. Dragseth, who died on June 30, 1937. Seven years later, she married George Irwin. Vicky died at age 89 on August 10, 2004. To say Vicki led a very active life in her community was an understatement. She did not believe her day was complete unless she had participated in at least three different clubs or meetings. Gardening was what Vicki did to relax. In fact, a few times after coming home late from a committee meeting, she used her car headlights to continue to weed her flower gardens. (Courtesy of Judy Dragseth Ellingson.)

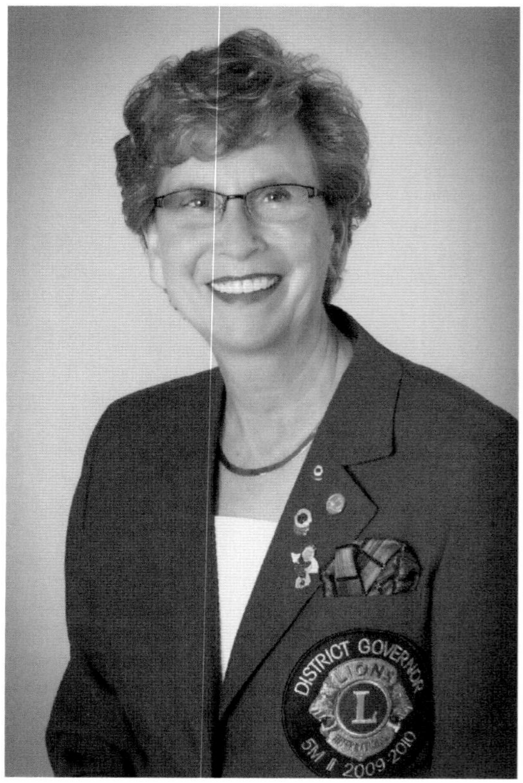

Jeannine Windels

In her leadership role as Lions district governor, Jeannine Windels has traveled 15,680 miles to visit 74 Lions Clubs and made 20 border crossings into Canada and back. The most rewarding part of her year as district governor was being able to meet people at club gatherings and learning firsthand about all their good works. One of the Lions' emphasis is ensuring people are provided with eyeglasses and eye care.

CHAPTER TEN

Volunteers Rock!

Where would small-town communities like Crookston be without the spirit of volunteerism? At first, volunteerism was limited by the hard work required to maintain day-to-day life. Nevertheless, early Crooksonites found time for church and school or civic activities. Neighbors in trouble, especially during spring floods, walked the dikes or helped use sandbags to protect homes.

The generation after the first settlers had easier lives. With more time on their hands, volunteerism was something that people had a desire to do, and they did so for a number of reasons. After the 1929 fifty-year anniversary of Crookston's existence, older Crookston residents recognized that something needed to be done to preserve the area's memories. Soon after, the Polk County Historical Museum was formed in the basement of the old courthouse. An appeal was made via the newspaper for old letters, photographs, and other memorabilia for the archives.

At about the same time, service clubs were formed. Lions, Rotary, Kiwanis, and Jaycees subscribed to the mission of serving people in the community and in the world. For the younger people, there were organizations like the Camp Fire Girls, Cub Scouts, and Candy Stripers. Nowadays, one way to volunteer, besides stocking the North Country Food Bank or serving at the kitchen of Care & Share, is to donate time listening to older people tell their stories. The older generations from the 1930s and 1940s have powerful narratives about what life was like in the old days. Back then, everyone seemed to be scraping-by especially during the Great Depression. Yet, even then, people helped one another. Another place to volunteer is at the Polk County Historical Society with volunteer coordinator Carol Solheim during the summer months.

Church was and is a place where volunteering of one's time for good purpose is encouraged. Bake sales and dinners are held as benefits to help others. Mission trips, like the one to help people after Hurricane Katrina, involve young people. At UMC, service-learning projects are a part of the curriculum. Students help around the community to make it a better place; many students join the Leo Club. Another example is helping to clean up and restore the former Carnegie library. It is not always about the bottom line and making money—the altruistic idea can be learned in order to help improve the community but also to benefit each individual who gives of their own time in serving others.

Bruno Jurchen, Keeper of History

Bruno Jurchen was born on October 8, 1911, and died on February 26, 1996. He recollected growing up in Roome Township near Eldred and attending only 35 days of eighth grade. He was forced to quit school to help with the family farm. They farmed with horses, and he witnessed the transition to the use of machines in farming. "While the horses were on the way out, the Depression hit—no credit, no rain, no crops, and no price. Oats were going for 6¢ a bushel and eggs for 6¢a dozen," he said. When Bruno died, he took a lot of what he knew about Crookston's history to his grave, but his efforts with the Polk County Historical Society preserved much of it as well.

On August 14, 1984, Bruno retired as historical society president. But that did not mean he did not keep working on his pet projects, such as saving the Carnegie library building from demolition and moving the log cabin to the museum. Bruno's fingerprints are literally all over the former Carnegie library building, plus the Glendenning Building, which he was able to get with the aid of Robert Kresl. Bob remembers sitting with Bruno at Robert's Restaurant, present-day Happy Joe's, and looking east in the direction where the old warehouse stood. He said it would be a perfect place to house all the artifacts that had been collecting in the old McKinley Elementary School building. They set about getting that building along with putting up pole barns to house the tractors, fire trucks, and other large implements. On January 11, 1994, Bruno was honored as "Keeper of History." As one examines the legacy of the PCHS, more and more things turn out to be the legacy of Bruno Jurchen. (Courtesy of Kathy Jurchen Pissoneault.)

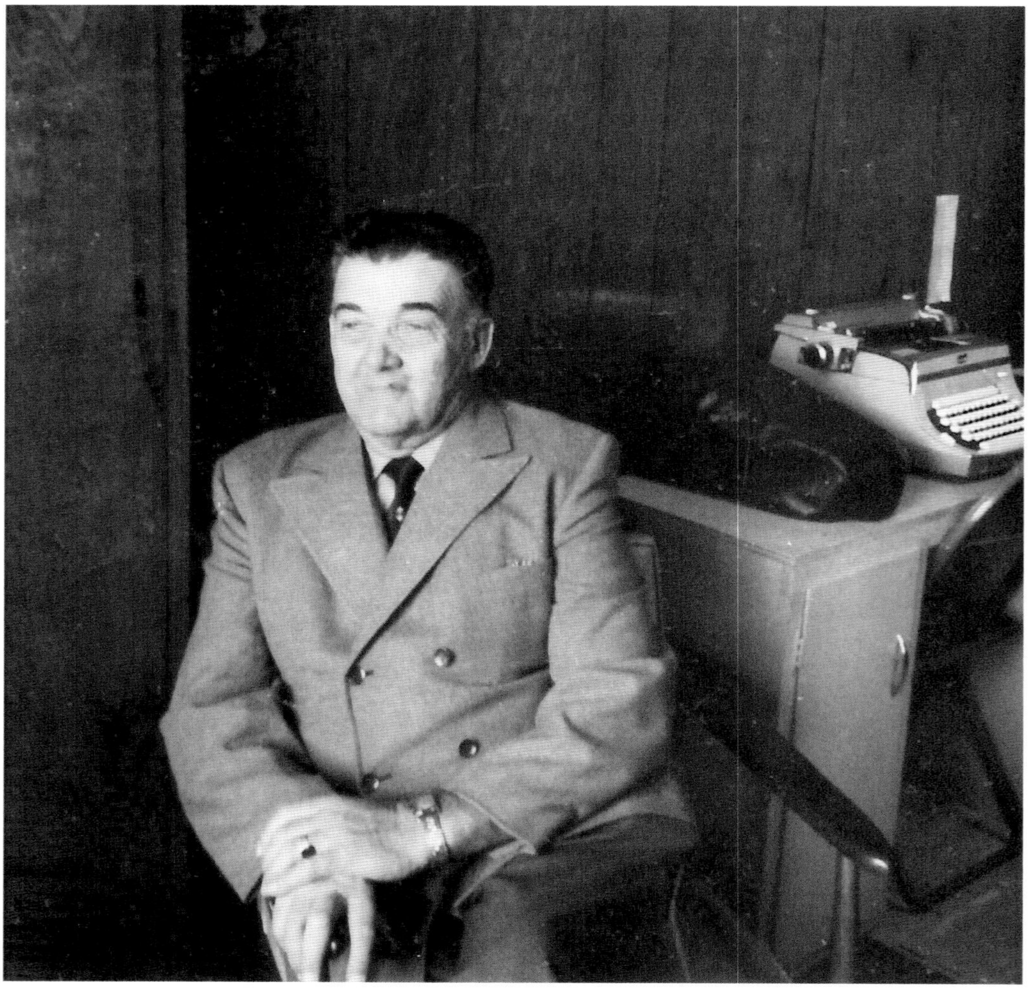

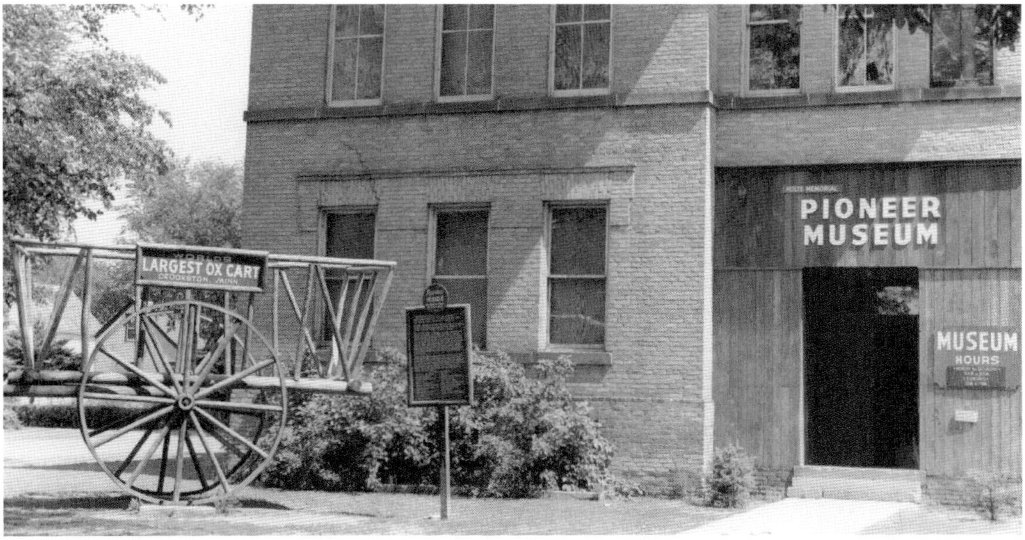

McKinley School's Transformation to Pioneer Museum
After the Polk County Historical Society started in 1933, the old courthouse basement was where artifacts were stored. Once the museum outgrew that space and the old McKinley Elementary School was no longer needed in the Jerome's Addition, board members of the historical society moved their things over to the bigger building. This was accomplished in the 1950s. At that point, the Old Pioneer Museum was dedicated and named after Henrietta Holte because of her significant accomplishments in preserving the Native American treasures she had collected over the years.

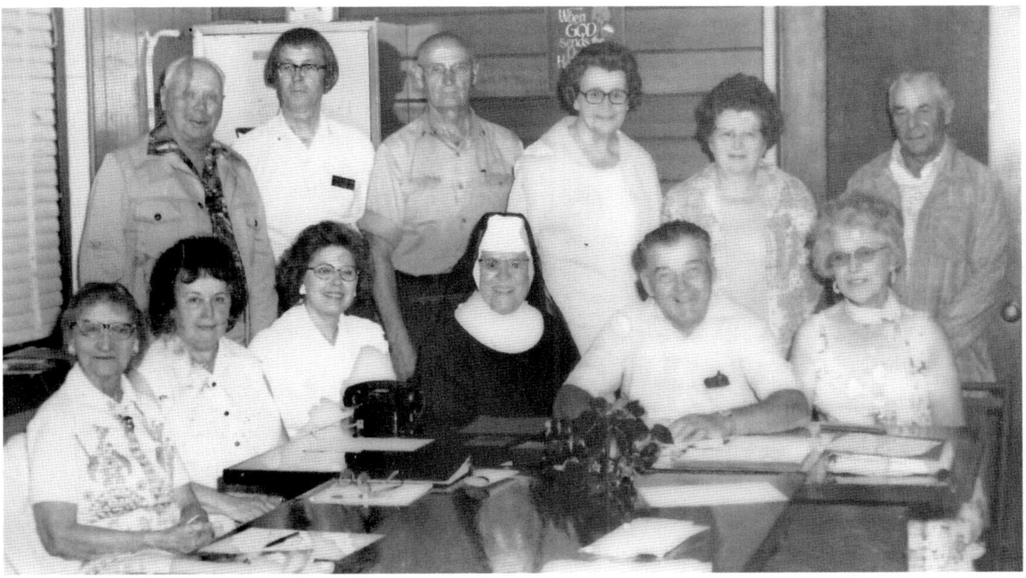

Polk County Museum Board of Directors
The Polk County Historical Society took on a very active role after a hiatus in the late 1950s. By 1975, there were many volunteers working on the Polk County Historical Society Board of Directors. Pictured are, from left to right, (first row) Ellen Pfeifer, Gwen Richards, Arlene Wagner, Sister Mary Magdelene, Bruno Jurchen, and Victoria Dragseth Irwin; (second row) Loren Parkin, Bruce Beresford, Clarence Swenson, Lillian Gorter, Marian Larson, and Albany Capistran.

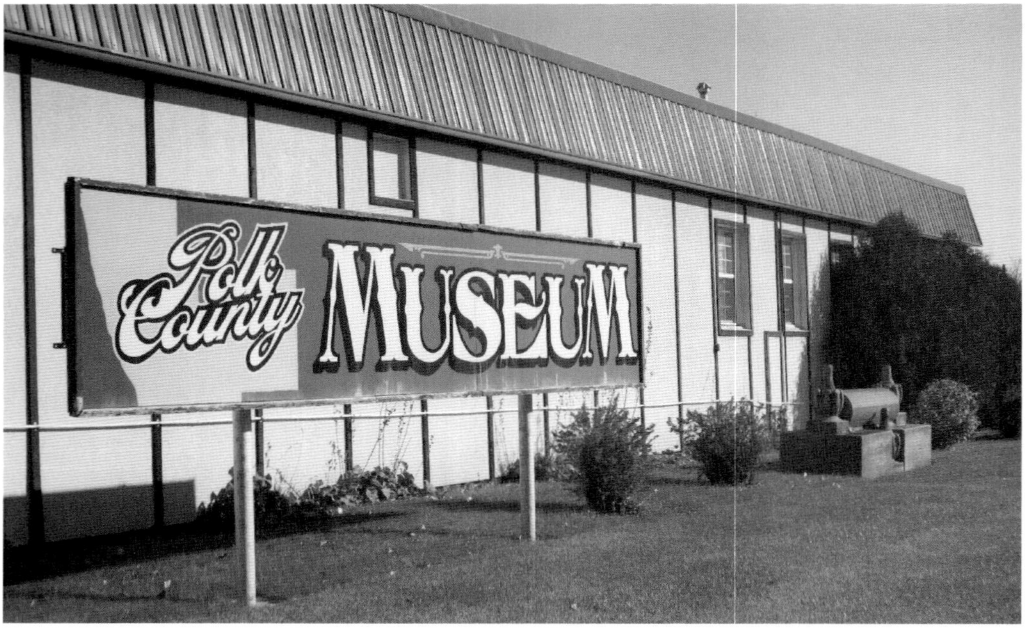

Polk County Historical Museum

The outside sign for Polk County Museum was painted by high school art teacher Rick McMenemy. The Polk County Historical Society Board obtained ownership of the old Glendenning Building and started remodeling it in 1976. The dedication of the new museum was on June 15, 1978. A railroad car has been added to the six-acre plot along with the old Hafslo Lutheran Church, at which Sen. Roger Moe was baptized and confirmed. (Courtesy of Steve Hannah.)

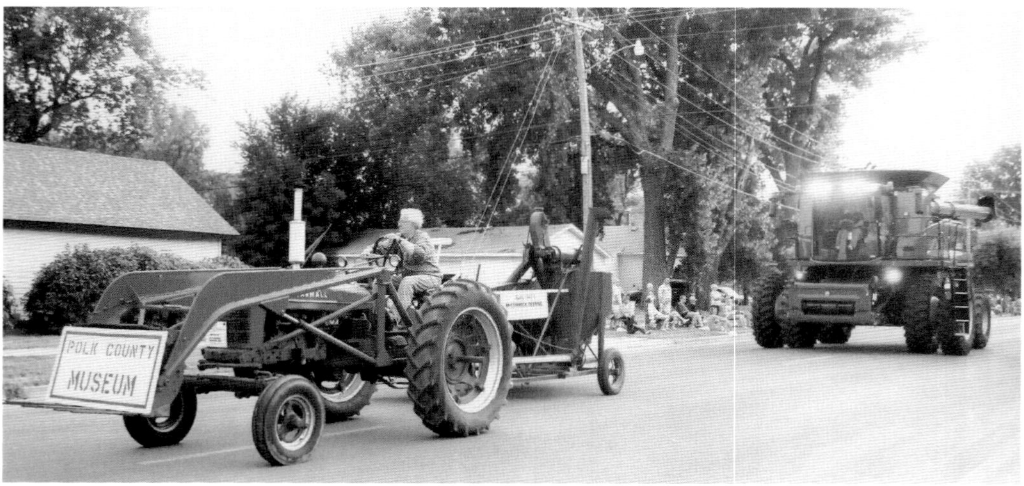

Cliff Nelson, Volunteer

During the annual 2013 Oxcart Day Torchlight Parade, Cliff Nelson, museum volunteer, drove a Farmall tractor, with a 1940s McCormick Deering combine, followed by a new combine (with its 45-foot header not attached). Cliff's Swedish grandfather struggled to survive in the early pioneer days. He walked 14 miles to Grand Forks for supplies and carried them home on his back. He traded a buffalo coat, a black silk dress, and a watch for a team of oxen and began plowing in the spring of 1878. (Courtesy of Twylla Altepeter.)

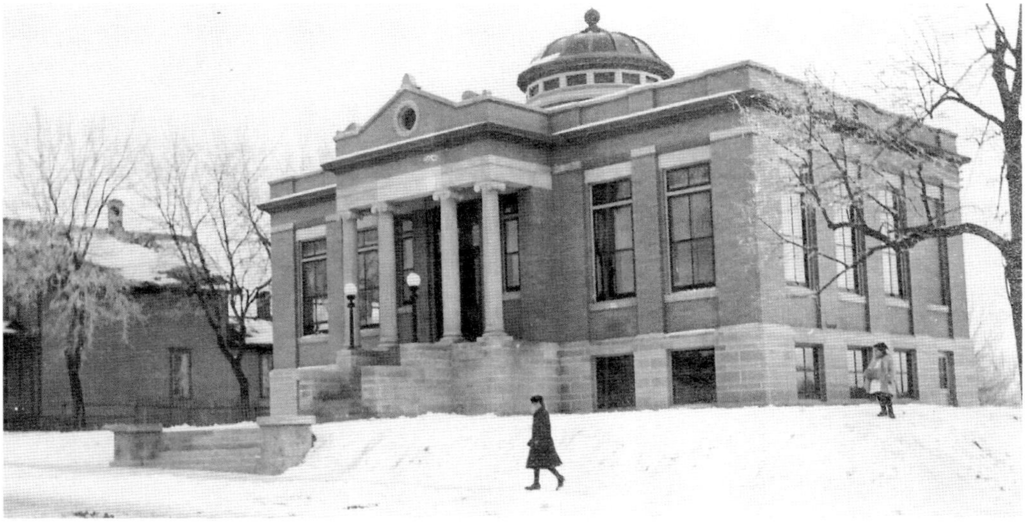

Repurposed Carnegie Library

This photograph of the library Andrew Carnegie gifted to Crookston was taken in 1908. In the 1970s, in an effort to save on heating costs, the dome that rose 30 feet high from the main lobby floor was taken out along with all the stained-glass windows that had a kaleidoscope look when the sun hit it just right. This structure was about to be demolished after the new Crookston library was built in 1985. The City of Crookston had no more use for this relic. Fortunately, Bruno Jurchen and others on the Polk County Historical Board saved it to serve as an archive for future researchers and genealogists. (PCHS.)

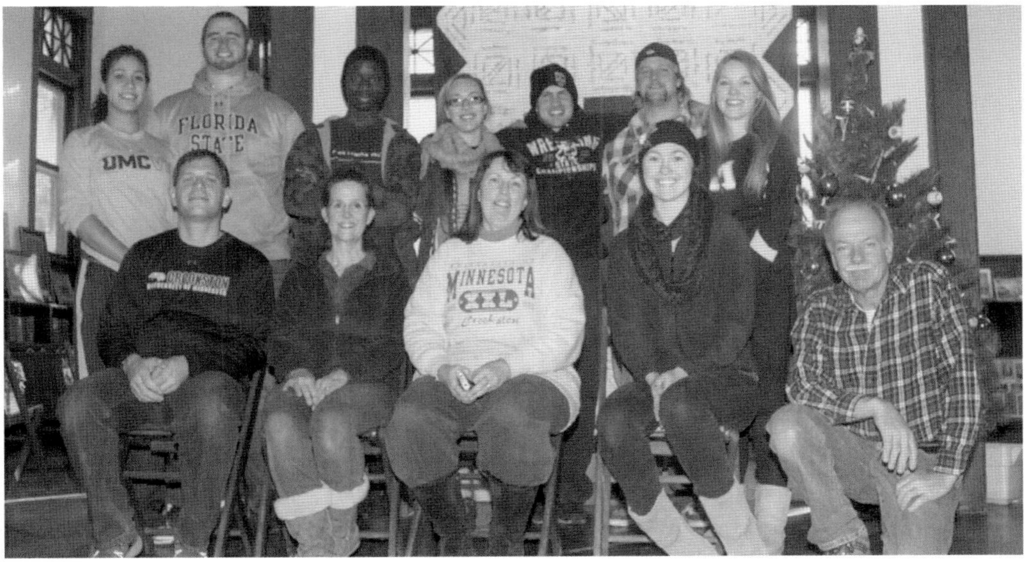

UMC Honors Student Volunteers

UMC students who are members of the Alpha Lambda Delta honor society make great volunteers at the former Carnegie library. They have donated money from their annual Pi run for the purpose of refurbishing the Carnegie building. They are, from left to right, (first row) Brian Dingmann, Elizabeth Tollefson, Kristina Gray, Amberly Pressel, and Steve Hannah; (second row) Alexandra Skeeter, Matthew Borowicz, Tim Adeniyi, Mary Mikutowski, Andrew Steinfeldt, Drew Selvestra, and Katie Sheetz. (Photograph taken by Steve Hannah.)

INDEX